HJ 88 99. DEV

Studies in Development Economics and Policy

General Editor: **Anthony Shorrocks**

UNU WORLD INSTITUTE FOR DEVELOPMENT ECONOMICS RESEARCH (UNU-WIDER) was established by the United Nations University as its first research and training centre and started work in Helsinki, Finland, in 1985. The purpose of the Institute is to undertake applied research and policy analysis on structural changes affecting the developing and transitional economies, to provide a forum for the advocacy of policies leading to robust, equitable and environmentally sustainable growth, and to promote capacity strengthening and training in the field of economic and social policy-making. Its work is carried out by staff researchers and visiting scholars in Helsinki and through networks of collaborating scholars and institutions around the world.

UNU World Institute for Development Economics Research (UNU-WIDER)
Katajanokanlaituri 6B, FIN-00160 Helsinki, Finland

Titles include:

Tony Addison, Henrik Hansen and Finn Tarp (*editors*)
DEBT RELIEF FOR POOR COUNTRIES

Tony Addison and George Mavrotas (*editors*)
DEVELOPMENT FINANCE IN THE GLOBAL ECONOMY
The Road Ahead

Tony Addison and Alan Roe (*editors*)
FISCAL POLICY FOR DEVELOPMENT
Poverty, Reconstruction and Growth

George G. Borjas and Jeff Crisp (*editors*)
POVERTY, INTERNATIONAL MIGRATION AND ASYLUM

Ricardo Ffrench-Davis and Stephany Griffith-Jones (*editors*)
FROM CAPITAL SURGES TO DROUGHT
Seeking Stability for Emerging Economies

David Fielding (*editor*)
MACROECONOMIC POLICY IN THE FRANC ZONE

Basudeb Guha-Khasnobis (*editor*)
THE WTO, DEVELOPING COUNTRIES AND THE DOHA
DEVELOPMENT AGENDA
Prospects and Challenges for Trade-led Growth

Basudeb Guha-Khasnobis, Shabd S. Acharya and Benjamin Davis (*editors*)
FOOD INSECURITY, VULNERABILITY AND HUMAN RIGHTS FAILURE

Basudeb Guha-Khasnobis and Ravi Kanbur (*editors*)
INFORMAL LABOUR MARKETS AND DEVELOPMENT

Basudeb Guha-Khasnobis and George Mavrotas (*editors*)
FINANCIAL DEVELOPMENTS, INSTITUTIONS, GROWTH AND
POVERTY REDUCTION

Aiguo Lu and Manuel F. Montes (*editors*)
POVERTY, INCOME DISTRIBUTION AND WELL-BEING IN ASIA
DURING THE TRANSITION

George Mavrotas (*editor*)
DOMESTIC RESOURCE MOBILIZATION AND FINANCIAL DEVELOPMENT

George Mavrotas and Anthony Shorrocks (*editors*)
ADVANCING DEVELOPMENT
Core Themes in Global Economics

Mark McGillivray (*editor*)
HUMAN WELL-BEING
Concept and Measurement

Mark McGillivray (*editor*)
INEQUALITY, POVERTY AND WELL-BEING

Robert J. McIntyre and Bruno Dallago (*editors*)
SMALL AND MEDIUM ENTERPRISES IN TRANSITIONAL ECONOMIES

Vladimir Mikhalev (*editor*)
INEQUALITY AND SOCIAL STRUCTURE DURING THE TRANSITION

E. Wayne Nafziger and Raimo Väyrynen (*editors*)
THE PREVENTION OF HUMANITARIAN EMERGENCIES

Machiko Nissanke and Erik Thorbecke (*editors*)
GLOBALIZATION AND THE POOR IN ASIA

Machiko Nissanke and Erik Thorbecke (*editors*)
THE IMPACT OF GLOBALIZATION ON THE WORLD'S POOR
Transmission Mechanisms

Matthew Odedokun (*editor*)
EXTERNAL FINANCE FOR PRIVATE SECTOR DEVELOPMENT
Appraisals and Issues

Laixiang Sun (*editor*)
OWNERSHIP AND GOVERNANCE OF ENTERPRISES
Recent Innovative Developments

Guanghua Wan (*editor*)
UNDERSTANDING INEQUALITY AND POVERTY IN CHINA
Methods and Applications

Studies in Development Economics and Policy
Series Standing Order ISBNs: 978–0–333–96424–8 hardback; 978–0–230–20041–8 paperback (*outside North America only*)

You can receive future titles in this series as they are published by placing a standing order. Please contact your bookseller or, in case of difficulty, write to us at the address below with your name and address, the title of the series and one of the ISBNs quoted above.

Customer Services Department, Macmillan Distribution Ltd, Houndmills, Basingstoke, Hampshire RG21 6XS, England

Development Finance in the Global Economy

The Road Ahead

Edited by

Tony Addison

and

George Mavrotas

in association with the World Institute for Development Economics Research of the United Nations University (UNU-WIDER)

First published 2008 by
PALGRAVE MACMILLAN
Houndmills, Basingstoke, Hampshire RG21 6XS and
175 Fifth Avenue, New York, N.Y. 10010
Companies and representatives throughout the world

PALGRAVE MACMILLAN is the global academic imprint of the Palgrave
Macmillan division of St. Martin's Press, LLC and of Palgrave Macmillan Ltd.
Macmillan® is a registered trademark in the United States, United Kingdom
and other countries. Palgrave is a registered trademark in the European
Union and other countries.

ISBN-13: 978—0—230—20248—1
ISBN-10: 0—230—20248—9

QM LIBRARY
(MILE END)

This book is printed on paper suitable for recycling and made from fully
managed and sustained forest sources. Logging, pulping and manufacturing
processes are expected to conform to the environmental regulations of the
country of origin.

A catalogue record for this book is available from the British Library.

A catalog record for this book is available from the Library of Congress.

2008011413

Printed and bound in Great Britain by
CPI Antony Rowe, Chippenham and Eastbourne

*To Eleni and Lynda, with thanks for
all their support*

Contents

List of Tables and Figures

Tables

Figures

Acknowledgements

The editors thank the hard-working staff at UNU-WIDER, and in particular Liisa (F'Art) Roponen for her consistent editing magic, and Adam Swallow, whose publishing drive has seen this volume completed.

Chapter 5 is reproduced with the kind permission of the OECD. *Financing Global and Regional Public Goods through ODA: Analysis and Evidence from the OECD Creditor Reporting System* by Helmut Reisen, Marcelo Soto and Thomas Weithöner, was published in September 2003 by the OECD Development Centre, OECD copyright 2003.

Chapter 9 was originally published in the *Swedish Economic Policy Review* (2006, vol. 13, no. 2, pp. 205–30) and is reproduced here with their kind permission.

UNU-WIDER gratefully acknowledges the financial contributions to the research programme by the governments of Denmark (Royal Ministry of Foreign Affairs), Finland (Ministry for Foreign Affairs), Norway (Royal Ministry of Foreign Affairs), Sweden (Swedish International Development Cooperation Agency – Sida) and the United Kingdom (Department for International Development).

Notes on the Contributors

Tony Addison is Professor of Development Studies and Director of the Brooks World Poverty Institute, University of Manchester, UK, and Associate Director of the Chronic Poverty Research Centre. He was previously deputy director at UNU-WIDER. His research interests include post-conflict reconstruction, the macroeconomics of development, and chronic poverty.

Peter Burnell is a Professor of Politics in the Department of Politics and International Studies, University of Warwick, UK. His main research interests, as demonstrated in many publications, are the international dimensions of democratization, specifically democracy promotion; the political economy of foreign aid; and politics and policy in Zambia.

Anthony Clunies-Ross is a retired economist attached to the University of Strathclyde in Glasgow, UK. Recent works include *Albania's Economy in Transition and Turmoil, 1990–97* (co-authored and -edited, Ashgate 1998), 'Resources for Social Development', a paper prepared for the ILO World Commission on the Social Dimension of Globalization (2002), and *Making the World Autonomous: A Global Role for the European Union* (Dunedin Academic Press, Edinburgh 2005).

Simon Feeny is currently a postdoctoral Research Fellow at RMIT University, Melbourne, Australia. His research interests include the allocation and effectiveness of foreign aid, and the achievement of the Millennium Development Goals.

Jeremy Heimans is a Research Associate at the University of Oxford's Global Economic Governance Programme, UK. He holds degrees from the Kennedy School of Government, Harvard University and the University of Sydney. He has acted a consultant to the OECD, the United Nations and the International Labour Organization's World Commission on the Social Dimensions of Globalization, and worked for international strategy consulting firm McKinsey and Company.

Renu Kohli is currently Senior Economist, International Monetary Fund, New Delhi, India. Her major areas of academic interest are macroeconomic policy issues, particularly exchange rates and capital flows in an open economy. She has recently published *Liberalizing Capital Flows: The Indian Experience* (Oxford University Press).

John Langmore has been an Australian MP and Director of Social Policy and Development in the UN Secretariat and is now a Professorial Fellow at the University of Melbourne, Australia. He is author of *Dealing with America: The*

UN, the US and Australia, and co-author of a UN report on global summits: *The United Nations Development Agenda.*

Robert Lensink is Professor of Finance and Financial Markets at the University of Groningen, The Netherlands. His main research interests include finance and development, corporate investments, and international finance. He has published several books, and more than sixty papers in international journals, such as the *Economic Journal, World Development, Journal of Development Studies, Journal of Public Economics, Journal of Money, Credit and Banking* and the *Journal of Banking and Finance.*

George Mavrotas is the Chief Economist of the Global Development Network. Previously he worked for UNU-WIDER as a research fellow and project director, and was a member of the Economics faculties of the Universities of Oxford and Manchester, UK. He has published extensively on development economics and development finance.

Mark McGillivray is Chief Economist of the Australian Agency for International Development. He was previously Deputy Director of UNU-WIDER. Mark is also honorary Professor of Development Economics at the University of Glasgow, an External Fellow of the Centre for Economic Development and International Trade at the University of Nottingham, and an Inaugural Fellow of the Human Development and Capability Association. His research focuses on aid effectiveness and allocation and measuring achieved human well-being.

Steven Radelet is a Senior Fellow at the Center for Global Development in Washington, DC. Previously he was Deputy Assistant Secretary of the US Treasury and a Fellow at the Harvard Institute for International Development. His research focuses on finance, debt, foreign aid and growth, and he is co-author of the leading textbook *Economics of Development.*

Helmut Reisen is Councillor at the OECD Development Centre, Paris, where he organizes the OECD Global Forum on Development; he is also Professor of Economics at Basel University, Switzerland. He writes on development finance, globalization and global governance, including a regular column in *Internationale Politik.*

Marcelo Soto is a Researcher at the Instituto de Análisis Económico, Barcelona, Spain. His research focuses on economic development and applied econometrics.

Helen S. Toxopeus is currently working as an Analyst at ABN AMRO Bank. Her research interests include financial services in developing countries, remittances and development economics. She was previously affiliated with the University of Groningen, The Netherlands, the UN

Department of Economic and Social Affairs (UN-DESA) and Postal Portals (www.postalportals.nl).

Thomas Weithöner is currently posted as Counsellor for Cultural Affairs to the German Embassy in Bucharest, Romania. Besides his diplomatic career, his main field of research remains institutional economics. His latest major publication, in the *Journal of International Money and Finance* (2006), investigates how country moral hazard can be eliminated by proper IMF policies.

Howard White works in the Independent Evaluation Group of the World Bank. He has published widely on the topic of aid effectiveness.

List of Abbreviations

ADB	Asian Development Bank
AfDB	African Development Bank
AfDF	African Development Fund
AIDS	acquired immune deficiency syndrome
APEC	Asia-Pacific Economic Cooperation
ARV	anti-retro viral
AsDF	Asian Development Fund
BSE	Bombay Stock Exchange
BWIs	Bretton Woods institutions
CarDB	Caribbean Development Bank
CCMs	country co-ordination mechanisms
CDI	Commitment to Development Index
CGD	Centre for Global Development
CIS	Commonwealth of Independent States
CPIA	country policy and institutional assessment
CREDIT	Centre for Research in Economic Development and International Trade, University of Nottingham
CRS	Creditor Reporting System, OECD
CTT	currency transaction tax
DFID	Department for International Development, UK
EBRD	European Bank for Reconstruction and Development
EC	European Commission
ECOSOC	Economic and Social Council, United Nations
EFA	Education for All initiative
EGDI	Expert Group for Development Initiatives
EITI	Extractive Industries Transparency Initiative
EU	European Union
FDI	foreign direct investment
FY	fiscal year
G8	Group of Eight leading industrialized nations (Canada, France, Germany, Italy, Japan, Russia, the UK and USA)
GAVI	Global Alliance for Vaccines and Immunization
GEF	Global Environment Facility
GFATM	Global Fund to Fight AIDS, Tuberculosis and Malaria
GNI	gross national income
GPGs	global public goods
HIPCs	heavily indebted poor countries
IBRD	International Bank for Reconstruction and Development

IDA	International Development Association
IDB	Inter-American Development Bank
IFAD	International Fund for Agricultural Development
IFC	International Finance Corporation
IFF	international finance facility
IFFIm	International Finance Facility for Immunization
ILO	International Labour Organization
IMF	International Monetary Fund
IPGs	international public goods
IRnet	international remittance network
ISPs	internet service providers
LAC	Latin America and Caribbean
LDC	least developed country
M&E	monitoring and evaluation
MCA	Millennium Challenge Account
MCC	Millennium Challenge Corporation
MDBs	multilateral development banks
MDGs	Millennium Development Goals
MDRI	Multilateral Debt Relief Initiative
MGFs	Multi-actor Global Funds
NEPAD	New Partnership for Africa's Development
NGOs	non-governmental organisations
NPV	net present value
NRIs	non-resident Indians
OA	official aid
ODA	official development assistance
OECD	Organisation for Economic Co-operation and Development
OECD-DAC	Organisation for Economic Co-operation and Development – Development Co-operation Directorate
OOF	other official flows
PBA	performance-based allocation
PPP	purchasing power parity
PRGF	Poverty Reduction and Growth Facility
PRSPs	Poverty Reduction Strategy Papers
REER	real effective exchange rate
RPGs	regional public goods
SARs	severe acute respiratory syndrome
SDRs	special drawing rights
SSA	Sub-Saharan Africa
SWAps	sector-wide approaches
TFP	total factor productivity

TIIC	Transparency International Index of Corruption
TRIPS	Trade-Related Aspects of Intellectual Property
TWG	Transitional Working Group
UN-DESA	United Nations Department of Economic and Social Affairs
UNDP	United Nations Development Programme
UNFPA	United Nations Population Fund
UNHCR	United Nations High Commissioner for Refugees
UNICEF	United Nations Children's Fund
UNRWA	United Nations Relief and Works Agency for Palestine Refugees in the Near East
UNTA	United Nations Regular Programme of Technical Assistance
UNU-WIDER	United Nations University – World Institute for Development Economics Research
WDI	*World Development Indicators*
WFP	World Food Programme
WHO	World Health Organization
WOCCU	World Council of Credit Unions
WTO	World Trade Organization

1
Development Finance in the Global Economy: The Road Ahead

Tony Addison and George Mavrotas

Introduction

Today, large volumes of global savings move through an increasingly integrated global capital market in search of investment opportunities. Capital is abundant. The developing world is receiving an increasing share of these flows, to the benefit of private investment – in production, trade and infrastructure – as well as to the balance of payments (with foreign direct investment (FDI) providing the most stable form of capital flow). Running alongside this story of private capital flow is one of increased official flows, official development assistance (ODA) having rebounded since its mid-1990s slump. And the flows of private and official capital run together at times, as with the international finance facility (IFF) which aims to leverage and front-load ODA by borrowing from international capital markets. The IFF, together with the French airline tax and proposals for global environmental taxes, the currency transaction tax (CTT) and the Global Premium Bond, constitute the new class of innovative financing mechanisms. Last, but certainly not least, the new philanthropy (increasingly in partnership with development agencies) is adding considerably to already well-established and growing flows from the charitable sector – and this source of capital has an especially close relationship with the goal of reducing poverty.

After many years of stagnation in the availability of finance for the developing world, the *aggregate* picture is brighter. But caution is also necessary. FDI is concentrated on a narrow range of countries (with China dominating), and while FDI into the smaller economies of Sub-Saharan Africa (SSA) is rising, it remains confined mainly to its traditional destination – the mining sector (which benefits growth but leaves economies undiversified). Private portfolio flows into equities and bonds are still concentrated on a narrow range of emerging markets, and while such flows into the so-called 'frontier markets' have risen in recent years – as investors' appetite for risk has increased – this is from a small base, especially in SSA. The good news on ODA is tempered by the fact that a significant part of the recent growth consists of debt relief.

Reducing the debt overhang of the heavily indebted poor countries (HIPCs) has been important to restoring their attractiveness to investors (Nigeria's international credit rating is now the same as Ukraine's) but many observers (including many poor countries) question whether debt relief represents a true net addition to their resources (and part of the jump in aid consists of cancelling the bad loans given to Saddam Hussein's Iraq). OECD-DAC warns that ODA could dip over the next few years, and this will imperil achievement of the Millennium Development Goals (MDGs) by 2015. And the effectiveness of aid is continually contested, most forcibly and recently by Bill Easterly (2006). Even among those favourably disposed to aid there are widely different views over the ability of poor countries to absorb and make good use of substantially larger flows (Mavrotas 2002; Killick 2005; Riddell 2007).

In summary, there is much to be positive about (especially when compared to the dismal decades of the 1980s and 1990s) but we are far from claiming victory in the battle to obtain more and better finance for the developing world, especially for the smaller and more vulnerable economies. There are ideas aplenty, and intellectual creativity in this area is certainly not confined to economists. The new international financial architecture raises many political and foreign-policy issues: finding the finance to tackle global environmental and health problems is recognized increasingly as being in everyone's interest; foreign aid is now viewed as an important part of the post-9/11 international security framework; and the balance of power in setting the international finance agenda is shifting, not only within the group of rich countries (as between the United States, Europe and Japan) but also between rich and poor countries, as China and India become increasingly important global actors. Political scientists and international relations specialists are now busy debating the implications of these trends both for the international financial architecture and for the global economy more widely.

 This book aims to provide an overview and assessment of where we stand in the debate, and where we need to go from here in constructing a system of international finance that serves the needs of poor countries and especially of poor people. It contains contributions by specialists in economics, international relations, and political science; and a number of the authors have been at the centre of the international policy debate. The book is part of a stream of UNU-WIDER work in this area since 2000, including the study by Griffith-Jones *et al.* (2001) on short-term capital flows; the 2001 conference on debt relief (Addison *et al.* 2004); the 2003 conference 'Sharing Global Prosperity'; the study led by Sir Anthony Atkinson on new sources of development finance undertaken for the UN General Assembly (Atkinson 2004); and the 2006 conference on aid policy. This stream of research activity was stimulated by the lead-up to the 2002 UN Financing for Development summit held in Monterrey (Mexico) and its aftermath, the associated (and intense) activity around the MDGs, and the desire to continue UNU-WIDER's long-standing work on the global economy and the developing world that has, since the 1980s, sought to understand the implications of rapid economic change (Calvo *et al.* 1989; Wyplosz 2001; Nayyar 2002).

This chapter provides an introduction to the main issues raised by the volume. The next two sections provide a short overview of development financing in order to place the individual chapters in an overall context, first discussing the changing picture for private financial flows and then official development finance as well as the new class of (innovative) sources of development finance. The penultimate section introduces the chapters in this collection, summarizing the main points of each, linking them together and to the earlier contextual discussion. In the concluding section we note that, while the development finance picture is now brighter than it was just a few years ago, much more action is necessary if this is not to be yet another false dawn.

Private development financing

Demographics shape global capital flows through the global savings rate and, since the population shares of the working young and the retired old vary across countries, the pattern of cross-border capital flows. Financing the pension and health costs of ageing societies, notably Europe and Japan but also increasingly China, is having powerful effects on international capital markets. For Northern-based pension funds this has led to a somewhat desperate search for yield as returns on the North's sovereign debt (which has the least risk of default) have fallen since the early 1990s, and particularly since the start of the 2000s, because of a strong growth in demand (amplified by a shift from equities to bonds by investors following the 1999–2001 sell-off in equity markets). A scenario is emerging in which ageing societies increasingly invest in the equity and bond markets of youthful developing countries, a potentially 'win–win' outcome for both; Northern investors get higher returns and the South gets more (and cheaper) capital. If this works well, it will create bigger and more liquid Southern markets for sovereign debt, equities, corporate debt and, eventually, municipal debt and property as asset classes for Northern (and Southern) investors. India's capital markets are already benefiting from this effect, although it is not without its costs (the speculation in these markets will no doubt lead to some booms and busts along the way). Optimists speak of a new era in which the need for concessional loans and grants from development agencies will decline rapidly, with ODA possibly becoming extinct (much to the satisfaction of those who question aid's effectiveness).

This mutually beneficial scenario is not, however, a done deal, and some very fundamental problems remain that are more difficult to overcome than the optimists allow. Perhaps the most important of all is that the recipients of increased private capital flows need effectively to turn these into investments that generate higher economic growth, and therefore deliver the higher returns global investors expect. Otherwise, they will go elsewhere in their search for yield. Global investors must also be sufficiently risk-taking to allocate a large enough share of their portfolio to the relevant asset categories to benefit significantly from any superior returns; for the moment they are willing to take on such increased risk, for reasons we discuss shortly (but this is far from being a given and the decision is much affected by the easing of global monetary policy since the start of the 2000s). Southern recipients must also improve corporate governance substantially to protect shareholder rights (otherwise equity investment will not be sustained), build better sovereign-debt management (a tough challenge for the poorer countries), and improve their macroeconomic management to cope with the real-economy effects of the capital inflows (thereby ensuring that they facilitate rather than undermine economic development). We can expect more use of derivative instruments by global investors to hedge currency and political risks; and innovation to reduce the costs of such hedging could do much to stimulate flows to the lesser-known and riskier countries.

But not all risks can be hedged (or are indeed observable, since many are asymmetric – as between lender and borrower). The political risks of investing in poor countries remain high (giving rise to insecure property rights) and to a degree unpredictable – including those associated with adverse global climate changes. So the world's capital markets are unlikely ever to achieve textbook perfection in which every investment need of poor countries is matched by willing global investors. Consequently there will remain considerable space for official flows. And the need for ODA could actually rise much further (even beyond that projected to meet MDG requirements) as the effects of global warming take their toll on the South (in particular, a greater variance of rainfall in Africa's agricultural margins, and increased flooding in the many densely populated and low-lying lands of Asia).

Alongside financial globalization, and interacting with it, are geopolitical changes of immense importance to everyone. China is in an especially interesting position. China is both a recipient of portfolio flows (its sovereign bond issues are regularly over-subscribed by Northern pension funds) as well as an increasing source, since it must cope with its own rapidly ageing population, including the effect on the ratio of workers-to-pensioners of the 'one-child' policy adopted in Maoist times (which in part explains China's very high personal savings rate). China is now attempting to invest its massive reserves through a specially created investment authority (initiated in 2007), and the country will no doubt become a big investor in the equity markets of the rest of the developing world. This will accentuate the decline in yields now occurring on emerging market investments, requiring all investors (including those in the North) to devote more of their portfolio to these markets (that is, to take on more risk) if they are to meet their overall targets for asset growth to match their liabilities. The growth in the latter greatly exceeds the projections made just a decade ago in the mid-1990s because the rate of improvement in life expectancy is rising every year (not just in the North but also in China), imposing on pension funds a 'longevity risk' (pension payments will go on much longer); a typical large or medium-sized company in the UK has a pension scheme with liabilities that are a quarter of its market capitalization.[1]

Not far behind China is India (a country that one of the chapters in this volume assesses in detail; see further discussion below). Both China and India now borrow very little (as a share of their total financing) from the World Bank, and nothing at all from the IMF (making India a net creditor of the Fund). Brazil has also stepped back from borrowing from the Bretton Woods institutions (BWIs). The fact that the world's three largest emerging economies have moved in this direction has further reduced the IMF's role (one borrower, Turkey, now accounts for much of the IMF's outstanding lending). This is not to say that the BWIs are unnecessary: the World Bank's financing of health and social protection in India provides much-needed sector support, for example. But it is to say that we have shifted rapidly from the world of just twenty years ago (or indeed ten, if we recall the Asian financial crisis) when the BWIs called the shots.

The present strength of the sovereign debt market is the result of abundant global liquidity (with real interest rates at historically very low levels in recent years). Consequently there is a danger that as the interest-rate cycle turns, and liquidity contracts, emerging markets will turn down as they did in the past (Addison 2007). The US Federal Reserve, the Bank of England, and the European Central Bank have all begun to tighten over 2006–7. Yet, despite some strains (a wobble in Ecuador's sovereign debt market and a sharp sell-off in Chinese equities in 2007) there is not as yet any sign of major trouble, and the compression in spreads of emerging market over developed country debt that has marked recent years is continuing. In some cases the fundamentals in emerging markets have improved sufficiently to attract further inflows even as US monetary policy tightens with, perhaps, the search for yield by investors from ageing societies putting some kind of floor under the market. Still, we should not be too sanguine: financial crises are twice as prevalent today as they were in that other era (pre-1914) of financial globalization (Eichengreen and Bordo 2001).

The financial services industry is, not surprisingly, in a golden era; it will constitute 10 per cent of global GDP by 2020 and the emerging economies are its fastest-growing markets (Goldman Sachs 2003). Financial services are also showing modest but respectable growth in the poorer countries, with more direct investment by foreign banks in joint ventures with local partners (thereby helping to recapitalize banking systems) propelled in part by an expanding middle-class demanding more insurance, banking and housing finance (with, in some countries, increased efforts to provide formal financial products to poor people as well; Mexico has several interesting initiatives). This offers more scope for connecting domestic and international capital markets to the benefit of poorer countries in securing a larger share of global portfolio flows (and perhaps to poor people, but this will not be accomplished without much institutional innovation and a large measure of private or public subsidy, at least initially). It also requires heavy investment in financial regulation to ensure that the increasing sophistication of financial sectors in poor countries does not undermine their macroeconomic stability when new financial institutions engage in imprudent borrowing and lending (see Brownbridge and Kirkpatrick 1999; Stiglitz 1999; Guha-Khasnobis and Mavrotas 2008; Mavrotas 2008).

The poorer and smaller countries are becoming better known to international investors since declining yields on emerging market debt – the consequence of large inflows in recent years and a reduction in the supply of such debt – have encouraged investors into 'frontier markets' (Addison 2007). This is paralleled by increased investment in equities in these countries as well. Traditionally, these markets were bypassed in favour of the bigger, better-known and deeper financial markets of countries such as Brazil, China, India and South Africa. Information asymmetries and high transactions costs have made it difficult for small, poor countries to tap into global capital markets, but this is starting to change. The large write-offs of HIPC debt have helped Ghana and Nigeria to raise their sovereign credit ratings (an effect we discuss further below). At the time of writing, twenty SSA countries have a sovereign credit rating (compared to only one in 1997), and many can now borrow commercially at interest rates less than half those of the past. And they have access to the international capital market on a scale unimaginable only a few years ago.

Their underdeveloped capital markets do, however, lack liquidity, and large flows can potentially destabilize poor economies (causing large changes in exchange rates that could undermine growth, for example); so, again, careful macroeconomic management – including, at times, the judicious use of capital controls – is necessary (Stiglitz *et al.* 2006). This must temper recent optimism, and there are dangers ahead that require careful navigation, not least re-running 'that '70s show' in which countries borrowed recklessly on the back of the 1970s commodity boom – only to see themselves saddled subsequently with enormous foreign debts (Collier and Gunning 1999). These had to be serviced on the back of meagre export earnings when commodity prices collapsed again in the recession of the 1980s.

So it is imperative that, this time round, the borrowed funds are used to fund infrastructure to diversify economies away from their traditional dependence on commodity exports. Getting the right infrastructure in place is no easy task, and one priority must be transport and communications infrastructure that facilitates more intra-Africa trade; the transport costs that countries face in trading with each other remain absurdly high, a problem that has been emphasized repeatedly for decades, but one for which there has been too little finance available.

At least today's financial markets offer more tools for hedging commodity price and exchange rate risks, and governments would be well-advised to use these, as the bonanza of cheap world capital cannot last for ever. At some point before 2012 global inflation will rise (perhaps as a result of China's seemingly insatiable demand for steel, copper and oil), requiring the major central banks to tighten interest rates: easy credit will then come to an end, risk premiums will jump (including those on emerging market debt), and countries that have not used their borrowing productively will be exposed to the chill winds of expensive credit again.

It is therefore worrying that, despite all the chatter about a 'new international financial architecture' over the last few years, we are no closer to its realization. There is still no institutional mechanism to manage private debt default, since the IMF's proposal for a sovereign debt restructuring mechanism fell by the wayside in 2003. And there are some very good ideas – such as GDP-indexed bonds and linking debt-service to commodity prices – that remain on the drawing board (Griffith-Jones and Sharma 2006). It is in the good times, when credit is easy and commodity prices are high, that we should be building a financial architecture that is robust for the bad times that inevitably arise.

Official development assistance

At the 2005 G8 summit in Gleneagles (Scotland) the UK extracted pledges from heads of state to add US$50 billion to annual aid flows up to 2010, with at least half the increase going to SSA. Moreover, the traditional mechanisms of ODA are now starting to connect to the debate around 'new' or 'innovative' sources of finance (discussed in the next section) specifically through the UK's IFF proposal promoted by HM Treasury (with the heavyweight political backing of Gordon Brown, UK Chancellor of the Exchequer at the time). The IFF will leverage additional money from the international capital markets (through a securitization process) to achieve a flow of US$50 billion from 2010 to the MDG target date of 2015 (Mavrotas 2004; Moore and Hulme 2004). Given the novel nature of its borrowing, one major issue has been how well the IFF fits into the fiscal frameworks of donor countries themselves; Eurostat has ruled that IFF borrowing need not be included in the government borrowing of EU member states (an important decision, since the latter is limited by the EU's stability and growth pact) but the IFF does not appear to be compatible with the budgetary procedures of Canada and the United States. An International Finance Facility for Immunization (IFFIm) is now in place and, aside from its inherent desirability, it also constitutes a pilot for an eventual IFF.

Two years on from Gleneagles, however, the promises were only half-delivered. ODA in fact fell by 1.8 per cent in real terms in 2005–6 (excluding debt relief to Iraq and Nigeria, which boosted the 2006 total: including this debt relief yields a fall of 5.1 per cent in real terms over 2005–6). Far from rising to meet the MDG goals, aid to SSA from OECD-DAC donors was constant in 2006, once debt relief to Nigeria is excluded out (OECD-DAC 2007). The UK, Spain and Sweden have increased their aid sharply, with the UK moving up to become the world's second-largest bilateral donor. But aid from many European countries is stagnant or has fallen (notably from Finland and Italy), while US and Japanese aid has also fallen. It seems that the predictions made during Gleneagles that donors were fudging their commitments have proved all too true, and the donor community has come in for some sharp criticism. Richard Manning, chair of OECD-DAC, made it clear that the problem is one of supply rather than demand: 'the promises will not be credible unless we begin to see substantial rises in 2007 and 2008. The shortfall reflected a lack of will in the rich nations, rather than Africa's inability to absorb more aid'.[2] Aid absorption itself remains a thorny issue, with wide differences of view (Killick 2005; Gupta *et al.* 2005; Easterly 2006; Guillaumont and Guillaumont-Jeanneney 2006; Heller *et al.* 2006; Bourguignon and Sundberg 2007; Riddell 2007). But one key dimension is the quality of fiscal management and the ability of countries to translate additional resources into effective pro-development (and pro-poor) infrastructure and services; this is at the core of questions over whether aid can be scaled up by shifting from traditional project aid to budgetary support (McGillivray and Morrissey 2004; Mavrotas 2005; Koeberk *et al.* 2007).

Meanwhile, as many of Africa's traditional Western donors stall, new players have come into the arena, buoyed up by their large-scale accumulation of foreign-exchange reserves. Once itself a large net recipient of aid, China is becoming a major aid donor in Central Asia, the poorer countries of South-East Asia and especially in Africa; at its 2006 Africa summit (attended by forty-eight African leaders) China pledged US$5.5 billion in aid to the region, and could be Africa's largest bilateral donor by 2010. Not surprisingly, China's new prominence as a donor is receiving mixed reviews. Optimists look to the large-scale infrastructure projects that China's aid is capable of funding, especially in easing the transportation of Africa's commodity exports which are now in high demand (a return to China's donor role in the 1970s when, in a very different political context, it funded the Tanzam railway linking Zambia to Dar es Salaam's port). China's funding of African infrastructure rose from US$700 million in 2003 to US$2–3 billion per year over 2005–6 (Naím 2007: 96). Pessimists go so far as to claim that China's aid represents a threat to Africa's healthy sustainable development. China could use its enormous reserves to contribute to the next replenishment of the International Development Association (it gave nothing to the last IDA replenishment in 2005) thereby dispelling some of the accusations that it is following the well-trodden path of Western donors in using its aid largely for commercial and diplomatic gain. As Richard Manning emphasizes, what is needed is a constructive dialogue between DAC and China, and other 'emerging' donors, to encourage their take-up of DAC procedures and norms (Manning 2006). As a permanent member of the UN Security Council, China has a duty to set an example in ensuring that *all* aid is used for development purposes.

Debt relief constitutes a significant part of the recent ODA increase following the HIPC Initiative (later 'Enhanced') and then the Multilateral Debt Relief Initiative (MDRI) arising out of the Gleneagles decision to cut debt further. Whether much of this debt would ever have been repaid, and therefore whether it actually represents a true addition to ODA, remains a contested point (for a critique, see Eurodad 2006). Nigeria has also cut its commercial debt. In March 2007, Nigeria redeemed most of the debt owed to its commercial creditors (the London Club) in a deal that Nenadi Usman, the finance minister, said would 'free Nigeria from its historic debt overhang' (which in the late 1990s amounted to US$35 billion, equivalent to 60 per cent of GDP).[3] The last US$500 million has been bought back, and there are high hopes that Nigeria's sovereign bonds can now achieve an investment-grade rating. Although a politically unpopular decision at home (much of the debt was incurred by Nigeria's feckless military rulers with little thought to the future), recent debt buy-backs will lower the country's risk premium and make it easier to finance the budget – including much needed spending on basic health services, primary education, and pro-poor infrastructure (all of which are needed to haul Nigeria out of deep poverty).

Similarly, at the time of writing, Ghana is expected to raise up to US$750 million in 2007 from the international capital market, and overall the prospects for the region's poorer borrowers have improved significantly after completion of relief under the Enhanced HIPC Initiative and the MDRI. While eight African countries continue to languish at pre-decision point status under the HIPC Initiative (Central African Republic and Sudan, for example) debt relief is unlikely to do much to resolve their urgent political problems (the genocide in Sudan's Darfur region, in particular).

Having only just eliminated their HIPC debt (largely the legacy of past concessional aid loans to fund structural adjustment), why are countries in a hurry to borrow commercially? One reason is that aid is an uncertain way of funding the public budget, and the time since Gleneagles has not inspired confidence that aid is anything but a fickle friend.[4] And so African countries are turning to commercial borrowing, taking advantage of a world that is, at least for the moment, abundant in capital looking for a return. This provides an excellent opportunity to finance Africa's enormous investment backlog not only in 'hard' infrastructure but also in human capital. With the midpoint of the MDGs now upon us (as at June 2007) Africa is far behind on the education and health-care investments it needs to get close to the 2015 targets, and borrowing to achieve these targets is all too necessary, given the many broken promises of the aid 'community'.

New sources of development finance

What are now called 'new' or 'innovative' sources of development finance have attracted increasing attention since the start of the 2000s, following initial work done around the time of the 2002 UN Financing for Development Summit in Monterrey (Clunies-Ross 2004) and in part stimulated by frustration at the fall in ODA in the 1990s and the need to finance the MDGs as set out at the 2000 UN Millennium Summit. At the start of the decade, a panel chaired by President Ernesto Zedillo of Mexico calculated that roughly US$50 billion was necessary in addition to existing annual ODA flows to achieve the international development goals (subsequently the MDGs) (UN 2001). Interest in these new sources of development finance has also grown in response to the pressing need for more global public goods, especially in peacekeeping (reflecting the intense pressure on the peacekeeping resources of the UN and regional bodies such as the African Union), health (in the light of new pandemics such as SARS and avian influenza as well as the continuing HIV/AIDS crisis) and global climate change – concern for the latter accelerating in 2005–6 especially (on global public goods, see Kaul *et al.* 2003). In 2000, the UN General Assembly called for a rigorous follow-up study to the Zedillo report, and this was undertaken by UNU-WIDER in association with the UN Department of Economic and Social Affairs, and led by Sir Anthony Atkinson of Oxford University (Atkinson 2004). A study by the French government (Landau 2004) considered additional proposals, including a tax on airline fuel that has become a cornerstone of French action in innovative finance. Innovative finance has also become an issue for political co-operation between Europe and the larger emerging economies; thus in September 2004, the Governments of Brazil, Chile, France and Spain convened a heads of state meeting at the UN on an 'Action Against Hunger and Poverty Initiative'.

One 'old-new' source – and still in many ways the best known – is the currency transactions tax (CTT), originally known as the 'Tobin tax' after the economist James Tobin (who argued for the tax as a way to stabilize the extreme fluctuations in exchange rates that followed the breakdown of the Bretton Woods system in the 1970s). Tobin himself rejected the use of the tax in its modern financing-for-development guise, but it has proved to be a remarkably resilient idea within global civil society (see, for example, Pätomaki and Sehm-Pätomaki 1999) despite intense criticism from many economists. The CTT would be applied to foreign exchange transactions including the spot, forward and future markets as well as swaps and other derivatives. Countries that host major centres of international finance (notably New York, London and Frankfurt) do not favour the CTT, and even France has been lukewarm.

How much the CTT and other such sources of finance could raise remains an open question, depending as it does on the tax rates used, compliance, and the willingness (or otherwise) of national authorities to sign on. The

UNU-WIDER study assessed the relative merits of global environmental taxes (specifically, a carbon-use tax) and the CTT, as well as frameworks for international taxation more generally, and found that comparatively low tax rates could mobilize large revenues (Atkinson 2004). The CTT could generate US$15–28 billion per year (Nissanke 2004), and taxing hydrocarbon fuels could generate another US$50 billion (Sandmo 2004). Note that, to make an effective dent in global carbon emissions, the tax rates would have to be significantly higher than those used in the UNU-WIDER calculations, and while such taxes do have 'double dividends' – reducing adverse global climate change in the case of carbon taxes as well as raising revenue – they remain controversial, as the recent 'Stern Report' points out (Stern 2006).

The UNU-WIDER assessment informed the report of the French government (Landau 2004) as well as the 2004 'Action Against Hunger and Poverty Initiative' of the governments of Brazil, Chile, France and Spain. UNU-WIDER's findings were well received by the developing-country and European members of the UN General Assembly (although the developing countries did affirm that innovative sources of finance need to be *additional* to ODA) but the United States remains opposed to global taxes, arguing that they infringe national sovereignty (Addison *et al.* 2005a, 2005b). The present US administration's position is in part bound up with its reluctance to be swayed by scientific evidence on global warming, and therefore its extreme reluctance to sign up to any comprehensive action, be it the Kyoto protocol or global environmental taxes. But this reluctance is steadily being chipped away, not least by the state government of California, which is now taking global climate change very seriously. More fundamentally, global taxes raise issues of who will run the necessary tax authority; the UN would seem to offer the best home, but if the UN took on this role it would represent a large shift of power from its constituent (nation-state) members. Innovative finance in synergy with action on global climate change could become an avenue for recasting the UN's global role, although the practical and political issues that must be overcome remain formidable, but it is hoped not insurmountable.

Aside from global taxes, the remaining ideas in the innovative finance area are a mixed bag. The UK's IFF (a blend of ODA leveraged by private capital markets), which we have already discussed; the creation of Special Drawing Rights (SDRs) for development purposes (donor countries making their SDR allocation available for poorer countries) a long-standing idea but one that has been given a recent boost; innovations using IT to scale up charitable donations for development, especially for micro-enterprises; the Finnish proposal for a global lottery; and a global premium (prize) bond for poverty reduction. Others have looked to remittances, which now amount to US$80 billion per annum (matching annual aid flows), and while this is a very old flow there are new proposals to reduce transaction costs for poorer households and communities by creating new financial services for them to bypass the reliance on traditional (but high-cost) money-transfer services (Solimano 2004). One of the chapters in this volume focuses on the development impact of remittances.

One important side-effect of the boom in information technology businesses and global financial services is the creation of new wealth, a portion of which is going into global philanthropy, with the Bill and Melinda Gates Foundation and the Google Foundation being the largest of the new players. Innovation in service delivery is central to these new philanthropic models, as is public and private partnership. A good example is the current effort to supply cheap Coartem (a highly effective malaria drug) to Africa. Novartis, which makes Coartem, has waived the patent restriction and supplies it at cost price to public health authorities in Africa, the Global Fund to Fight AIDS, Tuberculosis and Malaria (GFATM), and other donors. The Gates Foundation is working with GFATM and the World Bank to cut the cost further by subsidizing the supply chain by some US$300 million per year. This, together with Novartis's production subsidy, constitutes a major external resource transfer straight into an area of key priority, since at least a million Africans die of malaria every year (many of them under five years old).

Development philanthropy by individuals and corporations can be increased by tax incentives and matching private donations with public funds: the UK's Treasury offers a range of tax incentives for corporate and private giving, including a Payroll Giving scheme, for example (HM Treasury 2003; Micklewright and Wright 2004). Being voluntary, private and corporate philanthropy is one area where the present US administration is supportive, and the United States has a long and fine philanthropic tradition. Microfinance is now increasingly internationalized through the work of NGOs such as the Microloan Foundation and Five Talents, building on the much-deserved success of the Grameen Bank. The market for ethical financial products is also growing, as more individuals and companies seek to incorporate ethical investments into their portfolios. Ideas for hybrid products – those that appeal to both self-interest and altruism – are also around. Addison and Chowdhury (2004) assess the prospects for a global development lottery that could perhaps mobilize US$6 billion per annum by taking a portion of the world gambling market (a US$1 trillion per year business). While some might (reasonably) question the ethics of financing development in this way, the urgency of meeting the MDGs (and the shortfall in ODA) may overcome such qualms. One alternative, is a global premium (prize) bond, which has the characteristics of a lottery but where investors do not lose their stake, making it an attractive ethical investment product in a way that a pure lottery is not (Addison and Chowdhury 2004). In summary, global philanthropy (both large and small) – often exploiting the enormous leverage available from global financial markets – could take the centre stage of development finance into the 2010s.

The worlds of finance and environmental change also intersect increasingly; 2007 saw the first debt-for-carbon swap when the United States agreed to exchange US$12.6 million of Costa Rica's US$93 million debt for carbon certificates (covering some 10 per cent of the country's debt to the US). This looks promising for a future with more capital flows to poor countries as rich countries seek to offset their carbon footprints by investing in sustainable forestry and alternative energy. Africa could benefit from this, given its great tropical forests with their rich biodiversity – a global public good that needs preserving for the benefit of all humanity.

In summary, the various proposals in the innovative finance area involve varying combinations of private and public action: global philanthropy requires no government approval as such (although tax concessions can stimulate it further) and the IFF's implementation may be undertaken unilaterally or by a small subset of countries. A lottery for development purposes could be introduced by individual countries without co-ordination, as could a global premium bond. Creating SDRs for development purposes requires ratification by 100 IMF members (85 per cent of the voting power of the Fund), and global taxes would require a complete new institutional structure; hence these are the measures least likely to make progress in the current international political environment. There is a great deal of exciting talk about innovative sources of development finance, but it may just remain just that: talk. With the exception of the IFFIm and the French airline fuel tax, no further action has been taken. A cynic would say that some of the rich world's politicians advance bold new schemes in development finance when they are most keen to distract attention away from their lack of political success in the mundane (but vital) task of raising ODA.

Overview of this volume

This book addresses many of the most important issues in development finance. The discussion ranges from economics to politics to political economy, reflecting as it does the interaction of economic and political considerations in driving financial flows, both private and public, to developing countries. In this section we summarize briefly the main issues and approaches taken by each chapter.

Despite the promise of increased private capital flow, aid remains a major source of development finance for the poorest countries. But in framing aid policy it is crucial to understand the history of aid – that is, how we got to where we are today. Chapter 2, by Peter Burnell, provides the reader with a fascinating journey into the history of aid since the end of the Cold War, and its revival in recent years. The author explains the reasons why aid was down but definitely not out in the early 1990s following the collapse of the Soviet Union, and the changing perceptions about the importance of aid as an instrument of *realpolitik*.

The chapter then details the reasons why aid has staged something of a recovery in recent years, by focusing on two crucial factors and, at the same time, two potentially competing 'drivers', namely globalization and poverty, and security concerns following the events of 11 September 2001. Burnell argues that reports circulating in the 1990s claiming that foreign aid was in terminal crisis, were premature, and that while there is still a strong recognition that some countries continue to need aid because they are poor, traditional political factors play a large part in translating need into *effective* demand. Therefore, according to Burnell, the size and shape of the market for aid are political constructs. Furthermore, questions about whether economic progress, even if it does reduce poverty, will solve the kind of problems related to globalization and the post-9/11 era – and *how* aid might best contribute – continue to be controversial in development studies and among aid practitioners. This takes Burnell into the discussion of an important category of foreign aid that emerges from the new environment for aid – namely, democracy assistance or political development aid. The chapter concludes by arguing that aid for democratization considered in the 1990s to be an instrument for addressing indirectly socioeconomic weakness and improving development aid's effectiveness – making it a positive feature in a bleak decade – is increasingly seen as problematic. The author concludes by arguing that, for now, aid's resurgence should target pro-poor development rather than democratic reform, although the likelihood is that old-fashioned determinants of *realpolitik* will continue to get in the way, so that 'notwithstanding all the new spirit informing an increase of support for aid to both development and democracy, there could still follow a very familiar hangover'.

One of the central debates in the area of development aid is related to the developmental role of multilateral aid as compared to the bilateral assistance. Mark McGillivray, Simon Feeny and Howard White argue in Chapter 3 that from a development perspective, bilateral aid was often seen as bad (or just plain ugly) during the years of the Cold War. Multilateral aid, on the other hand, had a better reputation in the sense that it went to countries in greatest need, was generally of better quality and was more orientated towards development. Since the end of the Cold War, bilateral aid has recovered some of its reputation and is perceived to have become more developmental. But are these common perceptions in fact correct? The chapter provides a quantitative assessment of whether multilateral aid is more developmental than bilateral aid, and whether bilateral aid has become more developmental, relative to multilateral aid, since 1990. The authors employ a range of indicators of the development orientation of the two types of aid, including the degree of support for low-income countries, the division between grants and loans, the extent of concentration and indices of donor performance with respect to inter-country allocation. They find that, contrary to common wisdom, it is difficult to conclude that multilateral aid is more developmental than bilateral aid, or that the relative degrees of orientation to development of these broad categories of aid have changed appreciably since the early 1990s.

There are now many ideas on the table of ways to raise additional resources from new ('innovative') sources of development finance. But getting these ideas implemented is in many ways a much tougher process than thinking them up, and our earlier discussion indicated that each measure requires very different levels of political support and co-ordination among countries; some can be introduced by small coalitions of countries (or indeed unilaterally) while others need considerable international unanimity. In Chapter 4, Anthony Clunies-Ross and John Langmore discuss strategies to move forward, in particular the importance of developing-country governments building effective alliances with each other, and with campaigning NGOs and sympathetic research organizations, to press the case for innovative finance. They emphasize that, for such alliances to work, they must be sufficiently institutionalized (preferably with a high-level secretariat) to negotiate forcefully with the rich world regarding development finance, and to forge common ground with groups in the rich world over areas of common global concern. They note a considerable degree of consensus within the European Union and between this and the larger developing-country governments. While the process is subject to frequent stalling, the chapter concludes that measures seen as visionary at the time of the Monterrey summit are now debated in terms of possibilities for their practical implementation. At least some progress has therefore been made.

One factor that is changing the global political landscape is rising international concern over adverse global climate changes (Stern 2006). The need to increase spending on goods with wide social effects that transcend national boundaries has therefore become more urgent since the start of the millennium. Yet there is also a continuing need for aid to fund traditional development projects and programmes, and for this aid to rise to meet the MDGs (Sachs 2005). But how much needs to be allocated to funding 'new' global public goods and how much for 'traditional' ODA? Chapter 5 by Helmut Reisen, Marcelo Soto and Thomas Weithöner organizes its analysis around three classes of public goods based on a taxonomy from the theory of public finance. An international public good (IPG) is a public good that provides benefits that cross the national borders of the producing country; a regional public good (RPG) is an international public good that displays spillover benefits to countries in the neighbourhood of the producing country; and a global public good (GPG) is an international public good that benefits consumers across the world (although not all necessarily to the same extent). Using data from the OECD Creditor Reporting System (CRS) the chapter then attributes ODA to the provision of global public goods, regional public goods and traditional aid over the period 1997–2001, and models donors' interest in the provision of international public goods. The authors find a strong empirical relationship between the provision of international public goods, and donors' income and budget balances. They also discuss and assess empirically possible crowding-out between international public goods and ODA, concluding that an increase in spending on such goods is unlikely to reduce the flow of aid to the poorest countries.

If traditional forms of development finance are not enough, or it takes time to increase them substantially to meet the MDGs, then other sources of finance must be found; this is the focus of Chapter 6, by Jeremy Heimans. These have emerged as important and increasingly popular new mechanisms for financing development and other global priorities. Multi-actor Global Funds (MGFs), such as GFATM, are distinctive because they are administered and financed by multi-actor coalitions of governments, international organizations, the private sector and civil society. They also operate independently of any single institution and are tied to a particular issue or policy area. The author argues that, while MGFs have become increasingly popular in recent years, little is known about the way they operate, whether they are desirable as instruments for financing major international initiatives, and what implications they might have more broadly for global governance. The chapter assesses the desirability of MGFs as instruments for international financial mobilization, resource allocation, and as a form of experimentation in global governance. Heimans argues that MGFs hold considerable promise as focal points for generating additional public and private resources to address urgent global problems and to finance global public goods. They may be more operationally nimble than traditional mechanisms and capture some of the benefits of collaboration among different actors. However, he concludes that MGFs may also result in a less coherent response to global problems, duplicate existing structures, and may be only weakly accountable democratically.

Although official capital flows such as ODA remain the dominant type of development finance for many low-income countries, private capital flow in all its forms is becoming more important, especially for the fast growers in transition from low-income to middle-income status. Managing the macroeconomic effects of private capital flows is challenging, as we discussed earlier. In Chapter 7, Renu Kohli assesses India's sharp swing in external financing from ODA to private capital following the 1990 crisis and the subsequent economic liberalization. The chapter demonstrates that external resources have increased, and that the greater role of private capital flows has required more macroeconomic discipline to deal with the increased vulnerability of the economy to negative capital account shocks, volatility and other risks associated with private capital flows. Kohli's analysis also reveals that, in India's case, private capital flows are, in contrast to official flows, associated with a real exchange rate appreciation, expansion in the domestic money supply, and stock market growth, liquidity and volatility. Integrated financial markets also expose the economy to correlated risks (with different types of private flows having varying degrees of volatility and predictability) requiring the development of sound and efficient domestic financial institutions with the capacity to intermediate private flows effectively. The author concludes that this transition points to the importance of developing 'self-protection' policies to mitigate the risks while at the same time extracting the static and dynamic gains that private capital flows can bring (the externalities arising from FDI, for example).

Issues related to the selectivity of foreign aid have attracted a lot of attention from researchers and policy-makers alike (see McGillivray 2003 for a comprehensive discussion). The World Bank study *Assessing Aid* (World Bank 1998) and the work of Burnside and Dollar (2000) and Collier and Dollar (2002) have been very influential in policy circles in recent years, and many donors have adopted the 'country selectivity' approach emanating from this work. Although the World Bank study, and in particular the aid–policies–growth empirics on which it is based, has received its fair share of criticism (see, for example, Guillaumont and Chauvet 2001; Hansen and Tarp 2001; Easterly *et al.* 2004; Antipin and Mavrotas 2006) many donors have none the less embraced the country selectivity argument in their aid policies.

A recent example is the Millennium Challenge Account (MCA) introduced in 2004 by the US administration of President Bush in 2004, and evaluated by Steve Radelet in Chapter 8. The MCA is designed to provide substantial new funding to a select group of low-income countries that, in the administration's view are 'ruling justly, investing in their people, and encouraging economic freedom'. Radelet argues that, while the MCA is a promising new programme, much work needs to be done to turn that promise into reality – and it is quite possible that the programme will never reach its potential. The chapter discusses the potential impact of the Millennium Challenge Corporation (MCC) that runs the MCA on USAID and the relationship between the two aid organizations in the United States. Radelet argues that there exist a number of important issues needing to be clearly addressed in this case and if not resolved carefully through planning and coordination, the difficulties in operating two foreign assistance programmes from two very different parts of the US government could significantly undermine both the MCA and USAID programmes. And this echoes similar concerns expressed by others on the MCC–USAID *modus operandi* with calls to merge the two aid agencies to improve the performance of US development aid.[5] Radelet stresses that the MCA's potential for success depends very much on its willingness to co-operate with recipient governments and other donors in reducing administrative burdens on countries. If the United States stridently insists on using its own unique proposal format and reporting systems, the MCA will set back recent efforts to improve co-ordination. If, however, there is a serious effort to establish rigorous procedural norms that a majority of donors can accept, the MCA will be a step in the right direction of improving donor harmonization and overall aid performance.

The legacy of the concessional lending that supported structural adjustment in the 1980s and the early 1990s was the HIPC debt problem that bedevilled the issue of financing for poor countries in the late 1990s; much energy was wasted denying the scale of the problem, thereby delaying the debt write-down that was inevitable. Tony Addison, in Chapter 9, discusses how the poor-country debt crisis arose as a result of low growth (policy mistakes, but also the big structural constraints of infrastructure and health that still impede Africa's take-off), uncoordinated donor-lending (no single lender would have lent as much as the myriad of uncoordinated donors), and the absence of a market that could mark down official debt's value (thereby recognizing the impossibility of paying it back).

The chapter then assesses the state of play with the HIPC Initiative and MDRI; the HIPCs that have reached their completion points account for 64 per cent of the HIPC Initiative assistance to be delivered by creditors, so substantial progress has been made. The chapter then turns to the development and poverty impact of debt relief, discussing the debt over-hang and fiscal effects. Addison argues that the quality of the fiscal system is crucial; debt relief will not have its expected benefits unless we see an improvement in the ability of public expenditure management to transfer the resources released by debt relief into quality infrastructure and services for the poor, and to mobilize additional resources from equitable (fair) taxation. The chapter also discusses the respective roles of economics versus international politics in driving the amount of debt relief granted: what started out as a process in which economic considerations dominated (albeit that the debt sustainability criteria of HIPC were too constraining) turned very much into a process in which donor governments were pushed along by debt campaigners, culminating in the debt cancellation agreed at Gleneagles. This success notwithstanding, Addison argues that debt relief's development benefits will prove disappointing unless fiscal institutions (which are at the core of state-building itself) improve dramatically. The chapter concludes by emphasizing the importance of getting poor countries connected effectively to the international capital market, where they can share in the growth of global portfolio flows and FDI.

Away from the world of official flows, one of the most noteworthy developments is the accelerating pace of globalization and migration (both legal and illegal) that is boosting remittances. The growth in this financial flow looks firm for the future and likely to continue to outpace ODA (remittances are already much larger). Remittances are generally viewed as having many positive development dimensions: they support both consumption and capital investment (especially in small-scale projects) in receiving countries; the external transfer is not mediated through the potentially problematic fiscal institutions of governments (as in the case of ODA in the form of budget support or debt relief); and they are a less fickle form of capital flow (thereby inducing some stability in the current account). Chapter 10, by

Helen Toxopeus and Robert Lensink, sets out to examine one crucial additional effect, namely that they stimulate financial-sector development and thereby growth. This has been much discussed, but until now there has been little empirical investigation. From their econometric analysis, Toxopeus and Lensink find that financial inclusion is an important effect, and that remittances raise economic growth through this route. They point to the need for better databases on remittances (particularly on flows through informal financial channels) so that we can draw more robust conclusions on their development impact (and in particular their impact on poverty). And they also highlight the need to disaggregate the characteristics of migrants who send remittances to understand better who does not use the formal financial system and why; this is especially important for understanding the remittance behaviour of poorer migrants.

Conclusions

For much of the last thirty years or so – since the post-Second World War boom collapsed under the weight of the 1970s oil shocks – the global economy has not worked well for most poor countries, or for many poor people. China is the big exception, but China is large enough to take on the global economy on its own terms, deploying a combination of external orientation and state-led development (while at the same time enjoying the benefits of an enormous domestic market). This puts it in a different class from small and highly vulnerable economies such as Bolivia, Guinea-Bissau and Papua New Guinea (to name just three examples from the main regions of the developing world). So, despite the rapid and large increase in flows of trade, finance, and technology across the global economy, the very poorest countries have mainly had very low access to the finance necessary for development. Private portfolio flows into equities and bonds have been limited to a narrow range of emerging markets, and FDI is highly concentrated in a narrow range of countries (China, in particular). And while policies have to be 'right', a lack of finance has limited the ability of many countries to invest in diversifying their trade, to access new technologies, and to achieve poverty reduction. This has in turn diminished returns from policy reform.

This picture is starting to change. Global liquidity is ample at present, pushing investors into parts of the world they previously avoided, in their search for yield. High prices for many (but not all) commodities are raising the export earnings of primary producers, in Africa especially, thereby improving their debt sustainability, and this together with debt relief has improved their sovereign credit ratings. A new page has opened in Africa's debt history and, for once, it looks like a positive story – in which the region begins to access the international capital market in ways that could fund development and poverty reduction. After years of stagnation, aid flows have started to rise again, and were given a political push by the 2002 Monterrey summit and the 2005 Gleneagles G8 meeting. There are now in addition plenty of innovatory ideas around to expand finance. These include the use of Global Funds, the US Millennium Challenge Account, the UK's International Finance Facility, and proposals for global taxation, the expansion of SDRs, and ways to encourage the flow of private finance (both FDI and portfolio flows). The separation between private and official flows is becoming much less marked, especially in initiatives involving the new philanthropy. So there are grounds for optimism.

Yet plenty can still go wrong. Eventually the credit cycle will turn, interest rates will rise, and global liquidity will contract. The risk tolerance of global investors for the bonds and equities of small and poor economies will turn down. Using borrowing to achieve development remains a tough job for many countries; careful choices must be made over the sectors in which to invest to achieve effective diversification away from dependence on only a few primary commodity exports. Fiscal systems must be overhauled so that sovereign borrowing as well as ODA is deployed effectively into public investments with the highest returns for growth and into the areas of human capital formation – primary education, basic health care, safe water and sanitation – that most benefit the poor. None of this can be taken for granted, as it involves building the state itself, with all the necessary institutions. And while there are many bright ideas for innovation in development finance, getting the political will together is another matter; the present US administration is far apart from Europe (and in denial over the human-made nature of climate change, which stymies proposals such as a carbon tax) and collective action by the developing world is far from assured. So while the development finance picture is now brighter than it was just a few years ago, much more effort is needed if this is not to be yet another false dawn.

Notes

1   'Everyone Wants a Solution to Longevity Risk', *Financial Times*, 1 May 2007.
2   'G8 Pledge on Aid to Africa Threatened as Spending Falls', *Financial Times*, 4 April 2007: 1.
3   Nenadi Usman cited in *Financial Times*, 2 March 2007.
4   On aid volatility, see Fielding and Mavrotas (2005).
5   See, for example, Carol Lancaster (2006), who concludes that: 'To make US foreign aid more effective in supporting development in poor countries, the two large aid agencies – USAID and the Millennium Challenge Corporation – should be merged into a new development agency. It is no secret that the MCC – set up by the Bush administration to provide aid to countries deemed 'good performers' – has struggled to get up and running.'

References

Addison, T. (2007) 'International Finance and the Developing World: The Next Twenty Years', in G. Mavrotas and A. Shorrocks (eds), *Advancing Development: Core Themes in Global Economics*, Basingstoke: Palgrave Macmillan for UNU-WIDER.

Addison, T. and A. Chowdhury (2004) 'A Global Lottery and Premium Bond' in A. B. Atkinson (ed.), *New Sources of Development Finance*, Oxford: Oxford University Press for UNU-WIDER.

Addison, T., H. Hansen and F. Tarp (eds) (2004) *Debt Relief for Poor Countries*, Basingstoke: Palgrave Macmillan for UNU-WIDER.

Addison, T., G. Mavrotas and M. McGillivray (2005a) 'Aid, Debt Relief, and New Sources of Finance for Meeting the Millennium Development Goals', *Journal of International Affairs*, 58(2): 113–27.

Addison, T., G. Mavrotas and M. McGillivray (2005b) 'Development Assistance and Development Finance', *Journal of International Development*, 17: 819–36.

Antipin, J.-E. and G. Mavrotas (2006) 'On the Empirics of Aid and Growth: A Fresh Look', WIDER Research Paper 2006/05, Helsinki: UNU-WIDER.

Atkinson, A. B. (ed.) (2004) *New Sources of Development Finance*, Oxford: Oxford University Press for UNU-WIDER.

Bourguignon, F. and M. Sundberg (2007) 'Absorptive Capacity and Achieving the Millennium Development Goals', in G. Mavrotas and A. Shorrocks (eds), *Advancing Development: Core Themes in Global Economics*, Basingstoke: Palgrave Macmillan for UNU-WIDER.

Brownbridge, M. and C. Kirkpatrick (1999) 'Financial Sector Regulation: Lessons of the Asia Crisis', *Development Policy Review*, 17(3): 243–66.

Burnside, C. and D. Dollar (2000) 'Aid, Policies and Growth', *American Economic Review*, 90(4): 847–68.

Calvo, G., R. Findlay, P. Kouri and J. Braga de Macedo (eds) (1989), *Debt, Stabilization and Development*, Oxford: Basil Blackwell for UNU-WIDER.

Clunies-Ross, A. I. (2004) 'Development Finance: Beyond Budgetary "Official Development Assistance"', *Michigan Journal of International Law*, 26(1): 389–410.

Collier P. and D. Dollar (2002) 'Aid Allocation and Poverty Reduction', *European Economic Review*, 45: 1470–500.

Collier, P. and J. Gunning (eds) (1999) *Trade Shocks in Developing Countries: Volume 1 – Africa*, Oxford: Oxford University Press.

Eichengreen, B. and M. Bordo (2001) 'Crises Now and Then: What Lessons from the Last Era of Financial Globalization?', Paper prepared for a conference in honour of Charles Goodhart at the Bank of England, 15–16 November.

Easterly, W. (2006) *The White Man's Burden: Why the West's Efforts to Aid the Rest Have Done So Much Ill and So Little Good*, New York: Oxford University Press.

Easterly, W., R. Levine and D. Roodman (2004) 'New Data, New Doubts: A Comment on Burnside and Dollar's "Aid, Polices and Growth (2000)"', *American Economic Review*, 94(2): 774–80.

Eurodad (2006) *EU Aid: Genuine Leadership or Misleading Figures?*, Brussels: Eurodad.

Fielding, D. and G. Mavrotas (2005) 'The Volatility of Aid', WIDER Discussion Paper 2005/06. Helsinki: UNU-WIDER.

Goldman Sachs (2003) 'Dreaming with the BRICs: The Path to 2050', *Global Economic Paper 99*, London: Goldman Sachs.

Griffith-Jones, S. and K. Sharma (2006) 'GDP-Indexed Bonds: Making it Happen', UN-DESA Working Paper 21, New York: UN-DESA.

Griffith-Jones, S., M. F. Montes and A. Nasution (eds) (2001) *Short-Term Capital Flows and Economic Crises*, Oxford: Oxford University Press for UNU-WIDER.

Guha-Khasnobis, B. and G. Mavrotas (eds) (2008) *Financial Development, Institutions, Growth and Poverty Reduction*, Basingstoke: Palgrave Macmillan for UNU-WIDER.

Guillaumont, P. and L. Chauvet (2001) 'Aid and Performance: A Reassessment', *Journal of Development Studies*, 37(6): 66–87.

Guillaumont, P. and S. Guillaumont Jeanneney (2006) 'Big Push versus Absorptive Capacity: How to Reconcile the Two Approaches', Paper presented at the WIDER development conference on Aid: Principles, Policies and Performance, Helsinki, 16–17 June.

Gupta, S., R. Powell and Y. Yang (2005) 'The Macroeconomic Challenges of Scaling Up Aid to Africa', IMF Working Paper 05/179, Washington, DC: IMF.

Hansen, H. and F. Tarp (2001) 'Aid and Growth Regressions', *Journal of Development Economics*, 64: 547–70.

Heller, P. S., M. Katz, X. Debrun, T. Thomas, T. Koranchelian and I. Adenauer (2006) 'Making Fiscal Space Happen! Managing Fiscal Policy in a World of Scaled-Up Aid', WIDER Research Paper 2006/125, Helsinki: UNU-WIDER.

HM Treasury (2003) 'Corporate Challenge: Strengthening Community Involvement', London: HM Treasury. Available at: http://hm-treasury.gov.uk.

Kaul, I., P. Conceição, K. Le Goulven, and R. U. Mendoza (eds) (2003) *Providing Global Public Goods: Managing Globalization*, New York: Oxford University Press for UNDP.

Killick, T. (2005) 'Don't Throw Money at Africa', *IDS Bulletin*, 36(3): 14–19.

Koeberk, S., J. Walliser and Z. Stavreski (2007) *Budget Support as More Effective Aid?*, Washington, DC: World Bank.

Lancaster, C. (2006) 'Bush's Foreign Aid Reforms Do Not Go Far Enough', *Financial Times*, 20 January.

Landau, J. P. (2004). 'Groupe de travail sur les nouvelles contributions financières internationales: rapport à Monsieur Jacques Chirac Le Président de la République' (The Landau Report), Paris. Available online.

Manning, R. (2006) 'Will "Emerging Donors" Change the Face of International Cooperation?', *Development Policy Review*, 24(4): 371–85.

Mavrotas, G. (2002) 'Foreign Aid and Fiscal Response: Does Aid Disaggregation Matter?', *Weltwirtschaftliches Archiv*, 138(3): 534–59.

Mavrotas, G. (2004) 'The International Finance Facility Proposal', in A. B. Atkinson (ed.), *New Sources of Development Finance*, Oxford: Oxford University Press for UNU-WIDER.

Mavrotas, G. (2005) 'Aid Heterogeneity: Looking at Aid Effectiveness from a Different Angle', *Journal of International Development*, 17: 1019–36.

Mavrotas, G. (ed.) (2008) *Domestic Resource Mobilization and Financial Development*, Basingstoke: Palgrave Macmillan for UNU-WIDER.

McGillivray, M. (2003) 'Aid Effectiveness and Aid Selectivity: Integrating Multiple Objectives into Aid Allocations', Summary paper presented at the joint OECD-DAC/Development Centre Experts' Seminar on Aid Effectiveness and Aid Selectivity: Integrating Multiple Objectives into Aid Allocations, Paris, March.

McGillivray, M. and O. Morrissey (2004) 'Fiscal Effects of Aid', in T. Addison and A. Roe (eds), *Fiscal Policy for Development: Poverty, Reconstruction and Growth*, Basingstoke: Palgrave Macmillan for UNU-WIDER.

Micklewright, J. and A. Wright (2004) 'Private Donations for International Development', in A. B. Atkinson (ed.), *New Sources of Development Finance*, Oxford: Oxford University Press for UNU-WIDER.

Moore, K. and D. Hulme (2004) 'The International Finance Facility – Reaching the MDGs without Spending More?', *Journal of International Development*, 16: 887–95.

Naím, M. (2007) 'Rogue Aid', *Foreign Policy*, 159: 95–6.

Nayyar, D. (ed.) (2002) *Governing Globalization: Issues and Institutions*, Oxford: Oxford University Press for UNU-WIDER.

Nissanke, M. (2004) 'Revenue Potential of the Tobin Tax for Development Finance: A Critical Appraisal', in A. B. Atkinson (ed.), *New Sources of Development Finance*, Oxford: Oxford University Press for UNU-WIDER.

OECD-DAC (2007) 'Development Aid from OECD Countries Fell 5.1% in 2006', Paris: Organisation for Economic Cooperation and Development – Development Cooperation Directorate.

Pätomaki, H. and K. Sehm-Pätomaki (1999) *The Tobin Tax: How to Make It Real*, Helsinki: The Network Institute for Global Democratisation.

Riddell, R. (2007) *Does Foreign Aid Really Work?*, Oxford: Oxford University Press.

Sachs, J. (2005) *The End of Poverty: How We Can Make It Happen in Our Lifetime*, London: Penguin.

Sagasti, F., K. Bezanson and F. Prada (2005) *The Future of Development Financing: Challenges and Strategic Choices*, Basingstoke, Palgrave Macmillan for the Expert Group for Development Initiatives (EGDI) of the Swedish Ministry for Foreign Affairs.

Sandmo, A. (2004) 'Environmental Taxation and Revenue for Development', in A. B. Atkinson (ed.), *New Sources of Development Finance*, Oxford: Oxford University Press for UNU-WIDER.

Solimano A. (2004) 'Remittances by Emigrants: Issues and Evidence', in A. B. Atkinson (ed.), *New Sources of Development Finance*, Oxford: Oxford University Press for UNU-WIDER.

Stern, N. (2006) *The Economics of Climate Change: The Stern Review*, Cambridge: Cambridge University Press.

Stiglitz, J. (1999) 'Responding to Economic Crises: Policy Alternatives for Equitable Recovery and Development', *The Manchester School*, 67(5): 409–27.

Stiglitz, J. (2002) *Globalization and its Discontents*, London: Penguin.

Stiglitz, J., J. A. Ocampo, S. Spiegel, R. Ffrench-Davis and D. Nayyar (2006) *Stability with Growth: Macroeconomics, Liberalization and Development*, New York: Oxford University Press for the Initiative for Policy Dialogue.

UN (2001) *Report of the High-Level Panel on Financing for Development* (Chair, Ernesto Zedillo), New York: United Nations.

World Bank (1998) *Assessing Aid: What Works, What Doesn't and Why*, Oxford: Oxford University Press.

Wyplosz, C. (2001) *The Impact of EMU on Europe and the Developing Countries*, Oxford: Oxford University Press for UNU-WIDER.

2
Foreign Aid Resurgent: New Spirit or Old Hangover?

Peter Burnell

Introduction

The analysis in this chapter proceeds from a summary of aid's decline in the 1990s and its recent recovery, to an explanation highlighting two potentially competing agendas: first, globalization and poverty; and second, post-9/11 and other new security concerns. The subsequent sections assess the contribution of political development aid to aid's reviving fortunes, and argue that confused and imperfect understandings over the relationships between socioeconomic and political variables only make more likely a situation where *realpolitik* is a major determinant of aid, so that notwithstanding signs of aid's recovery, its developmental impact will remain insecure.

Foreign aid – down but not out

Official development assistance (ODA) peaked in the early 1990s, and subsequent trends appeared to confirm predictions of inexorable decline. All major donors reduced ODA relative to gross national income (GNI); by 2000, the DAC states were providing a smaller share (0.22 per cent) than at any time since the late 1940s, moving further away from the 0.7 per cent target the UN General Assembly adopted in 1970. Over the decade of the 1990s, annual ODA flows in real terms declined by around 10 per cent, and by 40 per cent to Sub-Saharan Africa, which has the highest concentration of least developed countries.[1] Although lower-middle- and upper-middle-income countries retained their share – around a third of ODA – the proportion going to least developed countries fell from around 36 per cent to 29 per cent. Only a few countries, such as China and Tanzania, remained relatively unscathed. Mozambique embarked on post-civil-war reconstruction and witnessed a substantial aid decline. India and Pakistan, formerly sizeable aid recipients, experienced considerable declines, although Vietnam became a major new beneficiary. In Latin America, newly stabilized El Salvador was a notable loser.

The reasons behind the trends are well known. Pre-eminent was the collapse of the Soviet Union. This reduced US support dramatically, for both bilateral and multilateral ODA, which was driven between 1945 and 1990 (with the United States as top donor) by national security and geopolitical strategic concerns. In Japan, the largest ODA provider for most of the 1990s, financial and economic deterioration caused popular and government support to ware as the decade wore on. Germany's willingness to continue its historically large ODA budgets was undermined by the financial, economic and political costs of reunification. The European Union (EU), while vying to become one of the world's leading donors by volume (together with member states' bilateral aid, the EU accounts for just over half of all ODA), became more preoccupied with its own internal agenda: enlargement to the east (which could drain EU finances), deeper political integration, and preparations for the single currency. Aid budgets were a soft target, as member states sought to restrain public spending to satisfy the convergence criteria for monetary union. In the UK, where the incoming Labour government in May 1997 endorsed the Conservative Party's animus against overt increases in direct taxation, pressure to allocate more resources to domestic social policy was trailed as a political priority. The newly rich countries of East Asia showed no inclination to share the burden of international assistance, let alone fill the gap left by large former donors such as Saudi Arabia and the Soviet Union. Then came the Asian financial crisis (1997), generating requests for massive external financial support from the International Monetary Fund (IMF).

A widespread perception set in that there was growing 'aid fatigue' among the public, articulated by both the political left and the more influential right, fuelled by doubts about aid's effectiveness even with respect to the ethically-rooted development objectives. Furthermore, in many countries, the increasingly onerous foreign debt overhang appeared to confirm these doubts, suggesting that new aid, particularly loans, would only compound the problem. And an ideology of international political economy that privileges *private* capital flows and trade over aid became increasingly influential, locating responsibility for development in the developing and transition economies themselves. In the late 1990s, dramatically increased foreign corporate investment and commercial bank lending to a few developing countries in East Asia (primarily China) and Latin America made ODA look increasingly insignificant. Certain favourable developments made aid look less essential in any case. For example, peace became the norm in Central America. It was expected that post-apartheid South Africa would provide an engine of growth for all of southern Africa. A more stable Middle East involving peace between Israel and the Palestinians seemed to be a real possibility after the 1991 Gulf War. All in all, aid's future was judged to be 'precarious' as recently as 2000 (Hopkins 2000: 423).

New spirit

Recent developments suggest that trends have finally turned the corner. Thus, prior to the international conference on 'Financing for Development' (Monterrey, March 2002) the Bush administration unexpectedly revealed proposals to increase its bilateral aid, linked to economic policy and governance conditionalities. The increase involved an extra US$10 billion over 2004–6, of which US$5 billion would be in 2006 (subsequently a new government agency – the Millennium Challenge Corporation – was announced, that would be responsible for distributing the funds). This 'Millennium Challenge Account' followed an EU pledge to increase ODA by up to US$7 billion annually by 2006. EU member states agreed to raise their contribution to, at minimum, the EU's current average (0.33 per cent of GNI), entailing an extra €22 billion and raising the average to 0.39 per cent. The combined US and EU pledges would raise the DAC ODA/GNI ratio from 0.22 per cent to 0.24 per cent (assuming annual real income growth averages 2.5 per cent) – still a long way from the 0.33 per cent of 1990–2. Of course, the US pledge, implying in real terms an increase in aid of around 40 per cent by 2006 compared to 2003, still leaves aid's share of the federal budget and GNI at historically low levels (Shapiro and Birdsall 2002). And, as time passes, slow progress on implementation because of familiar problems of poor co-ordination and rivalry among different bureaucracies in the government tarnishes the picture. Nevertheless, President Bush, in a state-of-the-union address in 2003, again surprised his detractors by increasing by US$10 billion to US$15 a 5-year emergency plan for AIDS relief in Africa and the Caribbean (although indicating that only US$1 billion of this was for the UN's Global Fund). This put pressure on European leaders to consider a matching commitment.

It is difficult not to see these various pledges as a form of competition to avoid the moral 'low ground', with implications for the respective desires to influence international policy towards development co-operation in multilateral forums especially. Also, after the events of 11 September 2001, the US administration began to court diplomatic support for its global campaign against terrorism, and was conscious of criticism of its increasingly unilateralist tendencies and weak aid contribution to 'international burden sharing'. (The US's proportional share has fallen continuously since the early 1960s, and at 0.11 per cent of GNI at the time of writing, with only 0.02 per cent going to the least developed countries, the US compares unfavourably with all other DAC donors, despite regaining from Japan the position of largest donor). Moreover, even modest promises are not always kept (in July 2003 the relevant US House of Representatives sub-committee trimmed the administration's aid appropriations request, but reapportioned AIDS funding to the UN Global Fund), and look insignificant compared to the challenge posed by world poverty or in relation to US defence expenditures or OECD domestic agricultural subsidies. After all, the UN's Millennium Development Goal of halving by 2015 the proportion of people living in extreme poverty is reckoned to require at minimum a doubling of world aid. And disagreements persist over funding the IDA, whose interest-free loans are crucial to the poorest countries that cannot attract international private capital, with the US wanting the World Bank to convert at least half of its lending into grants. Concerned commentators say this will erode its funding base (repayments by borrowers to the IDA were US$13 billion between 1992 and 2001); ultimately dependence on, and political vulnerability to, major donors would increase, especially given continuing US opposition to developing-country demands for greater voting rights on the Bank's board. Meanwhile Japan, hitherto the top donor, far from showing more inclination to exercise global leadership over aid's overall direction, is set to make further reductions in its ODA. The EU too still has difficulty in agreeing and applying rigorously a coherent vision for its development co-operation. EU aid implementation remains notoriously bureaucratic.

Nevertheless, it would be difficult to deny that the climate for aid has improved. Observers interpreted the Millennium Challenge as a signal that the US is becoming more open to persuasion that aid *might* be developmentally efficacious in certain circumstances. In the words of Jeffrey Sachs, the 'US is waking up from a 20-year sleep in the development field. We can forgive them not immediately knowing everything that has been happening during their slumbers' (*Financial Times*, 25 March 2002). Of course, the publications mill on aid never did stop working overtime (nothing attracts attention quite like the manner of its passing), but there does now seem more enthusiasm to move the debate forward. One example is the endeavour to unlock 'added value' in our understanding of complex development and aid issues by combining interest in ODA's effectiveness with the analytical framework offered by public goods theory. The demand for international/global public goods of all descriptions – which, according to one estimate, accounts for only 9 per cent of aid (a further 30 per cent is allocated to national public goods) – looks bound to increase, thus fuelling demands for much more aid.[2] Indeed, major issues where aid is invited to contribute range ever more widely, from meeting refugee and humanitarian crises (in the 1990s a significant growth area for aid) to combating illicit drugs production and trafficking, checking the spread of communicable diseases, and addressing environmental threats – all features of the new security agenda. Target-setting remains in fashion too: the UN 'World Summit on Sustainable Development' (September 2002) agreed to halve the number of people without access to sanitation facilities and safe water to one billion by 2015. This will require help from aid.

Economists, too, have regained the courage to reassert some good news about aid, contrasting with the emphasis in previous years on doubts and reservations. The positive association between aid inflows and economic growth has been restated, noting that even aid not directed into investment can still benefit welfare and development. Poverty has definitely moved centre-stage in the discourse and the policy rhetorics. For example, a joint statement of the EU Commission and Council in 2002 enshrined poverty reduction as the main objective of its development aid. The World Bank's *World Development Report 2000–01: Attacking Poverty* was greeted favourably – 'in some ways this recent report really is a step forward' (Boer 2001: 288) – unlike the 1980s, when the Bank was widely held to be responsible for it being a 'lost decade for poverty'. Of course, the OECD's *Shaping the 21st Century: The Contribution of Development Cooperation* (1996) first provided a significant milestone, setting clear targets for global poverty reduction and social development. And then came the World Bank's *Assessing Aid. What Works, What Doesn't, and Why* (1998), reconfirming the view that ODA (more particularly, multilateral aid) is an effective instrument against poverty – so long as the recipient countries have the right political will, appropriate policies, institutions and governance. The calculations suggestion that additional assistance of US$1 billion would raise 284,000 people above absolute poverty, compared with only 105,000 people in the mid-1990s. There is now a standard requirement that governments write poverty reduction strategy papers, in consultation with civil society, for endorsement by the Bank and the IMF.

Finally, the end of the Cold War did more than liberate aid from some old political constraints. It provided an enabling environment for new political objectives and aid rationales, namely democracy, 'good governance' and human rights, to be sought directly via projects or programmes, and through adding political conditionalities to aid's other conditionalities. The belief that such political reform might serve economic liberalization in formerly statist and authoritarian regimes was particularly important for aid to retain US support. New dimensions in the academic study of aid came about, involving not just economists but also political analysts and international relations experts. New questions came into vogue, such as how the effectiveness of political aid can be measured, and whether the methodologies allow meaningful comparison with the returns to more conventional development aid. Are political conditionalities likely to be more successful than the mixed record of economic conditionalities?

So, despite the ill omens of the early 1990s, reports of aid's death were greatly exaggerated. The pledged flows and the mood music have been lifted, nowhere more so than in the UK, where both the status within government and the resourcing of the Department for International Development (DfID) increased under Blair's Labour government. The Chancellor of the Exchequer canvassed international support for more substantial debt relief to poor countries, endorsing calls for a doubling of world aid, and supporting for this purpose a proposed International Finance Facility that would leverage money from the private capital markets – immediately dubbed a 'modern Marshall plan'. By 2007 the UK was providing £6.7 billion in ODA, or 0.51 per cent of ODA/GNI. The UK is the second largest OECD-DAC donor, and at the end of

2007 announced an increase in its IDA contribution to make it the largest contributor.

Naturally, for aid's most enthusiastic proponents, these developments can never promise enough. But approval for aid at the highest levels and lively public debate are an improvement on hostility (the situation during Thatcher's premiership) and stale debate, or no debate at all. Even contributions such as the suggestion that the World Bank has undergone a 'tragic deterioration',[3] and is now in crisis, can be interpreted in a positive light. They reflect the somewhat myopic position of right-wing bankers and economic purists, expressing regret for defensible Bank initiatives to consult representatives of poor communities, incorporate competent NGOs in the policy process, and address gender and environmental considerations – developments that many aid supporters believe can be profoundly beneficial.

Explaining recent developments

Explaining aid's revival could easily get caught up in theoretical debates over the relative importance of structure and agency, ideas and interests, the push and pull of endogenous and exogenous forces. A full audit of influential factors would have to tease out relationships between demand- and supply-side forces as mediated by formal and informal institutions, both private and public sector actors at national, international and subnational levels. Here, only two factors – and the tensions between them – will be visited: globalization, and the consequences of 9/11.

Globalization and poverty

The concept of globalization and its historical origins are contentious issues. Contemporary usage varies from simple propositions about increases in world trade and foreign direct investment to ideas about the increased interconnectedness of peoples more generally and supra-territorially. Different social science disciplines offer different perspectives; globalization's meaning and significance are contested even *within* disciplines or subdisciplines – international relations, for example. That said, there are implications for aid.

One side of the debate rejects World Bank confidence in the declining number of people in absolute poverty and inequality among households. Instead, it maintains that globalization's effects are unequal and there are losers (whatever the unit of analysis – households, larger social groups, whole countries, or regions), both relative and absolute, chiefly in the developing and postcommunist worlds. Even in countries such as China, where the numbers in absolute poverty are declining, increased inequality can be highly significant if it really is the case that relative poverty is disempowering for the least well-off. Substantial inequality increases the rate of economic growth required to improve the condition of the poorest. Wade (2001) goes even further than the claim that world income distribution is becoming more unequal. He argues that incomes in the lower deciles of world income have probably fallen abso-lutely since the 1980s, and the number of people in absolute poverty has probably increased.[4] Whatever is the true picture now, what is beyond doubt is that over fifty countries experienced negative economic growth between 1990 and 2001, including many that saw social development in retreat.

The realistic option in all this is not to try to reverse the tide of glob-alization, but rather to make intelligent use of policy instruments so as to optimize its effects, capture the benefits and reduce or compensate for the harmful consequences. This implies a role for concessionary transfers. They can support the casualties of globalization (peoples whose livelihoods are dis-rupted) and societies so peripheral that they will not experience the potential benefits or make progress in isolation either (around two billion, mainly very poor people, are reckoned to live in countries that are neither globalizing nor developing). In addition, there is now a greater appreciation of how increased poverty and immiserization are often linked to violent conflict. The surge in peace settlements in conflict zones seen immediately after the end of the Cold War turned out to be yet another false dawn. The expected duration of conflicts appears to be longer than previously thought, therefore the scope for humanitarian intervention and sustained programmes of assistance in post-conflict reconstruction and development has increased.[5] Timor-Leste is already eligible. Post-Mugabe Zimbabwe can expect to see a dramatic increase in ODA; Sri Lanka too has been promised several billion dollars in return for progress in building peace.

There are several different issues here; needless to say, if assistance is to help, then different forms must be directed to different situations. There remains much analytical work to be done to refine our understanding of how different kinds of intervention can achieve the desired effects. Over the years, researchers have accumulated plenty of case lore about what does *not* work well, or may not work at all. But assured knowledge about the secrets of success and the identity of transferable solutions, or ones that can be replicated and scaled up, remains elusive. 'The road to hell is paved with good intentions' is a staple reflection among specialists in international devel-opment co-operation, applicable even to the NGOs. Even so, awareness of the negative side of globalization still strengthens the case for international assistance – whether the reasoning is grounded in morality and justice, or in the security of the rich world (more on that below). Only critics who believe considerably more radical action is required, such as reversing globalization or abolishing capitalism, disagree fundamentally.

The events of 11 September 2001

It has become *passé* to say the events of 11 September 2001 (9/11) 'changed the world', altering both the way we understand contemporary politics and the prospects for global stability and peace. The consequences for aid are only now unfolding, and they are positive and ambiguous.

Heightened sensitivity to international terrorism followed by the invasion of Iraq in 2003 and concern about the proliferation of weapons of mass destruction have provoked a return to the kind of foreign policy behaviour associated with old-fashioned *realpolitik*. The consequences of 9/11 included, *inter alia*, immediate US offers of bilateral debt relief to Pakistan, culminating in the cancellation of US$1 billion (out of US$2.8 billion) and relaxation of aid sanctions imposed in 1990 (in response to fears about nuclear proliferation). Japan was pressed by the US to show solidarity by lifting aid sanctions. Pakistan, of course, was (and remains) critical to US counter-terrorism objectives in Afghanistan and inside Pakistan and Kashmir (hence President Bush's offer, in June 2003, of a US$3 billion package of financial and military assistance). At the time of the invasion of Afghanistan, autocratic former Soviet republics in Central Asia were made offers of US aid in return for the use of military bases. Turkey seemed well placed to capitalize on planned US preparations for the invasion of Iraq, until the chances of a deal collapsed amid recriminations – but not before the US reputedly offered Turkey a choice of either US$24 billion (US$4 billion in grants and the balance in loan guarantees) or a US$6 billion lump sum grant (including US$2 billion in military sales/forgiveness of military debts) (*Financial Times*, 20 February 2003).[6]

Issue linkage between Islamic fundamentalist hostility to the US and the conflict between Israel and the Palestinians is a contentious subject. But to combat the former and play a key role in the latter, the US will probably maintain substantial assistance to 'moderate regimes' such as that in Egypt (a major recipient of US aid since the Camp David Agreement of 1978) and, now, Jordan. In this theatre at least, aid's usefulness as a bribe or reward in exchange for political concessions has not gone away. Israel's indebtedness to the US for 'security assistance' of around US$3 billion annually (including US$1.8 billion in military aid) – increasing to a request in 2003 for US$4 billion grant aid plus US$10 billion in loan guarantees – is legendary. It seems unlikely to decrease. The deteriorating situation in the Middle East has generated further opportunities for large-scale humanitarian and post-conflict reconstruction assistance. In late 2003, donors were called on to provide US$2 billion in emergency assistance for the Palestinians alone: between 60 per cent and 75 per cent are reckoned to be surviving on less than US$2 a day. Substantial aid will have to be part of any political deal to create an internationally recognized Palestinian state, just as it eventually dawned on the US administration that the reconstruction of Iraq will need massive financial support, well beyond Iraq's limited ability to pay.[7]

Afghanistan itself poses a dynamic new aid frontier, promised up to US$4.8 billion in grants (plus loans) by international donors for 2002–6. In March 2003, Pakistan chipped in US$100 million to rebuild transport and trade links. Eventually, very much larger sums will be needed, if the Afghan authorities can create the absorptive capacity to make productive use of the funds. Elsewhere, the US administration seems set to increase security assistance to the authorities in Colombia, in what looks like 'mission creep' from the original campaign of supporting counter-narcotics operations to waging war against 'left-wing terrorism'. In Africa, US diplomatic initiatives appear to link offers of aid to secure long-term access to oil (African supplies to the US average around two-thirds of the crude oil obtained from the Persian Gulf) and co-operation in fighting anti-US terrorism there. It is difficult to believe that neither the US nor France included aid packages in their efforts to gain the support of African 'swing state' members of the UN Security Council over voting on a second resolution on Iraq prior to the invasion.

Yet, to many eyes, the events of 9/11 seemed to confirm the security case for the rich world to be more proactive in tackling world poverty, in what could be a clear case of mutual benefit involving the poor. Prime Minister Tony Blair told his hosts in Ghana, 'There are times in politics when it is possible to do what was thought to be impossible a short time before. This is such a time. Let the developing and the developed world create together that decent prosperous future.'[8] One view is that a society's economic progress may increase the appetite for, and means to threaten, international violence. But a different and frequently expressed view is that extreme poverty, resentment at gross international inequalities, and despair all provide fertile ground for forms of 'anti-system behaviour' – whether targeting rich countries directly or operating indirectly through the intervening variable of violent domestic conflict. Frances Stewart (2001: 33) expressed it thus: 'It is clearly fairly easy for leaders, such as Bin Laden, to mobilize the economically deprived against the economically privileged non-Moslem world.'[9] What is most important here is not whether poverty is in fact the main cause of something such as international terrorism (or the other 'new security' threats) – clearly a complex and debatable claim – or, even, the state of perceptions among the international aid bureaucracies. Instead, it is that reasoning like this is being used in high places to shape and justify present-day commitments to aid; at a minimum it has acquired strong presentational credentials.

The problems posed to the rich world by 'rogue states' and fragile or failing states (of which there are several) also now loom much larger in public debate than in, say, 1995, when first the US Marines and then a United Nations force withdrew from the chaos in Somalia. President Bush, after first maintaining that the US would not be drawn into providing support for nation-building or state reconstruction in countries such as Afghanistan, then took a contrary line over Iraq. It seems the 'logic of neoimperialism is too compelling', given the dangers to global security of non-involvement (Mallaby 2002: 6). Also, the connections between poverty and several of the other conditions that are now construed as global or regional security threats – large-scale movements of illegal migrants and (even) legitimate asylum-seekers, internationally organized crime, the rapid transmission of disease across borders, and so on – are now widely recognized. Such concerns presently affecting EU countries in their relations with the Maghreb could well increase now that the EU has enlarged to the east, bringing proximity to struggling economies in Belarus and Ukraine that much closer.

Almost everywhere, the political dimensions in aid relations are never far from the surface. Take, for example, in Sub-Saharan Africa, the idea of a New Partnership for Africa's Development (NEPAD), which Blair warmly welcomed. It appears to suggest an African willingness to acknowledge Africa's share of responsibility for improving Africa's economic and political prospects. The idea of a mechanism for self-regulatory peer review in Africa seems central to the proposal. In return, there would be more aid and trade concessions; the G8 summit in June 2003 secured conditional pledges to Africa worth £4 billion annually (Kofi Annan called the outcome 'a turning point in the history of Africa and indeed the world' [*The Independent*, 28 June 2002][10]), all of which makes African reluctance to criticize openly Zimbabwe's flawed presidential election of March 2002 look like an inauspicious omen (the Common Market for Eastern and Southern Africa observer mission proclaimed that it was conducted credibly, freely and fairly). And then, in November 2002, President Mbeki announced that peer review should be restricted to economic aspects of governance. Of course, the anti-capitalist/anti-globalization protestors see NEPAD as being irrelevant in any case – just another elite-formulated, top-down initiative that can only fail.

In sum, while recognition is still very strong that some countries continue to need aid because they are poor, old-fashioned political factors play a large part in translating need into *effective* demand – into donor support for aid and influencing their aid resource allocations – in particular, bilateral disbursements. Thus the size and shape of the market for aid are a political construct. Furthermore, questions about whether economic progress, even if it does reduce poverty, will solve the kinds of problems raised in this section – and *how* aid might best contribute – continue to be controversial in development studies and among aid practitioners. The past tendency for 'magic bullets' to disappoint the hopes that were at first vested in them now inclines observers to be cautious, nowhere more so than in respect of political development aid.

Political development aid: from rise to dénouement?

If aid generally (or aid volumes more specifically) now faces a more promising future than seemed likely just a few years ago, then it is ironic that political development aid – more specifically democracy assistance – could be a partial exception. A significant increase in 'international co-operation for democratization' (the politically more correct term) followed the collapse of the Soviet Union.[11] In political science, the 'new institutionalism' claims that politics matters: it is no mere epiphenomenon, or dependent variable, of 'deeper' economic and social structures. Thus political institutional reform, engineered or underwritten by international assistance, can make a difference to the way countries are governed, irrespective of their economic situation. That, in turn, will lead to improved economic management of those countries, and so their prospects of enjoying economic, social and human development will also increase. This clutch of beliefs provided some intellectual underpinning to political development aid. Bush's address on national security strategy outlined to Congress on 20 September 2002 declared that the US will 'use our foreign aid to promote freedom and support those who struggle non-violently for it, ensuring that nations moving towards democracy are rewarded for the steps they take' (*Financial Times*, 21/22 September 2002). Subsequently, Bush proposed to spread democracy and freedom throughout the entire Middle East.

However, there is always a lag between the inauguration or expansion of new kinds of activity and the devising of suitable methodologies to evaluate results and appraise performance. The story so far with regard to democracy assistance is not wholly encouraging. The evidence to date underlines the difficulties facing attempts to promote any or all of the following: a rigorous respect for the rule of law (by power-holders in particular); a durable system of competitive party politics that steers between single-party dominance and unstable hyper-pluralism/factionalism; a sustainable increase in the strength and vitality of a supportive version of civil society; and inter-communal trust and co-operation in societies where deep-seated divisions exist. Even the limited objective of consolidating judicial autonomy seems elusive, unless many more fundamental changes in the social, cultural and political context are secured. With respect to democracy, aid practitioners are still very far from establishing a consensus on 'best practice'; analysts now question seriously even some of the basic concepts, including the kinds of democracy and civil society that are being encouraged. Problems similar to those that have long beset more conventional ODA are endemic – for example, issues concerning relations with partners in civil society projects – formerly the repository of great hopes, just like the NGOs in socioeconomic development work. Establishing 'ownership' (or should it be authorship?) and preventing dependence are typically proving to be problematic, as are the idea and practice of 'partnership'. The sequence of events in Iraq after the fall of Saddam have only added to the growing scepticism about 'doing democratic development' – both with respect to Iraq itself and the 'domino effect' that reform there was supposed to have on the rest of the Arab world.[12] Of course, suspicions in that region about barely concealed 'hidden agendas' involving US economic imperialism and Israel's territorial objectives do not help. They reinforce a perception in some quarters that the West's commitment to democratization – whether by means of democracy projects or through aid conditionalities – is both unprincipled and unreliable.

In the political economy of aid, political conditionalities represent one of the more obvious sites where power and wealth meet. The calibration of an optimal mix of support for political projects/programme with those 'positive conditionalities' (inducements of economic development/financial aid in return for improvements in democracy, human rights, 'good governance') and the 'negative conditionalities' (threatened ODA sanctions in the event of non-compliance) remains, at best, experimental. The *economic* conditionalities that became the norm in the 1980s were conceived on the grounds that it was essential to get economic policies and institutions 'right'. By the 1990s, this was overtaken – or overlayered – by the view that an essential (albeit not sufficient) requirement could be to 'get the politics right' first. The simple view was that sound economics would take over afterwards, and facilitate poverty reduction thereafter, although both these inferences remain controversial. So, enter political conditionalities, albeit with some confusion over whether priority should be given to promoting democracy, or human rights, or 'good governance', and over the tensions between these three objectives or among their constituent parts.

Alas, just as some economists now dismiss economic conditionality's effectiveness, or argue that measuring compliance is problematic (as well as worries about adverse social effects), and instead recommend targeting aid on states already committed to 'good' policies and institutions,[13] so good grounds also exist for scepticism about political conditionalities. Against this background, NEPAD may be interpreted in one of two ways, neither of them complimentary. One view is that NEPAD represents a tacit acknowledgement by the West that political conditionalities do not work, and some alternative, more consensual approach to levering political change is indicated. Another is that it represents a final attempt to strengthen conditionality, by invoking the threat of collective punishment (aid sanctions) even against the region's more economically and politically liberal states should their leaders fail to bring obdurate colleagues such as Mugabe into line. Neither interpretation removes serious problems with political conditionality on both the donor and recipient sides.

Donor side

By comparison with economic conditionalities, it is even more difficult to formulate political objectives of conditionality in clear, agreed language that will allow progress/regress to be measured objectively and to furnish a sound basis for judging policy compliance. Fine-tuning the conditionalities in subsequent 'rounds' is an even more imprecise art than with respect to economic targets/objectives/conditionalities. More significant, our understanding of the relationships between the stipulations typically associated with political conditionalities and their wider political impact (anticipated and actual), and of the temporal dimensions and sequencing are far more tentative than what we think we know about the management of public financial and economic affairs.

The absence of a true counterpart to the central enforcement mechanism and co-ordination that the Bretton Woods institutions provide on economic conditionalities does not help. Of course, their Articles of Agreement rule against political goals. And given that states in the 'international community' frequently privilege the high politics of bilateral diplomacy over collective action, it is inevitable that contradictions and inconsistencies arise in the political demands they make through their aid relations – sometimes at the expense of pro-democracy goals. Here, the EU is no exception: members will hide behind the EU's collective stance to 'talk tough', as when spelling out conditions to the seventy-nine Africa-Caribbean-Pacific partner states in the Cotonou Agreement, but individually sometimes default on EU solidarity when pursuing bilateral relations with favoured states.

So, democracy promotion faces strong competition from the donors' other foreign-policy interest, including both commercial or national economic interests and strategic geopolitical concerns. Democratic conditionalities even have to compete with other kinds of political conditionalities. The UK government's (failed) bid to make EU ODA conditional on recipient co-operation in controlling illegal migration is one example.[14] The US faces choices over whether to maintain good relations with (semi-)authoritarian regimes that co-operate in fighting terrorism, or pressing them to become more like liberal democracies – choices made all the sharper by the divided counsels over whether it is poverty, or political oppression, that provides the most significant breeding ground for terrorism. After all, there are cases where democratization could mean states becoming more responsive to pro-Palestinian sentiments: Pakistan's parliamentary elections (October 2002) amplified the political voice of Islamists. In Indonesia's new democracy, there is the potential for Muslim parties to hold the balance of power in the elected parliament. The West's reaction to the Bali nightclub atrocity in October 2002 provided weight to the military and other security forces (given US aid) notwithstanding continuing human rights abuses (in Aceh province, for example). Unlike small, debt-distressed, least developed countries – such as Zambia – that have few bargaining resources, little pro-democracy pressure is exerted on China, easily the largest aid recipient in the 1990s, from either Japan (the major donor) or an increasingly friendly US administration.

The clash of donor political imperatives is unavoidable and, of course, need not always be a cause for concern. For example, in post-conflict environments (where the risk of conflict recurring is disproportionately high) the entrenching of civilian rule, evidence of political stabilization and state reconstruction might – should – take precedence over the niceties of democracy. Electoral irregularities may be condoned, as in Nigeria's presidential elections in February 1999 and April 2003; and even the postponement of elections can seem appropriate. EU aid support to Macedonia provides a different example.[15] But just as often the situation looks more like incoherence in the policy process, or serious disagreements over strategy between major donors, or inside entities such as the EU or the US administration. Thus, for example, Bush's robust line against the 'axis of evil' was criticized for undermining putative reformers in Iran; in Egypt, the US's war on terrorism has offered a pretext to the government to silence dissent.

Recipient side

In responding to aid conditionalities, autocrats self-evidently will be more inclined to make economic rather than political concessions where the latter obviously threaten their interest in retaining power. Many ruling elites have shown themselves adept at neutralizing the potential domestic political fall-out from structural economic adjustment, such as by externalizing the responsibility for painful economic measures. Semi-authoritarian rulers have appeared to concede to donor political pressure for multiparty elections, for example, but by frustrating the very purpose – the substitution of a more legitimate, accountable government. Irrespective of whether conditionality is understood primarily to be a coercive instrument, a bribe, an exchange or an exercise in persuasion, the chances of achieving 'ownership' look more remote for democratic rather than economic conditions, in respect of these regimes. By comparison, economic policy conditions have not infrequently been adopted where they could be used to further the interests of the power-holders – the privatization of state enterprises to rent-seekers in the ruling elite being a typical example.

Finally, many political conditionalities could be largely redundant in any case, not just for non-aid-receiving countries such as Saudi Arabia, but where the main threats to democracy or democratization come from actors largely beyond the control of elected governments. In some cases, this can mean the military and security services; in others, terrorists and guerrillas/freedom fighters; or some debilitating combination of very fragile state structures and non-state actors. The exact relevance of aid-supported pressure to democratize will vary with whether the chosen perspective is short- or longer-term. So, for example, in respect of the EU's offer of €1 billion for reconstruction in Afghanistan, the EU Commissioner for External Affairs expressly ruled out specific conditions despite the EU's desire to see fiscal transparency, an end to opium poppy cultivation, and a more ethnically mixed government.[16] In countries such as Pakistan, strengthening the state's ability to govern, maintain order and collect taxes can look as attractive as promoting democracy. And we should not forget that democratization – or interventions designed to enable democratization – can be highly destabilizing, and produce some profoundly anti-democratic effects.[17] Far from drawing on the 'democratic peace' hypothesis (namely, democracies are peace-loving, and so a world made up of democracies will be stable and secure), attempts to force the pace of political change could transform even some non-Islamic countries into greater risks to security, because of the internal turmoil it brings – another reason, then, for being more restrained. For a time in 2002, certain European governments considered the idea of delaying World Bank funding to Pakistan, but note the reason: not to apply pressure for political liberalization/democratization, but to press for greater efforts to control cross-border terrorism *vis-à-vis* India. The US rejected even this limited idea, fearing it might destabilize President Musharraf's leadership (*Financial Times*, 7 June 2002).

The reality is that attaching political conditionalities to aid may well be more effective at promoting some political objectives (partial liberalization or conversion of authoritarian into semi-authoritarian regimes) than others such as democratic consolidation. It is not simply that donors 'tend to have a natural bias in favour of the incumbents whom their funding buttresses' (van de Walle 2002: 74). But 'consolidation', whether understood as democratic 'deepening' or as democracy's longevity, requires the internalization of democratic values by society. Attempts at imposition are misguided, unless the indigenous political culture and possibly the social and economic conditions too change in ways that make democracy's advance possible. Again, the example of post-Saddam Iraq provides confirmation. Possibly political conditionality could be more effective at retarding complete democratic reversal by would-be autocrats than at promoting sustainable democracy. Yet examples such as President Mugabe (with some assistance from Libya) suggest that nowhere will it deter leaders determined to get their way, even though the country might desperately need ODA.[18] Given the limitations of politically conditioned aid, in certain circumstances other kinds of leverage offer much greater purchase – for example, the 'carrot' of EU accession inducing democratic reform in transition economies.

Big debates, familiar conclusions?

This analysis questions the judgement of many in the 1990s that ODA is in terminal decline. It does not set out to defend aid against its critics. Nor does it claim that in future there will be impressively sustained growth in the real volume of aid or its quality. The increasingly heavy financial burden of the US's involvement in Iraq could hit its willingness to commit to ODA elsewhere. And Japan could be set to reduce its UN funding if its ambitions for a permanent seat on the Security Council are thwarted.

But, with hindsight, it is clear that the context of multiple driving forces and plural objectives that has long characterized aid is just as pronounced as ever. After all, that fact combined with the vested interests that cause numerous governmental, inter-governmental and non-governmental institutions to defend their own corner, helps to explain aid's survival. New frontiers for ODA have opened up; and there remains much scope to make the debt relief under the HIPC initiative more liberal. And policy-orientated economists and development practitioners continue to explore ways of further strengthening the developmental case for aid.

That said, there are two unresolved debates running through the meld of aid policy's political determinants. The first considers that either socio-economic development leads ultimately to democratization – which provides a strong case for development assistance, or democratization can be a condition for socioeconomic development – which appears to suggest the use of aid to promote democracy. The second unresolved debate considers that either the main threats (not just international terrorism) to global security originate in poverty/social malaise and consequential domestic violence – and so aid should address the socioeconomic roots through conventional ODA – or these threats owe much to the domestic political conditions. The latter could make a change of political regime a prerequisite, preferably to be brought about voluntarily or by 'soft power' (including aid's political conditions) rather than by force. In every case, clearly, there is a chain of causal assumptions that creates several points at which the argument might conceivably break down in practice and frustrate the overall effect. In particular, we are not now so confident that aid can produce democratic progress. The record of democratic assistance and the chances of making aid political conditionality effective have both tended to be disappointing.

Moreover, there are some 'no-go areas' and some comparatively unpropitious terrain for both democratization and the promotion of democracy (the Middle East may be an example) and for political conditionalities (India's decision in mid-2003 to 'drop' twenty-two government donors was a response to political criticism by donors). Other, more effective, methods for securing political change exist, but they do not necessarily promise democracy, and they can have adverse economic and social consequences. In some instances, continued co-operation with (semi-)authoritarian regimes retains its attractions, in the short term at least. Perhaps, then, aid should concentrate on pursuing pro-poor development, with just the possibility that where development takes place, it will deliver a bonus in the form of benefits to democracy and/or security, the latter directly and/or indirectly.

Regardless of what credit is given to alms-racing in securing the West's victory in the Cold War and defeating communism, there can be no doubting that *realpolitik* heavily compromised aid's ability to advance developmental goals in the past. Put differently, if correcting or compensating for globalization's more adverse social effects had really been given priority, then ODA's regional, country and sectoral allocations, and the terms and conditions under which it was supplied would all have been very different. Quite plausibly, the future will not look very different. On the one hand, recent aid initiatives connected to security issues illustrate how global estimates of the market for aid can be a hostage to political fortune. They can be affected drastically by sudden political events. Favourable political developments in, say, North Korea, Myanmar and Cuba could dramatically increase effective demand and absorptive capacity even for development aid. On the other side, reduced attention to some very poor, stable and peaceful countries could be part of the opportunity cost of doing more to address new international security concerns. Perversely, such countries might be marginalized even further. Moral hazard could creep in, if major donors appear to favour countries where they have a paramount concern with their own security interests. Thus, while in general weakness is not a (negotiating) strength, there are instances where it might serve as such, leading to patterns of aid allocation at variance with a concentration on effective pro-poor development. Emergency food and energy aid to near-nuclear North Korea is illustrative. North Korea's total economic collapse no less than its achievement of nuclear power status would have serious consequences for South Korea and much farther afield. Given North Korea's current political leadership and the potential for instability, the chances that collapse and nuclearization could happen together present an especially powerful case for international assistance. The regime in North Korea has not been slow to try to capitalize on this.

Thus, while at one level aid's prospects look brighter now, it is premature to say that the judgement future historians will pass on the present era will be any kinder than the often damning reports that social scientists have produced in the past. For one thing, history tells us that promises of more aid do not always materialize. For another, aid's political drivers mean we cannot be certain that ODA will be substantially reallocated to countries with policy environments that favour pro-poor development. Economists advise us that, in countries with weak institutions, an increase in badly-designed aid can actually harm the prospects for sustainable development – and frustrate effective democratic governance. Nevertheless, that may well not be sufficient to prevent some aid going to some such countries. Conversely, political neglect will mean that some societies that most need help (in Africa, for example) will not get the amounts and kinds of assistance they need. That aid has always been, *inter alia*, a political instrument harnessed to the pursuit of national interests by rich, powerful states is hardly news. But its significance for a resurgent aid industry should not now be underestimated either. Notwithstanding all the new spirit informing an increase of support for aid to both development and democracy, there could still follow a very familiar hangover.

Notes

1 Data in this paragraph from *The DAC Journal* (2001: 68).
2 See te Velde (2002). Poverty reduction is just one of the global public goods; others include peace and environmental goods.
3 Cited in *Financial Times* (28 August 2001).
4 The relationships between economic openness, growth, poverty and inequality are all in dispute, but there seems to be little doubt that international inequality 'is of staggering proportions ... And the only available data show world inequality to be increasing' (Wade 2001: 39). White's view of the data is that the real income of the poor fell between 1988 and 1993 (White 2001: 334).
5 See Collier *et al.* (2003).
6 Turkey apparently first asked for US$92 billion, and then US$30 billion. Subsequent offers by the US included an US$8.5 billion bridging loan ahead of the

disbursement of US$6 billion in grants, of which US$4 billion would be for the economy (*Financial Times*, 27 February 2003).

7   Coalition Provisional Authority views reported in *Financial Times* (25 June 2003). US Congress voted US$2.4 billion for Iraq's reconstruction in April 2003.

8   Tony Blair, quoted in *Financial Times* (9/10 February 2002).

9   According to Michel Camdessus, Managing Director of the IMF, at least a third of the separate discussion during the 'retreat' among heads of state at the Monterrey conference (2002) was devoted to the possible link between poverty and terrorism (*The Courier* 2002: 6). Jessica Mathews (2001: 9), president of the Washington DC-based Endowment for International Peace, says, 'it is clear that the new US interest in aid and development stems from the anti-terrorism connection'.

10   European leaders and Canada pushed unsuccessfully for larger sums. The same summit promised £13 billion over ten years for a programme to destroy Russia's unwanted nuclear stockpile.

11   See Burnell (2000); and Carothers (1999).

12   See Ottaway (2003).

13   See *Journal of Development Studies* (2001).

14   Floated in advance of an EU summit in June 2002, there was strong opposition from inside the cabinet and from some EU governments such as France.

15   Following a highly critical evaluation by independent consultants commissioned by EuropeAid (set up by External Affairs Commissioner, Chris Patten), donors including the EU approved US$515 million of new aid – more than double the predicted amount – at a pledging conference on 12 March 2002. This aid was intended to bolster an August 2001 peace deal reached between Macedonia's government and ethnic Albanian 'rebels', which looked close to collapse.

16   Chris Patten, 'I don't think there is any country where you would be mechanistic about conditionality' (cited in *Financial Times*, 21 May 2002).

17   See, for example, Huntington (1996) and Snyder (2000).

18   UK Foreign Office Minister for Africa, Baroness Amos, replying to MPs asking for even just one example of British influence in Zimbabwe before or since the March 2002 presidential elections: 'I cannot give … that kind of assurance … We are all deeply frustrated' (*Financial Times*, 15 May 2002). She later told the National Press Club in Pretoria that the Zimbabwe situation was causing foreign investors to 'think NEPAD a lost cause' (cited in *Financial Times*, 1 April 2003). Baroness Amos was subsequently appointed Secretary of State for International Development.

References

Boer, L. (2001) 'Attacking Poverty: Rediscovering the Political Economy', *Third World Quarterly*, 22(2): 288.

Burnell, P. (ed.) (2000) *Democracy Assistance*, London: Frank Cass.

Carothers, T. (1999) *Aiding Democracy. The Learning Curve*, Washington, DC: Carnegie Endowment for International Peace.

Collier, P., L. Elliot, H. Hegre, A. Hoeffler, M. Reynal-Querol and N. Sambanis (2003) *Breaking the Conflict Trap. Civil War and Development Policy*, Washington, DC: World Bank and Oxford University Press.

Courier, The (2002) 'ACP-EU Development Cooperation', *The Courier*, 192, May–June: 6.

Financial Times (various issues): 28 August 2001; 9/10 February 2002; 25 March 2002; 15 May 2002; 21 May 2002; 7 June 2002; 21/22 September 2002; 20 February 2003; 27 February 2003; 1 April 2003; 25 June 2003.

Hopkins, R. (2000) 'Political Economy of Foreign Aid', in F. Tarp (ed.), *Foreign Aid and Development: Lessons Learned and Directions for the Future*, London: Routledge.

Huntington, S. P. (1996) 'Democracy for the Long Haul', *Journal of Democracy*, 7(2): 3–13.

Journal of Development Studies (2001) Special issue on 'Changing the Conditions for Development Aid: A New Paradigm?', *Journal of Development Studies*, 37(6).

Mallaby, S. (2002) 'The Reluctant Imperialist: Terrorism, Failed States, and the Case for American Empire', *Foreign Affairs*, 81(2), March/April pp. 2–7.

Mathews, J. (2001) 'Carnegie Endowment Policy Brief, Special Edition 18', Washington, DC: Carnegie Endowment for International Peace.

OECD (1996) *Shaping the 21st Century: The Contribution of Development Cooperation*. Paris: OECD. Available at: http://www.oecd.org/dataoecd/23/35/2508761.pdf.

OECD (2001) 'Development Cooperation 2000 Report', *The DAC Journal*, 2(1): 68.

Ottaway, M. (2003) 'Promoting Democracy in the Middle East', Carnegie Endowment for International Peace Working Paper 35, Washington, DC: Carnegie Endowment.

Shapiro, I. and N. Birdsall (2002) 'How Does the Proposed Level of Foreign Economic Aid under the Bush Budget Compare with Historical Levels?', Washington, DC: Center for Global Development's Center on Budget and Policy Priorities. Available at: www.cbpp.org/3-14-02foreignaid.htm.

Snyder, J. (2000) *From Voting to Violence. Democratization and Nationalist Conflict* New York/London: W. W. Norton.

Stewart, F. (2001) 'Horizontal Inequalities: A Neglected Dimension of Development', WIDER Annual Lecture 5, Helsinki: UNU-WIDER.

te Velde, D. W. (2002) 'Aid Financing for International Public Goods?', ODI Opinions, February. Available at: www.odi.org.uk/opnions.

van de Walle, N. (2002) 'Africa's Range of Regimes', *Journal of Democracy*, 13(2): 74.

Wade, R. (2001) 'The Rising Inequality of World Income Distribution', *Finance and Development*, 38(4): 39.

White, H. (2001) 'National and International Redistribution as Tools for Poverty Reduction', *Journal of International Development*, 13: 344.

World Bank (1998) *Assessing Aid. What Works, What Doesn't, and Why*, Policy Research Report (November), Washington, DC: World Bank.

3
Multilateral Development Assistance: Good, Bad or Just Plain Ugly?

Mark McGillivray, Simon Feeny and Howard White

Introduction

Bilateral development assistance (aid) has been criticized heavily for well over forty years, in particular during the Cold War period. To many, bilateral aid was just plain ugly. Bilateral donors were not so concerned with the developmental impact of aid, or ensuring that it was allocated equitably according to the relative needs of recipient countries. Instead, they were more concerned about whether their aid generated commercial export opportunities, propped up certain governments, promoted stability in strategically important countries, ensured support in international forums, could be used to induce desired behaviour from recipient countries and so on. There was, of course, diversity among bilateral donors. Not all were plain ugly. But recognizing that no bilateral aid agency can ignore broader foreign-policy interests, some were thought to be simply bad or approaching good. Unfortunately, these agencies often administered small aid programmes, so that bilateral aid was on balance somewhere between bad and plain ugly. Since bilateral aid constituted the majority of aid flows, some attributed the ambiguity over the overall developmental effectiveness of aid – whether it increased growth and by implication reduced poverty – to the overall ugliness of bilateral flows.

Multilateral aid has been viewed rather differently. Multilateral agencies were thought to be able to pursue more easily purely developmental criteria and allocate aid more equitably among recipient countries. Multilateral aid was thought to be more effective, and there were widespread calls for the share of multilateral aid in total aid to increase, with donor governments being pressured to provide more aid via multilateral agencies. This is not to say that multilateral agencies were exempt from criticism. Some were accused of ideological bias, World Bank projects were often criticized, and World Bank and IMF-supported structural adjustment was in many circles roundly condemned. But while the activities of some multilateral development agencies were considered to be bad, on balance multilateral aid was thought to be quite good. Compared with bilateral aid, it was considered to be unambiguously good.

Times have certainly changed since the demise of the Cold War. Bilateral agencies are now thought to be freer to pursue developmental objectives. The allocation of their aid among recipients is thought to be based less on overt commercial, political and other self-interest criteria. The effectiveness of aid is thought to have increased as a partial consequence of this shift. There is real evidence that bilateral donors are taking steps to improve the developmental effectiveness of their aid programmes. But what about multilateral aid? Some multilateral agencies are still criticized. The World Bank has not totally changed its spots, but they are not as prominent as once was the case, and the IMF in some circles is as unpopular as ever. But there are claims that the poverty focus of multilateral aid has increased, that it is less fragmented and better co-ordinated than bilateral aid, and that it remains more effective and more developmentally orientated. If this is truly the case, then concerns regarding greater 'bilateralism' in aid policy, with greater proportions of global aid being allocated through bilateral agencies and less through multilateral agencies, should be taken seriously.

This chapter provides a quantitative assessment of multilateral aid from a developmental perspective. It is concerned specifically with the question of whether multilateral aid is more developmental than bilateral aid, and whether bilateral aid has become more developmental, relative to multilateral aid, since 1990. The basic premise of the chapter is that multilateral aid is under threat. By this, it is meant that donor governments will, over time, gradually provide substantially fewer funds to multilateral development agencies, instead switching funding to their own bilateral development assistance agencies, over which they have more control. As a result, multilateral agencies will have to reduce the scale of their programmes substantially in developing countries. This premise might indeed be wrong. But its contemplation leads us to a possible defence of multilateral aid. The strongest case for a defence of multilateral aid is that it is more developmental than bilateral aid, that it is of better quality developmentally, and has a greater positive impact on human well-being in developing countries. This impact obviously includes poverty reduction as a first priority, as the Millennium Development Goals (MDGs) emphasize. Multilateral aid in recent years is, in general, good, and certainly bad. It is absolutely not plain ugly; this dubious distinction goes to United States' aid. There is, however, sometimes significant variation in the quality of aid by multilateral agencies, not surprisingly. Overall, this chapter finds that a strong case for the defence of multilateral aid does not exist. A weaker case exists, in the sense that it is not significantly less developmental than bilateral aid.

Aid and financial flows to developing countries, 1960–2002

The level of development aid has grown solidly since the early 1960s. The most commonly used measure of development aid is the OECD's

Development Assistance Committee (DAC) concept of official development assistance (ODA). A definition of this concept is provided below. ODA flows to all developing countries amounted to US$22.7 billion. By 2002, the level of ODA had risen by two and a half times that amount, to US$56.9 billion.[1]

Figure 3.1 charts total, bilateral and multilateral ODA from 1960 to 2002. Bilateral ODA is that provided by country members of the DAC. From 1964 to 1978, the real level of bilateral aid trended downwards. It fell to its lowest level for the entire period 1960–2002 in 1978, when an amount of US$23.8 was disbursed. Bilateral aid grew at a steady rate from 1978, reaching US$42.9 billion in 1991, its highest level for the period 1960–2002. It fell dramatically between 1992 and 1997, reaching US$29.5 in 1997. Since 1999, bilateral ODA has trended upwards, reaching US$39.3 billion in 2002. The level of multilateral aid has followed a much more stable trend since 1960. It trended upwards from 1960 to the mid-1980s, recording positive yearly growth in almost all years during this period. The annual average real growth rate of multilateral aid during this period was 1.1 per cent. The trend since the mid-1980s was less stable, with negative growth in number of years being recorded. During 2000 to 2002, multilateral aid grew at a faster rate, reaching its peak for the period 1960–2002, of US$17.6, in 2002. Multilateral aid grew at a real annual average of 8.7 per cent during the period 1964–2002, almost six times the rate of growth in bilateral ODA over the same period of 1 per cent.[2] Total ODA, given the trend in multilateral aid, has followed virtually the same trend as bilateral ODA since the late 1970s. It

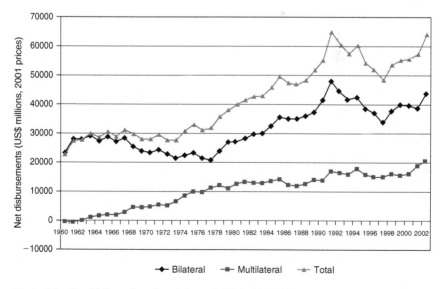

Figure 3.1   Total bilateral and multilateral ODA, 1960–2002

Table 3.1 Total net disbursements of total official and private flows by type, 1971–2002 (rounded per cent)

	1971–80	1981–90	1991–2002
All developing countries			
Official development assistance (ODA)	36.7	50.8	43.6
Bilateral	29.0	38.3	30.9
Multilateral	7.7	12.5	12.7
Other official flows (OOF)	8.7	6.6	4.3
Private flows	50.7	38.2	47.7
Grants from NGOs	3.9	4.4	4.8
Total	100.0	100.0	100.0
Sub-Saharan African countries			
Official development assistance (ODA)	59.5	77.8	88.3
Bilateral	42.0	52.9	54.2
Multilateral	17.5	24.9	34.1
Other official flows (OOF)	11.2	14.4	0.2
Private flows	29.3	7.9	11.5
Grants from NGOs	n.a.	n.a.	n.a.
Total	100.0	100.0	100.0

peaked at US$58.3 billion in 1991, dropped to US$43.2 billion in 1997, and climbed to US$56.9 billion in 2002, its second-highest level since 1960. The annual average real growth rate of total ODA over the period 1961–2002 is 2.5 per cent.

Aid flows provide the bulk of official flows to developing countries. The DAC recognizes as 'aid' flows to developing countries and multilateral institutions from official agencies which satisfy two criteria: (i) to be intended primarily for development purposes (which rules out both military aid and export credits); and (ii) to be highly concessional, defined as having a grant element of at least 25 per cent.[3] The DAC maintains a two-part list of 'eligible recipients'. Flows meeting the above criteria to countries in Part I are deemed to be ODA, and those to the richer countries in Part II are called official aid (OA). Other official flows (OOF) are official transactions for which the main objective is not development, or if it is, the funds are insufficiently concessional to qualify as ODA or OA. The main items of OOF are export credits, official sector equity and portfolio investment, and debt reorganization at non-concessional terms.

Table 3.1 shows the changing pattern in the importance of different financial flows to developing countries since 1971. For developing countries as a whole, the importance of total ODA and bilateral ODA as a source of financing increased during the 1980s, but fell during the 1990s, although

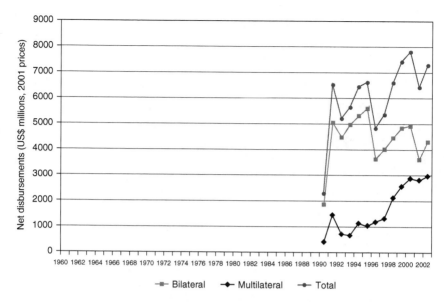

Figure 3.2 Total bilateral and multilateral OA, 1960–2002

they still remained higher than in the 1970s. An explanatory factor in the changing importance of financial flows is the reduction in private flows to developing countries during the debt crisis of the 1980s. Other official flows and grants from NGOs to developing countries have remained fairly stable since the late 1970s. However, the importance of multilateral aid has increased over this period, and since 1991 has accounted, on average, for almost 13 per cent of total flows to developing countries. The table also shows the great importance of ODA to Sub-Saharan Africa (SSA). ODA to SSA accounted for almost 90 per cent of total flows to this region since 1991, demonstrating that many of these SSA countries are unable to attract private capital flows. Multilateral aid to these countries is more important than to developing countries as a whole, accounting for over a third of total ODA since 1991. We return to the vital issue of aid to SSA below.

Figure 3.2 shows OA flows since 1990. There is much less year-on-year stability in the volume of these flows, again caused largely by the volatility of bilateral flows. Total OA have grew from US$2.3 billion in 1990 to US$7.9 billion in 2002. Multilateral OA increased from US$416 million in 1990 to US$2.9 billion in 2002. OA flows are combined with ODA flows in Figure 3.3 to show total official aid for the period 1960–2002. Given that OA flows are fairly small compared to ODA, year-on-year changes and trends in OA largely follow those shown in Figure 3.1.

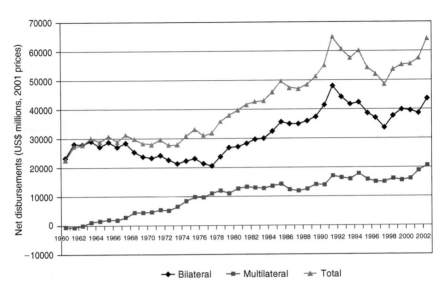

Figure 3.3   Total bilateral and multilateral aid, 1960–2002

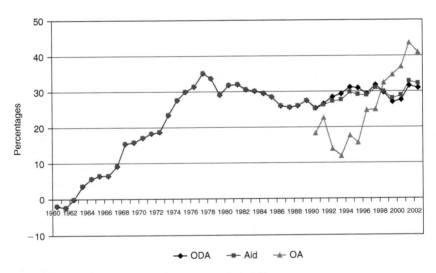

Figure 3.4   Multilateral shares in total aid, 1960–2002

Shares of multilateral aid, ODA and OA are shown in Figure 3.4. The shares in total aid and ODA increased dramatically during the 1960s and much of the 1970s, reaching 35 per cent in 1977. This is the highest share for the period 1960–2002. It then trends downwards, falling in most years until 1990. It

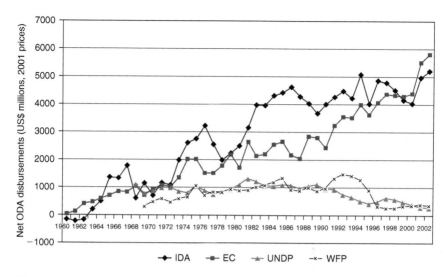

Figure 3.5 Multilateral ODA, largest four agencies by volume, 1960–2002

then trends upwards from 1990, with falls in 1998, 1999 and 2002 notwithstanding. In 2002, the share of multilateral aid in total aid was 32 per cent. The multilateral share in total OA has increased sharply since 1991, despite falls in some years. The multilateral share in OA in 2002 was 41 per cent.

The largest multilateral agencies in terms of aid volume since 1960 are the International Development Association (IDA) of the World Bank Group, the European Commission (EC), the United Nations Development Programme (UNDP) and the World Food Programme (WFP). These agencies have provided 65 per cent of total multilateral ODA since 1960. The IDA and EC are by far the largest agencies in terms of volume, providing 29 per cent and 23 per cent, respectively, of total multilateral ODA. Multilateral OA is dominated by the EC: 95 per cent of OA flows since 1990 have emanated from the EC.

Trends in ODA volume, ODA share and OA volume for these four big multilateral agencies are shown in Figures 3.5, 3.6 and 3.7, respectively. IDA and EC ODA volumes have trended upwards since 1960, despite often falling from one year to the next. In 2002, IDA and EC ODA volumes were US$5.2 billion and US$5.8 billion, respectively, the highest in any year since 1960. The EC share in total multilateral ODA has trended upwards since the early 1980s, reaching a 1960–2002 period peak of 34 per cent in 2001. IDA shares have been more volatile, trending downwards since 1997. UNDP and WFP ODA volumes and shares in total multilateral ODA have trended downwards since the early 1970s. For both agencies, ODA volumes were substantially lower in 2002 than in the late 1960s and mid-1970s. Indeed, for each agency, 2002

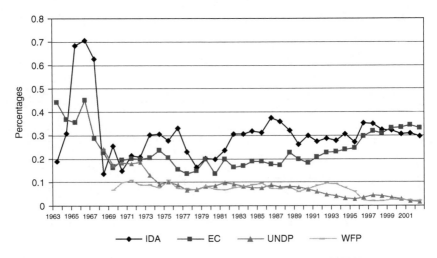

Figure 3.6   Shares in multilateral ODA, largest four agencies, 1963–2002

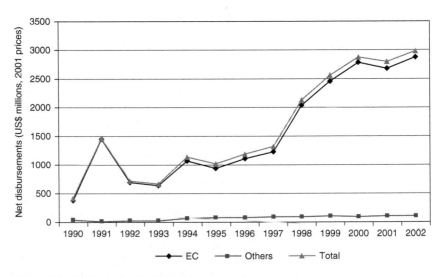

Figure 3.7   Multilateral OA, 1991–2002

volumes are approximately a third and a half, respectively, of the average volumes for these early years. For example, UNDP ODA volumes were US$837 million in 1970 and US$265 million in 2002. WFP ODA volumes, for the same years, were US$582 and US$338.

Figure 3.8 shows per capita official aid flows, obtained by dividing total aid (ODA plus OA) by total developing-country population, in each year for

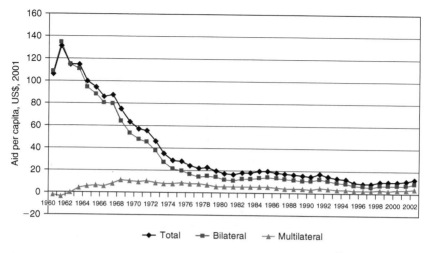

Figure 3.8 Aid per capita, 1960–2002

the period 1960–2002. A dismal picture is painted. Total and bilateral aid per capita has fallen, from one year to the next, in 28 and 32 years, respectively, during the period 1961–2002. As a result, total per capita aid fell from a peak of US$131 in 1961 to just US$13 in 2002. Similarly, bilateral per capita aid fell from a peak of US$134 in 1961 to US$9 in 2002. Multilateral per capita aid, while much smaller in magnitude and also falling for most of the period under consideration, has been more stable. It reached a peak of US$12 in 1968, and in 2002 was US$4. Since the mid-1980s it has hovered between US$3 and US$6.

Aid as a percentage of developing country GNI is shown in Figure 3.9. It follows a rather different trend from per capita aid, rising throughout the 1960s to the early 1990s. Total aid rose from 2 per cent of GNI in 1960 to 1.6 per cent of GNI in 1991. It trends downwards from 1991, falling to 1.2 per cent in 1997, but then recovering slightly to reach 1.4 per cent by 2002. Bilateral and multilateral aid follow similar trends. In 2002, bilateral and multilateral aid were 0.9 per cent and 0.4 per cent of developing-country GNI, respectively. For the period 1960 to 2002, bilateral aid and multilateral aid as percentages of developing country GNI reached their respective peaks in 1991 and 2002, recording levels of 1.14 per cent and 0.44 per cent, respectively. Perhaps the strongest message coming from Figure 3.9 does not so much relate to trends, as to the very small absolute amounts of aid, when expressed as a proportion of developing-country GNI. This has obvious implications for the effectiveness of aid.

Table 3.2 provides a comparison between the types of aid provided by bilateral and multilateral donors. Aid is disaggregated into aid grants and aid

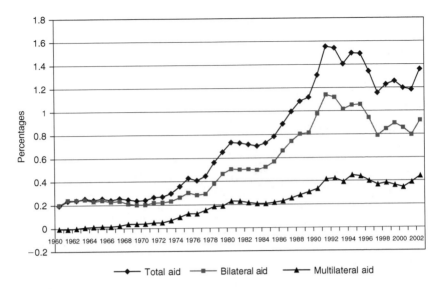

Figure 3.9   Aid as a percentage of GNI, 1960–2002

Table 3.2   Net ODA disbursements, by type and donor, 1971–2002 (period averages, rounded per cent)

	1971–80	1981–90	1991–2000	2001	2002
Bilateral					
Grants	65.5	77.2	89.1	94.6	94.8
Loans	34.5	22.8	10.9	5.4	5.2
Total	100.0	100.0	100.0	100.0	100.0
Multilateral					
Grants	50.0	52.4	53.7	55.2	51.2
Loans	50.0	47.6	46.3	44.8	48.8
Total	100.0	100.0	100.0	100.0	100.0

loans. For bilateral donors, the importance of aid grants has grown considerably since 1971, and accounted for almost 95 per cent of total bilateral aid in 2002. The share of grants in total multilateral aid is much lower in comparison to bilateral aid, and has remained fairly stable over the last three decades, accounting for roughly 50 per cent of total multilateral aid.

Table 3.3 provides a breakdown of bilateral and multilateral aid flows by region. Bilateral aid flows are widely dispersed across a number of regions. The most important region is SSA, accounting for a quarter of bilateral aid flows in 1980 and rising to almost a third by 2002. The proportion of bilateral

Table 3.3 Regional allocation of net ODA, 1980–2002

	Share of bilateral aid that is geographically allocatable (%)			Share of multilateral aid that is geographically allocatable (%)		
	1980	1990	2002	1980	1990	2002
North Africa	11.5	17.3	5.7	4.1	2.4	4.8
Sub-Saharan Africa	24.9	30.7	33.5	32.0	48.4	41.0
South America	2.7	4.1	5.8	3.1	4.0	2.4
Middle East	23.6	10.7	7.9	5.3	4.9	5.8
South & Central Asia	14.4	8.6	14.5	34.3	23.0	20.9
East Asia	9.1	14.6	14.6	9.4	10.1	8.3
Other	13.8	14.0	18.0	11.8	7.2	16.8
of which Europe	5.3	3.6	10.2	1.1	0.2	11.5
Total	100.0	100.0	100.0	100.0	100.0	100.0

aid allocated to European countries has increased since 1980, at the expense of countries situated in the Middle East and North Africa. In contrast, multilateral aid is concentrated in SSA, and South and Central Asia. The proportion of multilateral aid to SSA was 41 per cent in 2002 after climbing to almost 50 per cent in 1990. The proportion of multilateral aid to South and Central Asia has fallen from over a third in 1980 to a fifth in 2002. However, this region remains the second-largest recipient of multilateral aid.

Figures 3.10 and 3.11 provide a closer look at aid to SSA. Aid to this region is of great importance. It is now well-established that this region is clearly the poorest in the world, and one that has become poorer over the last decade. In 1990, 47 per cent of the population in SSA lived in conditions of extreme poverty, with an income of less than US$1 (in PPP terms) per day. By 1999, this percentage had risen to 49 per cent. It is widely believed that the principal Millennium Development Goal – reducing the proportion of people living in extreme poverty to half the 1990 level by 2015 – will certainly not be achieved in SSA. Even seemingly optimistic forecasts suggest the MDG poverty target will not be achieved in SSA until 2147, some 132 years late (UNDP 2003). Given that it is now reasonably well-established that aid works by increasing growth and, by implication, reducing poverty (Beynon 2001, 2002; McGillivray 2003b), the issue is of paramount importance.

Figures 3.10 and 3.11, against this background, are quite alarming and reveal information hidden by comparisons of aid shares for selected years. Total, bilateral and multilateral aid to SSA trended upwards until the early to mid-1990s. However, sharp declines are evident from the mid-1990s to 2000 or 2001. The share of multilateral aid to SSA declined between 1995 and 2000, indicating that this form of aid made the overall decline in aid

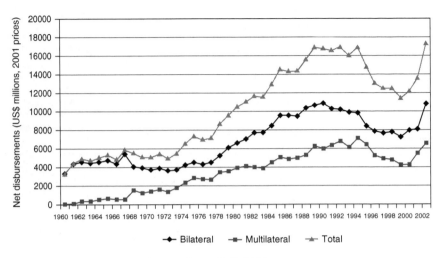

Figure 3.10   ODA to Sub-Saharan Africa, 1960–2002

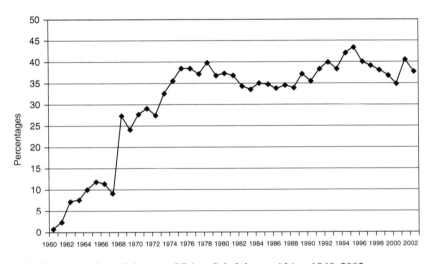

Figure 3.11   Multilateral share in ODA to Sub-Saharan Africa, 1960–2002

larger than would have otherwise been the case. Fortunately, ODA levels in 2002 recovered roughly to the levels of the early 1990s. Clearly, poverty is now much higher in SSA as a result of these declines; one is left to speculate as to the extent of poverty that might have prevailed without them.

That the share of multilateral aid allocated to SSA in 2002, compared to the early 1980s, has risen suggests that it is increasingly more pro-poor than bilateral aid. This is confirmed by Table 3.4, which provides information

Table 3.4 Allocation of bilateral and multilateral ODA by income groups (percentage shares of net disbursements)

	Low-income countries	Low middle-income countries	Upper middle- and high-income countries	Total
Total bilateral				
1971	68.1	22.5	9.4	100
1981	48.8	38.8	12.4	100
1990	53.4	37.2	9.4	100
2001	60.3	34.5	5.2	100
Multilateral				
1971	56.5	23.8	19.7	100
1981	78.5	17.9	3.6	100
1990	78.7	18.3	3.0	100
2001	70.9	23.1	6.0	100

on the allocation of bilateral and multilateral aid flows by income group. It reveals that multilateral aid is more pro-poor than bilateral aid, based on shares among income groups. The proportion of bilateral aid allocated to low-income countries fell from over two-thirds in 1971 to less than half in 1981. In 2001, low-income countries received just over 60 per cent of total bilateral aid. Until recently, upper-middle and high-income countries received approximately 10 per cent of bilateral aid, although in 2001 this fell to 5 per cent. About a third of bilateral aid is allocated to low-middle-income countries. In 1971, about 56 per cent of multilateral aid was allocated to low-income countries, while upper-middle and high-income countries received almost 20 per cent. However, since 1971, multilateral donors have become more pro-poor in their allocation of aid, and provide a far greater proportion of their aid to low-income countries than do bilateral agencies. Despite low-middle-income countries receiving a greater share of multilateral aid in 2001 than in 1991, over 70 per cent of multilateral aid was provided to low-income countries.

Major recipients of multilateral ODA and OA are provided in Tables 3.5 and 3.6, respectively. While the major recipients of ODA have changed over time, India, Bangladesh and Pakistan have consistently been major yearly recipients. Poland, Romania and Hungary were the largest recipients of multilateral official aid, although the Czech Republic, Bulgaria and Russia have also been large recipients during the 1990s. In comparison, the destination of bilateral OA is heavily influenced by protectorates of DAC donors. French Polynesia, New Caledonia and the Netherlands Antilles are all large recipients of bilateral official aid.

Table 3.7 provides a comparison of the bilateral and multilateral ODA commitments by sector during the period 1990 to 2002. The table shows that

Table 3.5   Major recipients of multilateral official development assistance, 1970–2002 (net disbursement, US$ millions, 2001 prices)

	US$	Share in total (%)		US$	Share in total (%)
1960			**1990**		
1. Madagascar	20.56		1. Bangladesh	1021.4	7.7
2. Congo, Dem. Rep.	1.97		2. India	663.2	5.0
3. Indonesia	1.1		3. China	587.2	4.4
4. Somalia	0.5		4. Pakistan	505.4	3.8
5. Niger	0.2		5. Kenya	453.7	3.4
1970			**2000**		
1. India	315.6	6.7	1. India	817.6	6.2
2. Mexico	263.6	5.6	2. Serbia Montenegro	536.4	4.1
3. Brazil	248.3	5.2	3. Bangladesh	502.7	3.8
4. Colombia	163.0	3.4	4. China	444.5	3.4
5. Pakistan	161.3	2.8	5. Vietnam	404.7	3.1
1980			**2002**		
1. India	2473.9	19.6	1. Pakistan	1343.9	7.6
2. Pakistan	679.9	5.4	2. Ethiopia	750.6	4.3
3. Bangladesh	589.0	4.7	3. India	651.4	3.7
4. Cambodia	376.8	3.0	4. Vietnam	491.5	2.8
5. Egypt	318.8	2.5	5. Congo, Dem. Rep.	436.1	2.5

Note: Shares for 1960 not provided because of negative total multilateral ODA.

over a-third of multilateral ODA commitments are allocated to 'social infrastructure and services', indicating that multilateral assistance might be more pro-poor than bilateral assistance. A higher share of multilateral aid is also allocated to 'economic infrastructure and services' and 'production sectors'. Part of the explanation for the differences is that more than 10 per cent of bilateral ODA commitments were allocated to 'action related to debt' in comparison to just 0.3 per cent for multilateral donors. Bilateral donors also allocate a greater share to emergency assistance and support for NGOs in comparison to multilateral donors.

Table 3.8 provides measures of the concentration of DAC bilateral aid and multilateral aid for the period 1990–6. There are valid concerns in the international aid community that the aid programmes of most donors are spread thinly over many recipients. There are good developmental grounds for concentrating the assistance of any given donor on a few countries. First, the staff of the agency, and the consultants working for them, build up expertise about a particular country. Second, concentration will reduce donor proliferation in developing countries, by which the scarce time and skills of government are taken up in satisfying the multiple demands of many different donors. In recognition of this problem, several donors have at various times sought to concentrate their aid on fewer countries (White 2002).

Table 3.6 Major recipients of multilateral official aid, 1991–2002 (US$ millions)

	Multilateral official aid					Bilateral official aid	
	1991	1996	2002	Share in 2002 (%)		2002	DAC share in 2002 (%)
Poland	72.70	286.33	770.64	24.0	Russia	1109.27	24.8
Romania	118.88	122.69	510.8	15.9	Israel	749.31	16.8
Hungary	514.8	96.77	430.45	13.4	French Polynesia	417.37	9.3
Czech Republic	187.05	57.09	342.23	10.7	Poland	388.57	8.7
Bulgaria	266.94	112.21	189.33	5.9	Ukraine	358.19	8.0
Russia	n.a.	186.78	152.53	4.7	New Caledonia	323.23	7.2
Slovak Republic	93.32	57.17	149.22	4.6	Bulgaria	189.22	4.2
Lithuania	n.a.	32.12	108.44	3.4	Romania	176.64	4.0
Ukraine	n.a.	24.94	79.21	2.5	Netherlands Antilles	94.24	2.1
Latvia	n.a.	29.95	58.83	1.8	Czech Republic	48.49	1.1
Estonia	n.a.	23.71	51.62	1.6	Hungary	40.32	0.9
Cyprus	n.a.	n.a.	27.62	0.9	Slovak Republic	39.15	0.9
Israel	n.a.	n.a.	4.57	0.1	Lithuania	35.98	0.8
Libya	n.a.	n.a.	4.57	0.1	Latvia	26.20	0.6
Belarus	n.a.	15.03	3.42	0.1	Belarus	25.98	0.6
Kuwait	n.a.	1.15	1.63	0.1	Cyprus	17.67	0.4
Part II, Total	1582.15	1545.57	3212.37	–	Part II, Total	4471.53	–

Table 3.7   ODA commitments by sector and purpose, 1971–2001, by donor

	Share of DAC bilateral aid 1990–2002 (%)	Share of multilateral aid 1990–2002 (%)
Social infrastructure and services	28.3	34.0
Economic infrastructure and services	18.6	27.1
Production sectors	10.4	16.8
Multisector (crosscutting)	5.7	8.4
Commodity aid and general programme aid	9.1	6.2
Action related to debt	10.3	0.3
Emergency assistance	6.1	2.8
Administrative costs of donors	4.8	2.4
Support to NGOs	1.9	0.2
Unallocated/unspecified	4.9	1.8
Totals	100.0	100.0

Table 3.8   Measure of the concentration of donor aid, 1991–96, percentages

	No. of countries receiving aid			Share in donor's aid of:		
	At all	>1%	>5%	Top recipient (%)	Top 3 recipients (%)	Top 10 recipients (%)
		Of donor allocation (%)				
DAC total	175	30	2	8	19	39
Multilateral aid						
AfDB	48	30	3	12	23	51
IDA	68	2	0	3	6	10
UNDP	162	32	2	7	17	33
EC	164	34	0	5	13	30
Multilateral aid total	173	29	2	6	16	37

Note: Shares calculated from total of that donor's aid allocation on a country basis.

Table 3.8 demonstrates that DAC and multilateral aid flows are widely, and reasonably evenly, dispersed across a large number of countries. Multilateral agencies provide aid to 173 countries. The largest recipient receives 6 per cent of total multilateral aid, while the ten largest recipients receive between them 37 per cent of the total. Aid provided by DAC donors exhibits a similar pattern of concentration. There are, however, considerable differences in the concentration of aid between multilateral donors. Not surprisingly, the African Development Bank (AfDB) provides aid only to its forty-eight members. Multilateral aid provided by the World Bank's IDA is more concentrated in comparison to multilateral aid provided by the UNDP or the EU. The latter two donors provide aid to over 160 countries in comparison to the IDA's sixty-eight.

Multilateral agency performance: further assessments

The preceding section looked at aid from a largely descriptive perspective, using data published by the DAC. There is a small, more analytical, literature which evaluates the quality of aid, from various donors, based on subjective criteria. The specific issue addressed concerns the manner in which aid is allocated among recipient countries. A very widely publicized critique of donor-country policies was released recently by the Centre for Global Development (CGD). This critique is based on values of the Commitment to Development Index (CDI) (Birdsall and Roodman 2003). The CDI is a multi-component index. One of its seven components relates to aid (Roodman 2003). While the CDI has been the subject of widespread criticism (which should be kept in mind below) it does provide information on multilateral aid that should not be ignored.

The aid component of the CDI evaluates the aid-giving performance of bilateral donors, including the 'aid-worthiness' of recipients. The underlying rationale for this is the notion of 'selectivity'. This notion is based on the premise that if aid is to maximize global poverty reduction – to be poverty-efficient – it should go primarily to those countries that use it best; that are most 'aid-worthy'. Put differently, this notion recognizes that the marginal poverty efficiency of aid differs across recipient countries, and the poverty-efficiency of donor aid programmes depends, therefore, on the countries that receive their aid. The Birdsall and Roodman (2003) approach is consistent with a view that the translation of aid into poverty reduction depends primarily on the quality of governance in recipient countries. They also recognize that the quality of governance is an increasing function of the per capita income (or level of economic development) of a country. Thus they define aid-worthiness in terms of country income levels and achievement in translating income-level achievements into quality governance. Those with low incomes per capita and high governance qualities relative to their per capita incomes are considered most aid-worthy, and vice versa. Selectivity weights for each recipient country are calculated on this basis.[4] Selectivity weights for each donor are then obtained, by taking the weighted average of selectivity weights for each recipient country to which they allocate aid.

Since donor countries provide aid not only bilaterally but also via multilateral agencies, Roodman (2003) provides information on average selectivity weights for multilateral agencies. The results are shown in Table 3.9. The agency with the highest average selectivity weight is – not surprisingly, given the low per capita incomes among the countries for which it is responsible – the African Development Fund (AfDF). This indicates that the AfDF provides a greater proportion of its aid to more 'worthy' aid recipients, in which the

Table 3.9   Multilateral agency performance in commitment to development index, 2001

Multilateral agency or donor country	Selectivity	Quality adjustment
AfDF	0.86	0.75
AsDF	0.77	0.49
CarDB	0.75	0.35
EBRD	0.60	0.60
EC	0.71	0.63
GEF	0.69	0.69
IBRD	0.77	0.77
IDA	0.82	0.57
IDB	0.75	0.17
IFAD	0.80	0.42
Montreal Protocol	0.74	0.74
Nordic Dev. Fund	0.80	0.78
Other UN	0.75	0.75
IMF	0.84	0.08
UNDP	0.80	0.80
UNFPA	0.78	0.78
UNHCR	0.75	0.75
UNICEF	0.79	0.79
UNRWA	0.72	0.72
UNTA	0.74	0.74
Rep. of Ireland	0.85	0.85
United Kingdom	0.84	0.79
United States	0.69	0.55
Japan	0.78	0.34
Multilateral agency average	0.69	0.56
Donor country average	0.77	0.68

Source: Roodman (2003).

development impact of these inflows is greatest. The agencies with the second and third highest weights are (not surprisingly) the IDA and (possibly surprisingly) the IMF. Table 3.10 also includes 'quality adjustment' data: ratios of reported (or actual) to discounted aid flows. The discount is based on a number of subjective criteria in addition to selectivity, including the level of donor administrative costs, interest repayments on previous years' aid and tying. Thus the ratio can be considered a broader measure of agency performance, broader than the one based on selectivity alone. UN agencies perform best in this regard, with the UNDP and UNICEF leading the way.

Table 3.9 also shows selectivity weights and quality adjustment ratios for the two best and worst performing donors, and averages for all multilateral agencies and all (DAC) donor countries (based on the latter's bilateral aid only) in terms of the quality adjustment. The two-top performing countries – the Republic of Ireland and the United Kingdom – exhibit better performance than most multilateral agencies. The UK exhibits the same assessed performance at UNICEF (each has adjustment ratios of 0.79), while the performance of the Republic of Ireland surpasses that of the UNDP. Indeed, the average (unweighted) performance of the DAC bilateral donor agencies exceeds that of their multilateral counterparts, based on both the selectivity weights and quality adjustment ratios. Bilateral aid is of better quality than multilateral aid, according to the aid component of the CDI.

A number of indices have been designed specifically for evaluating donor performance with respect to inter-recipient aid allocation. Reviewed in White and McGillivray (1992, 1995) and McGillivray (2003a, 2004), these indices have the following general form:

$$I_j = \sum_{i=1}^{n} w_i \frac{A_{i,j}}{A_j} \tag{3.1}$$

where I_j is the index for donor j, w_i is a weight relating to the 'developmental status' of recipient i, $A_{i,j}$ is aid to recipient i from donor j, and A_j is total donor j aid. Developmental status can be assessed in a number of ways, be it in terms of average income (income per capita), human development, the extent of poverty and so on. The interpretation of the general form of these indices is straightforward. The greater the share of aid allocated to countries with larger weight values, the higher the value of the index. If the weight is some measure of poverty in recipient i, for example, the greater the proportion of donor j aid allocated to recipients in which poverty is more prevalent, the greater the value of the index. Its maximum value is one, which would occur if the donor in question allocates all its aid to the country for which the weight takes the highest value. In the case of a poverty-based weight, this would occur if the donor gave all its aid to the country with the greatest prevalence of poverty.[5]

A number of variants of these indices have been used to evaluate bilateral and multilateral donors. McGillivray (1989, 1992) proposed a donor 'performance index', and applied it to data for the period 1969 to 1984. Rao (1994, 1997) proposed an 'equity index' and applied it to data for the period 1970 to 1993. McGillivray and White (1994) proposed what can be considered a 'concordance index' and applied it to data for the period 1974 to 1990. The McGillivray–White index is a little different in structure from Equation (3.1), although can still be considered as the sum of weighted aid shares. It is written as follows:

$$\Phi_j = 1 - \sum_{i=1}^{n} \left| \frac{\tilde{A}_{i,j} - A_{i,j}}{A_j} \right|$$

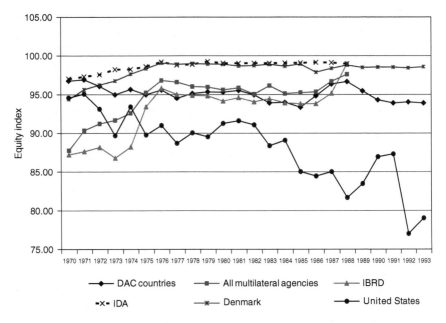

Figure 3.12   Rao equity index, 1970–93

where $\tilde{A}_{i,j}$ is a prescribed allocation derived from a non-linear optimization problem, taking in a range of variables, and $A_{i,j}$ is the actual amount of aid allocated to i. It follows that since the sum of $\tilde{A}_{i,j}$ equals $A_{i,j}$, the maximum value of Φ_j is one, which would occur if $\tilde{A}_{i,j}$ equals A_j for all i. The minimum value approaches minus one. More generally, the greater the value of Φ_j, the greater the performance of the donor.

Selected results of the McGillivray (1989), McGillivray and White (1994) and Rao (1997), studies are shown in Figures 3.12, 3.13 and 3.14. Rao's results tend not to differentiate donors significantly, although thus in fact found that bilateral aid marginally out-performed multilateral aid (see Figure 3.12) during the period under consideration. The IDA, however, out-performed all donors, exhibiting better performance than the best-performing bilateral donor, Denmark. The US exhibited the worst performance in most years under consideration, and by far the worst average performance for the entire period under consideration. McGillivray (1989) found that, while multilateral aid out-performed bilateral aid, it fell somewhat short of the performance of the best-performing bilateral donor, Belgium. The US was also the worst performer in the McGillivray study. The performance of this donor fell appreciably in the early 1970s, largely because of very large shares of its aid to Israel. McGillivray and White (1994), who only provide results for aggregated aid

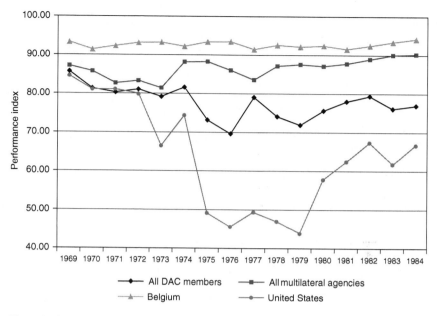

Figure 3.13 McGillivray performance index, 1969–84

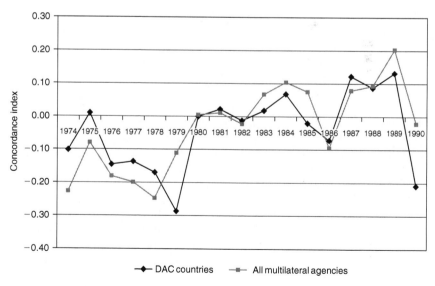

Figure 3.14 McGillivray–White concordance index, 1974–90

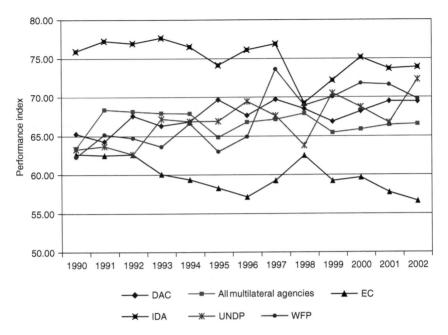

Figure 3.15   Income-weighted performance index, 1990–2002

flows, found that multilateral aid, on average, slightly out-performed bilateral aid. However, they found that for much of the 1970s the reverse was true. That multilateral aid on average out-performs bilateral aid is a result of substantial increases in multilateral performance in the early 1980s, which were sustained through the remainder of the decade.

Updated performance index values, weighted using PPP GDP per capita, the HDI and the US$2 per day poverty headcount are provided in Figures 3.15, 3.16 and 3.17, respectively. Population also appears in the weights. More precisely, the weights are the logarithm of ratios of population to GDP per capita, the HDI and the headcount, respectively. Thus, a donor's index value will be greater the higher the proportion of aid allocated to (i) countries with larger populations; and (ii) countries with either lower PPP GDPs per capita, lower HDIs or higher poverty headcounts. The use of the poverty headcount is justified on the grounds that countries with high HDIs or GDPs per capita can still have large numbers of people living in poverty. As such, the use of these indicators can overlook important information. The headcount provides a direct measure of the number of people living below the chosen poverty line, and as such is not subject to this criticism. Index values are for total DAC bilateral aid, total multilateral aid and the four big multilateral agencies – the EC, IDA, UNDP and WFP. The yearly sample of recipient countries varies according to

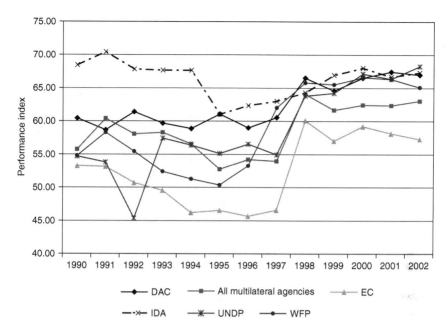

Figure 3.16 HDI-weighted performance index, 1990–2002

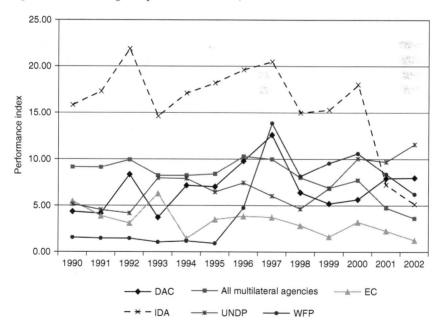

Figure 3.17 Poverty-weighted performance index, 1990–2002

weight data availability. For GDP per capita the sample size is 140 countries. It varies between 113 and 152 countries for the HDI, and between 37 and 55 countries for the headcount. The results based on the headcount (shown in Figure 3.17) should therefore be treated with caution.

Based on the income and HDI weights, two interesting results emerge. The first is that the DAC bilateral aid marginally out-performs total multilateral aid and that of the EC, UNDP and WFP. The second is that the IDA aid substantially out-performs all other aid under consideration: as such, it is the top-performing agency. These results are almost replicated using the poverty headcount as the weight, except that total multilateral aid out-performs bilateral aid, and EC aid is substantially out-performed by all other aid.

Finally, what does the research literature say about the developmental effectiveness of multilateral aid, relative to bilateral aid? There is a large and growing literature on the impact of aid on growth, and recent literature indicates that this impact is positive, ambiguities about the relevance of recipient country policies notwithstanding (Beynon 2001, 2002; McGillivray 2003a). Unfortunately, however, studies do not disaggregate aid in a way that highlights the impact of multilateral aid. This is a substantial gap in the aid effectiveness literature. The closest the literature comes to filling this gap has been the publication of a number of studies looking at the impact of aid on various public sector fiscal aggregates. A small number of studies (Heller 1975; Gang and Khan 1991; Khan and Hoshino 1992; McGillivray 2002) disaggregate aid into its bilateral and multilateral components. Mixed conclusions emerge. For example, Heller finds that there is little difference between the impacts of bilateral and multilateral aid on public investment, Gang and Khan find that a greater share of multilateral aid goes to development projects, and McGillivray finds that the impacts of bilateral and multilateral and differ according to whether a structural adjustment programme is in place. While these results are interesting in their own right, they do not permit one to infer much about the broader impacts of multilateral and bilateral aid, including impacts on poverty. The jury is still out (or is yet to be formed) on this issue.

Conclusion

This chapter has provided a quantitative assessment of multilateral aid from a developmental perspective. Its main objective was to establish whether multilateral aid is more developmental than bilateral aid, and whether bilateral aid has become more developmental, relative to multilateral aid, since 1990.

A number of specific findings emerged. First, measured using shares of aid allocated to country groups, multilateral aid has a greater poverty focus than bilateral aid, in that an increasingly larger share has gone to low-income countries and to those located in SSA. Therefore, multilateral agencies are doing more to achieve the MDGs, given the support provided to that region.

Offsetting this is the finding that declines in multilateral aid to SSA during the period 1995 to 2000 were greater than the declines in bilateral aid during the period. Second, measured using a number of donor performance indices, which look at the allocation of aid among individual countries rather than country groups, mixed evidence emerges regarding the poverty focus of the multilateral agencies. Based on per capita incomes and the HDI, bilateral agencies have, since 1990, collectively out-performed their multilateral counterparts. The reverse is true if the assessment is based on poverty headcount data. Third, based on CDI calculations, bilateral agencies collectively clearly out-perform multilateral agencies on a number of criteria, although some multilateral agencies perform as well as the best bilateral donors. Fourth, a greater share of bilateral aid is provided in the form of grants when compared to multilateral aid. While this share has increased since the early 1990s for bilateral aid, it has marginally decreased for multilateral aid. Finally, multilateral aid is marginally less concentrated than bilateral aid.

What do these specific findings tell us about the developmentalism of multilateral aid relative to bilateral aid? In short, it is difficult to conclude that multilateral aid is more developmental than bilateral aid. If anything, the reverse is the case. But it is also difficult to conclude that the degree of developmentalism of multilateral aid relative to bilateral aid has changed much since the 1990s. Can multilateral aid be defended on developmental criteria? To the extent that it is not significantly less developmental than bilateral aid, the answer would appear to be yes. The strongest case for a defence of multilateral aid is that it is more developmental than bilateral aid, that it is of better quality developmentally, and has a greater positive impact on human well-being in developing countries. Unfortunately, this case would appear to be rather difficult to make.

Acknowledgements

This chapter was originally prepared for the EU-LDC Network Conference 'Multilateralism at Risk – Beyond Globalisation', held in Brussels in April 2004. The authors are grateful to the conference participants for many useful comments. The usual disclaimer applies.

Notes

1 All data reported in this section of the chapter are taken from OECD (2004). All dollar amounts are in constant 2001 prices.
2 Calculations of growth rates which include those for 1961–4 are not reported here, given that multilateral ODA was negative in 1960–3.
3 The grant element is the grant equivalent divided by the face value, where the grant equivalent is the face value of the loan less the present value of repayments

discounted at 10 per cent. A grant has a grant element of 100 per cent, and a loan with an interest rate of 10 per cent has a grant element of 0 per cent.

4   Governance quality is measured using the indicator developed by Kaufmann, Kraay and Zoido-Lobatón (KKZ) (1999). This indicator is a composite of indicators of democracy, rule of law, bureaucratic regulation, government effectiveness and corruption.

The procedure is to fit the following governance regression equation to cross country data:

$$G_i = \alpha + \beta \ln Y_i + \mu_i \tag{3.2}$$

where G_i is the quality of governance of aid recipient i measured using the KKZ indicator, α is a constant term, β is a slope coefficient, $\ln Y_i$ is the logarithm of recipient i's purchasing power parity GDP per capita, and μ_i is a residual. The residual may be interpreted as that component of recipient governance quality which is not empirically accounted for by the constant term and the term $\beta \ln Y_i$. Countries with high governance qualities and low incomes per capita will have numerically larger residuals than those with low governance qualities. It follows that the larger the residual the better is governance relative to income, or the better recipient has performs in converting income into governance quality.

The selectivity weight for each recipient, W_i, is:

$$W_i = \mu_i - \beta \ln Y_i \tag{3.3}$$

provided β is positive (which was the case in fitting the governance regression equation to recipient country data), the selectivity weight is higher the higher the value of the residual and the lower is the level of income per capita.

Prior to adjusting aid for selectivity the weights are linearly transformed to range between 0.5 and 1.0, indicating lowest and highest worthiness for aid, respectively. Recipient selectivity weights are reported in Roodman (2003). Tanzania and Malawi have the highest weights (1.00 and 0.99, respectively), while Belarus and Russia have the lowest weights (0.50 each). Weights to countries receiving relatively large shares of Australian ODA are as follows: Papua New Guinea (0.75), Indonesia (0.66), Vietnam (0.76), Philippines (0.71), China (0.69) and Cambodia (0.87). Weights for 121 countries were calculated, based on data availability.

5   McGillivray and White (1992, 1995) look critically at a range of quantitative measures used to evaluate inter-recipient aid allocation. While none of these measures is problem free, the index defined by Equation (3.1), based on the application of McGillivray (1992), is consistent with a number of desirable properties. Moreover, as McGillivray (2003b, 2004) points out, it is advantageous over other measures in that it can easily incorporate weights that are non-income-based.

References

Beynon, J. (2001) 'Policy Implications for Aid Allocations of Recent Research on Aid Effectiveness and Selectivity', Paper presented at the Joint Development Centre/DAC Experts Seminar on Aid Effectiveness, Selectivity and Poor Performers, January, Paris: OECD.

Beynon, J. (2002) 'Policy Implications for Aid Allocations of Recent Research on Aid Effectiveness and Selectivity', in B. Mak Arvin (ed.), *New Perspectives on Foreign Aid and Economic Development*, Westport, Conn.: Praeger.

Birdsall, N. and D. Roodman (2003) 'The Commitment to Development Index: A Score-card of Rich-Country Policies', Technical Paper, Washington, DC: Center for Global Development.

Gang, I. N. and H. A. Khan (1991) 'Foreign Aid, Taxes and Public Investment', *Journal of Development Economics*, 34: 355–69.

Heller, P. S. (1975) 'A Model of Public Fiscal Behaviour in Developing Countries: Aid, Investment and Taxation', *American Economic Review*, 65: 429–45.

Kaufmann, D., A. Kraay and P. Zoido-Lobatón (1999) 'Governance Matters', World Bank Policy Research Working Paper 2196, Washington, DC: World Bank.

Khan, H. A. and E. Hoshino (1992) 'Impact of Foreign Aid on the Fiscal Behaviour of LDC Governments', *World Development*, 20: 1481–8.

McGillivray, M. (1989) 'The Allocation of Aid among Developing Countries: A Multidonor Analysis Using a Per Capita Aid Index', *World Development*, 17(4): 561–8.

McGillivray, M. (1992) 'Reply', *World Development*, 20(11): 1699–702.

McGillivray, M. (2002) 'Aid. Economic Reform and Public Sector Fiscal Behaviour in Developing Countries', CREDIT Discussion Paper 02/11, Nottingham: CREDIT.

McGillivray, M (2003a) 'Aid Effectiveness and Selectivity: Integrating Multiple Object-ives into Aid Allocations', Summary paper presented at the Joint OECD/DAC Development Centre Aid Experts' Seminar, 10 March, Paris: OECD.

McGillivray, M. (2003b) 'Descriptive and Prescriptive Analyses of Aid Allocation: Approaches, Issues and Consequences', WIDER Discussion Paper 2003/21, Helsinki: UNU-WIDER.

McGillivray, M. (2004) 'Descriptive and Prescriptive Analyses of Aid Allocation: Approaches, Issues and Consequences', *International Review of Economics and Finance*, 13(3): 275–92.

McGillivray, M. and O. Morrissey (2001) 'New of Evidence of the Fiscal Effects of Aid', CREDIT Research Paper 01/13, Nottingham: CREDIT.

McGillivray, M. and H. White (1994) 'Development Criteria for the Allocation and Aid and Assessment of Donor Performance', CREDIT Research Paper 94/7, Nottingham: CREDIT.

Rao, J. M. (1994) 'Judging Givers: Equity and Scale in Aid Allocation', *World Development*, 22(10): 1579–84.

Rao, J. M. (1997) 'Ranking Foreign Aid Donors: An Index Combining the Scale and Equity of Aid Giving', *World Development*, 25(6): 947–61.

Roodman, D. (2003) 'An Index of Donor Aid Performance', Technical Paper, Washington, DC: Center for Global Development.

OECD (2004) *International Development Statistics Online*, Paris: OECD-DAC.

UNDP (2003) *Human Development Report 2003: Millennium Development Goals – A Compact Among Nations to end Human Poverty*, New York: UNDP.

White, H. and M. McGillivray (1992) 'Descriptive Measures of the Allocation of Development Aid', ISS Working Paper 125, The Hague: Institute of Social Studies.

White, H. and M. McGillivray (1995) 'How Well Is Aid Allocated? Descriptive Measures of Aid Allocation: A Survey of Methodology and Results', *Development and Change*, 26(1): 163–83.

White, H. (2002) 'Long-run Trends and Recent Developments in Official Assistance from Donor Countries', WIDER Discussion Paper 2002/106, Helsinki: UNU-WIDER.

4
Political Economy of Additional Development Finance

Anthony Clunies-Ross and John Langmore

Introduction

The world needs more 'development finance' in order to facilitate faster growth in the economies of low- and middle-income countries, and for attending to the shorter-term basic material-welfare needs of poor people in poor countries. There are many purposes counting as urgent from a humanitarian point of view that depend on extra funding: vaccination, essential medicines, dehydration doses, clean and accessible water supplies, sewerage, teachers' pay, teacher training, emergency food stocks, and with all the transport and skills and administrative infrastructure to bring these benefits to fruition. And this is to take no account of the relevance of much of the same infrastructure, or of the immediate welfare benefits themselves, to economic growth and to the increased material capacity that these in turn will bring.

Extra development finance may come, first, as extra 'own-resources': in the form either of enhanced 'own-revenue' for the governments of developing countries, or of enhanced personal disposable income for those of their citizens likely to spend part of the addition on enlarging their productive capacity or ministering to the urgent needs of their families or communities. It may come, second, from voluntary donations, directly or through non-government organizations (NGOs). It may come, third, in the form of official development assistance (ODA), either bilaterally (government-to-government) or in the form of payments from governments to international institutions. Fourth, it may in principle come from the activities of international institutions themselves, or from taxes imposed by agreement on resources or activities that are held to be international in character, or from taxes or comparable levies that depend for their collection on international co-operation, so that in each of these cases the funds generated do not appear to belong naturally to any state or private person. Resources coming in any of these last ways may be called 'global-provenance funds'. Genuine possibilities exist for realizing finance in this fourth form, but their exploitation would raise the question of who would determine the disposal of the funds thus generated.

The Sachs Report (UN 2005) on strategies to achieve the Millennium Development Goals (MDGs) is concerned with action on a wider front than aid in these senses. And, over aid itself (in the sense of the third and fourth categories in the preceding paragraph), it adopts a selective approach, advocating heavy concentration on those recipient countries geared by the character of their governance to make good use of the resources provided. Even so, it advocates increasing aid provided by high-income countries from around 0.25 per cent of donor national income in 2003 to around 0.44 per cent in 2006, and 0.54 per cent in 2015. Millennium Project personnel calculate the difference between total ODA needs and existing annual commitments as US$48 billion in 2006, US$50 billion in 2010, and US$74 billion in 2015.

This chapter is concerned with any potential sources of additional development finance that have an international dimension: that depend on some form of cross-national activity.

The underlying question in the chapter is how political forces might be mobilized more effectively to secure, and to use effectively, additional development finance. The chapter is structured in three parts.

The first part considers the bearing of political arrangements and strategies on the opportunities for increasing development finance through cross-national activity. It looks at types of political strategy or presentational devices that might enable additional funds to be released; the obstacles that this enterprise faces; the bodies that are potential allies in its pursuit; some sources of funds that might be realized by exploiting potential support and attacking soft targets; and what particular tactics might be helpful or necessary for securing these funds.

The second part considers specifically how to deal with any large sources of funds that are recognized as being international in nature and not naturally the property of any state or person – the global-provenance funds – together with any other sources that the governments of the world are prepared to assign to international disposal. It considers the political problem of finding institutional means through which these funds, possibly flowing in amounts that dwarf existing multilateral development finance, might acceptably be allocated. The quest is motivated by the view that the allocating institutions may well have to be approved before there can be a decisive impetus for tapping large, innovative sources of funds for global disposal. The devices adopted will need to be widely deemed to be legitimate, to inspire a measure of confidence, and to be efficient in directing the funds to purposes recognized as having high priority. A proposal is made for one possible way of meeting these requirements. The third part of the chapter is a brief conclusion.

Raising finance

Preliminary

Development finance and its global enhancement constitute one of several major international 'development' issues for which existing institutions and practices are widely held to be inadequate. Others are trade, the physical and biological environment, stabilization, international debt, and direct foreign investment. The matter of development finance overlaps with these other concerns, and similar or overlapping ranges of political strategies and tactics may be available for them.

Suppose we believed that there was a desirable outcome, a desirable range of outcomes or a desirable direction of movement on any of these questions. It might be said then that we regarded that outcome, or one of those outcomes, or that direction of movement, as in the broadest sense a global public good: 'in the broadest sense' in that it might in that case be necessary to include as global public goods such objectives as equity across the world or the mutual responsibility of peoples for one another – in other words, to regard those objectives as being broadly good for all: those that give and those that take. But that is a matter of terminology. There is a narrower concept of global public goods that would exclude the satisfaction of such ideals.

Whatever terms are used, however, our belief that there are in any of these areas desirable and feasible objectives – objectives whose pursuit or achievement would be *possible* given the consent or positive commitment of certain people with power (in the context, mainly members of governments), and of whose desirability it seems that people generally have the potential to be persuaded – raises the question of how these objectives can be approached or achieved effectively. The question arising implies that there are obstacles that ostensibly might be removed, or gaps that ostensibly might be filled, so that the path toward the objectives might appreciably be cleared. In the main we are concerned with intergovernmental co-operation. It is principally governments that have to be drawn to take together the necessary action.

We could say that the obstacles (and hence the means of their potential elimination) might lie in one or more of four categories: attitudes, understanding, focus and process. 'Attitudes' would include both values and perceptions of personal or group interest. 'Understanding' would cover both factual knowledge and a grasp of causal connections: the facts and how the world works. 'Focus' would refer to a sufficiently clear view of a possible rule, or of a combination and sequence of actions, by which an objective might be advanced. And 'process' would denote the routine requirements of laws and constitutions that would have to be met if the required rules were to be instituted or the required combination and sequence of actions were to be followed.

Action under the first heading (to influence attitudes) would involve elo-
quence or persistence in moral persuasion, or forms of depiction of the
relevant needs and their satisfaction, or presentation of world views in which
universal mutual responsibility plays a part, in such a way as to alter the emotive responses of the relevant public. Under the second, it would entail the
assembly and presentation of relevant information and of a priori or empirical
analysis. Under the third, it would require, principally, imagination. Under
the fourth, ingenuity would need to be applied to local (national) institutional knowledge. These categories of necessary responses overlap, and in
any situation the effectiveness of one is likely to depend on the presence of
others.

Strategies and tactics exploitable in pursuit of objectives in these areas

The ten approaches listed below are not to be seen as alternatives. One or
more may be invoked as the occasion arises.

Highlighting 'win–win' opportunities

This would mean identifying and publicizing measures that would secure
what economists call 'Pareto improvements' for the major legitimate interests; that is, measures that would represent *win–win possibilities* for them, or
at least no sacrifices, even in the fairly short term.

Where it can be shown that the main recognized governmental partners in
any contemplated arrangement can all gain from it soon enough for the gain
to be politically relevant to them, the obstacles to the arrangement should
not, by ordinary reasoning, be difficult to remove. It will be a matter of
demonstrating the balance of advantages rather than asking for sacrifices.
The requirements for advance may well include progress in understanding,
in focus, and in attention to process. But the most difficult category of
movement – in attitudes – will not be necessary.

Such, it would seem, first, are a number of possible measures of international tax co-operation. Examples where there would be, or might be, gains
to fiscal authorities almost universally would be (i) the concerted imposition, at least by rich countries, of a withholding tax at a significantly high
rate on interest and other portfolio income accruing to foreign residents;
(ii) a co-ordinated whole-enterprise system of assessing the taxable income
of multinational firms with the total divided by formula among the countries of operation; and (failing that, or where it can not be fully applied)
(iii) tax liability in a multinational firm's country of residence (origin) for
its *whole* global income but subject to credit (not deduction from base, or
exemption) for tax paid in other jurisdictions. The governments of most or
all major countries, rich and poor, have the potential to gain fiscally – that
is, in government revenue, from the first two of these arrangements (Tanzi

1995; Avi-Yonah 2000). The third would be of clear benefit fiscally to the poorer host countries as a body over arrangements normally in place now, because it would remove any incentive they had to competitive tax reduction for the purpose of attracting multinational investment. It might or might not be of fiscal benefit to the countries that were predominantly sources rather than recipients of direct investment, depending in part on the provisions it would be replacing.

The obstacles, at least in the first two of these cases, are probably the lack of a widespread understanding of the effects of present arrangements, and of the alternative possibilities; lobbying by criminal or socially irresponsible private vested interests that may, among other actions, exert themselves to mis-represent the issues; the opposition of a few small states – some of them quite affluent – that profit from offering opportunities for tax evasion and tax avoidance, but might possibly be compensated, at least in part, for their loss; and bureaucratic-cum-political inertia or lack of imagination. (Some individuals would, of course, lose from these changes – as a result of having to pay the taxes that the law obliges or intends them to pay but which they would otherwise evade or avoid. But evasion and avoidance in this sense are generally both unfair and inefficient. The fiscal gain accruing to the authorities of most countries from closing these gaps would generally be in the interests of their peoples as normally considered.) Of the four areas of movement, it is thus mainly changes in understanding and focus that are required. Attitudes – values and perceptions of interest – need not shift. Argument and presentation of evidence would doubtless have an important part to play in breaking the factors of resistance, but the argument would be about cause and effect rather than about values.

A second example of what might very well be of value for the present purpose as a win–win (Pareto-type) improvement is the regular issue of Special Drawing Rights (SDRs) by the IMF. The primary purpose of SDRs, at the time of their institution in the late 1960s, was stabilization in a world in which a shortage of international reserve media was feared. Stabilization is still an important reason for expanding their supply: it would enable the currency reserves of all IMF member countries to be increased without cost to those countries. This is of particular value for developing countries because, for most of them, the expansion of their reserves would otherwise entail net costs; and they are the ones at greatest direct risk of currency crises, against which reserves form a defence. So, if their alternative to receiving SDRs would have been the same reserve levels, but at a cost, the issue of SDRs would constitute a direct real-income gain to them. If their alternative would have been lower reserve levels, the gain would come in the form of greater protection against currency collapse; and, because of the contagion that might arise from currency collapse in any single country, as was seen in the East Asian crisis of 1997–8, that enhanced protection would constitute a gain to the rest of the world as well. The modernized case for regular SDR 'allocation' has been argued by Clark and Polak (2002). On the potential income gain to developing countries as a body from regular SDR allocations within the range that has been considered in IMF circles as feasible, Clark and Polak cite a study by Mussa (1996), which estimates that a repeated annual 'allocation' of 36 billion SDRs would add to the income of developing countries, given a constant level of reserves held by them, amounts of the order of 1 billion SDRs in the first year, 2 billion in the second and so on; that is, a cumulative total addition to income of about 55 billion over the first ten years. (The value of an SDR is of a similar order to that of a US dollar, and has usually been higher since the 1980s.)

If the developing countries that had the potential for this income gain chose to enjoy it in full and did not use it to add to their reserves, this might constitute a corresponding cost for those parts of the world (effectively the rich countries) that would not benefit in the same way – but *only* in so far as the resources of those rich countries were already so fully employed that they would need to curtail their domestic demand in order to accommodate this increased spending power of the developing countries. In other words, it would represent a cost to them only in so far as extra demand for their exports would overstretch their economies, obliging them to reduce their own consumption or investment.

If, at the other extreme, the developing countries were to use all their SDR allocations to add to their reserves, this would involve no levy on the income of the rest of the world, even if the latter were operating at full capacity. It would contribute to the real global benefit of greater currency stability. It would, admittedly, to a small degree reduce the capacity of the countries issuing the main reserve currencies (principally the US dollar) for borrowing at low interest from foreign monetary authorities, but the reduction would be small, as Clark and Polak (2002) show, in relation to those countries' total short-term borrowing from the rest of the world. It is in any case questionable whether what appears now as an unlimited capacity for the reserve-currency countries to borrow from the rest of the world is, on a longer perspective, an unqualified boon to those countries themselves.

So there may be argument over whether, strictly speaking, the resumption of regular annual issues of SDRs would constitute a win–win improvement from the viewpoint of every state and its population, under every possible circumstance. But there is a strong presumption that increasing reserves, for any country likely to be subject to currency-flight, contributes to the global good of increased stability of income. And any costs accruing to any party from the enjoyment of extra real income on the part of developing countries as a result of the SDR allocations would be questionable, difficult to identify, and highly diffused.

So, for the purposes of its political prospects, resumption of SDR allocations may well count as a win–win improvement. There are likely to be no significant vested interests against this. No government has to allow in its budget for these benefits at the cost of alternative beneficial outlays. And no serious 'respectable' case can be made against it on the grounds of harm to any country or to the global system. Ignorance, prejudice, and possibly inertia, form the main obstacles. The machinery is all there, ready to be used. The key corrective ingredient needed is *understanding*.

An additional possible bonus to developing countries or other global concerns from regular SDR allocations has been advanced by Soros (2002). The SDRs received by countries with access at most favourable rates to short-term financial markets – roughly speaking, the rich countries – derive no net benefit from them. This is because they can borrow to increase their reserves at similar rates to those they can earn by holding SDRs. The proceeds from selling these SDRs (or, if the rules permit, the SDRs themselves), making up roughly 60 per cent of each SDR allocation, might be 'recycled' as development finance. However, because the original recipients would still have to pay interest on them at the (low) SDR rate, they would have to be recycled as low-interest (termless) loans rather than as grants if there was to be no net cost of the operation for these original recipients. These assets would still be useful as finance for any 'development' purpose that could cover the low servicing charges of the loan, but would otherwise involve borrowing at higher cost. An example might be reducing the burden of international debts incurred at higher interest rates.

Again, there would be no net cost to any party. It would simply be a case of use of the IMF's power to make funds available on more favourable terms to certain borrowers than the market would otherwise provide. There would appear to be no interests against this transformation.

Third, it may also be that improved arrangements for facilitating migrant-worker remittances, which might increase the capacity for development and welfare spending in poor countries, can be devised so as to be of little or no cost to most national authorities fiscally, and not to be against the identifiable interests of any party except, at most, certain financial intermediaries.

There are also possible cases, mentioned below under the heading 'Bargains' (page 81), in which the donor countries may be able to obtain what they regard as compensatory benefits from the recipients, and as a result, again, most or all of the parties can recognize themselves as gainers on balance from the deal, over and above any gain that may be held to flow from the global public good of equity and mutual responsibility.

However, most of the modes of obtaining additional development finance do have costs, fiscal or otherwise, that matter to the governments of the countries whose co-operation in supplying the finance is needed. In these cases, attitudes – that is, values or perceptions of interest – may have to move. At the same time, because these movements are probably the most difficult to generate, it is reasonable to seek ways of minimizing the attitudinal changes required.

Alliance and concentration

John Braithwaite (2004), drawing on Braithwaite and Drahos (2000), has brought to light important instances in which apparently weak parties in international economic negotiation have achieved their purposes through strategically exploited alliances and networking. The strategy required may involve the building of alliances (alliances that might include commercial enterprises and NGOs as well as governments); using assertively, but in a measured and graduated way, the powers of punishment and reward that the alliances have; concentrating the bargaining power, creativity and technical competence of the alliances at what are described as 'nodes' (briefly, times and places, already available or fixed by the allies themselves, at which they take opportunities to pursue their objectives); and in this process choosing, from among international forums, those that from time to time will be most favourable to the purpose pursued. 'The power of rich nations sometimes crumbles,' Braithwaite writes, 'because their own largest corporations and NGOs ... defect to the cause of poor nations. This allows, in an era of networked governance, for weapons of the weak to become formidable' (2004: 298).

Economic weight counts, so Braithwaite argues, but it is not the only factor in determining power and influence in international economic negotiation. Japan, with the second-largest affluent global economy, far ahead of those next in line, appears to have played a much less powerful role in global business regulation than France or Britain, less powerful in some cases even than some of the much smaller Scandinavian countries. Developing-country governments opposed to the projected Multilateral Agreement on Investment were able, with the help of NGOs in both rich and poor countries, to sink it in 1998. On the other hand, a small group of Washington lawyers, representing particular firms, were able to build up a coalition that could use the formation of the World Trade Organization (WTO) as an occasion for pushing through the TRIPS Agreement on intellectual property, an arrangement that much of the world soon came to deem as against its interests. As another example, proponents of an ozone-layer agreement were able, by enlisting Dupont, the largest US chemicals producer, which had potential interests in favour, to bring the US government on side and so to achieve, in the Montreal Protocol of 1987, the most successful global environmental treaty so far. All these are examples cited by Braithwaite. Success on the part of the ostensibly weaker parties in such instances may on balance have been good or bad. No general position need be taken on this question. The point is simply that such success has on certain terms been possible.

Another case, exemplifying a possibility to which the same Braithwaite paper alludes, was one in which it could be maintained that the developing-country governments involved signally failed to use the intrinsic bargaining power they had. This was the 1980s debt crisis, which involved as debtors so many middle-income-country governments, some of them, such as Brazil and Mexico, with considerable economic weight. Collectively, it could be argued, the debtor-governments could have inflicted more harm on the creditors, and indirectly on the states in which the creditors were based, than the creditors could have visited on the debtors. At all events, each side had potential weapons. The significant debtor governments numbered in the teens, with a small subgroup of them owing a large proportion of the debt. In contrast, the relevant creditors of Mexico and Brazil numbered around 500 and 800, respectively (Boughton 2001: 359, 377). Mobilization of the debtors would seem on the face of it to have been intrinsically much easier than that of the creditors. But it showed no sign of happening. With difficulty, the creditors of some particular debtor could sometimes be mobilized to reach a settlement that appeared to be in their collective interest. No serious attempt seems to have been made to mobilize the handful of large-debtor governments. The IMF staff, concerned above all to prevent a collapse of the international financial system, was fitfully able, with the help of some large creditors, to devise and maintain just-tolerable arrangements between each individual debtor and its creditors, with potential free-riders among the latter largely brought into line. The Paris Club of government concessional lenders and the IMF itself helped to seal the deals. Boughton's detailed history of these attempts has a heroic character. The show was very precariously and painfully kept on the road.

Yet debt *reduction*, other than in a few exceptional cases (notably that of Bolivia in 1986–7 and tentatively that of Mexico in 1987–8) (Boughton 2001: 484–91), did not come until the Brady bonds were instituted in early 1989. Debt reduction seems to have been critical in finally surmounting the crisis in some important cases (Boughton 2001: 499–531), and it might quite plausibly have been forced on the creditors, with the connivance of the multilaterals, some years before if the debtors had deployed their collective muscle. It had been advocated persuasively earlier by some members of the IMF staff and other highly reputable economists (Boughton 2001: 480), and had been supported in different forms by the governments of Japan (ibid. 480, n. 1) and France (ibid. 481, n. 1). In retrospect, the citadels of opposition to debt-forgiveness do not seem to have been secure.

Proverbially, if you (a handful of you) owe a trillion dollars to hundreds of creditors and cannot pay, it is the creditors who have the problem. But no use was made of this piece of folk wisdom. It is possible that myths about the power of international finance, 'dependency theory' and the like had promoted a victim-psychology and removed the hope of effective resistance.

It is easy to see why parties with punitive weapons at their disposal can sometimes be effective in pursuing their goals against otherwise powerful opposition if, and only if, they combine and co-ordinate their actions. What is less obvious is why intrinsically weak parties that have *no* convincing threats in their armoury can, as Braithwaite argues, sometimes prevail by concentrating their resources at appropriate points: not only whatever capacity for obstruction or harassment they possess, but also their creativity and expertise. It seems possible, for example, that the Jubilee movement over the late 1990s and early 2000s, with no obvious capacity for punishing opponents, has helped to push forward significantly the forgiveness of official bilateral debts of the 'heavily indebted poor countries (HIPC)'. If that is the case, we may ask how it is possible, when 'realist' analysis would appear to imply that governments will consistently pursue their national interests – and by implication that they will not change their views on the what their nations' interests are in response to outside persuasion, unless that persuasion comes with the offer of compensating concessions or with the credible threat of punishment.

The reason seems to lie in certain familiar features in the character of human beings, which they do not lose by becoming politicians or officials. Government decisions are not made by intelligent robots rigorously pursuing objectively-determined national interests. What constitutes the national interest in any instance is always a matter of opinion. Members of the political executive in any country may have differing views about it, or no firm views at all. Career diplomatic and economic officials and opinion-leaders in that country may differ among themselves, and on balance differ from the ruling politicians. Every government taking part in an international negotiation is therefore likely itself to be an arena, with some of its members and servants being uneasy about the currently dominant official line.

And we humans, including the politicians and officials negotiating internationally, are more or less 'moral' and 'reasonable' beings: moral in the sense of being inclined to respond to appeals from need vividly and forcefully presented, being moved in some degree by plausible claims of justice, and desiring on the whole to maintain good relations with those we meet (especially those we meet repeatedly and face-to-face); and reasonable in the sense of valuing consistency in statement and action, in having a capacity to be persuaded by argument and evidence, in accepting that we need reasons for opposing a plausible case that has been made to us, in sometimes recognizing when a dilemma or conflict of interest has been or can be circumvented, and in having some respect for intellectual dexterity. Hence appeals to justice and compassion, and the reasoned and striking presentation of evidence and argument, do not always fall entirely on deaf ears. It is not that all negotiators are incapable of ignoring plausible arguments based on justice and compassion, or on strong evidence. It is rather that ignoring such arguments costs many people an effort: we have to suppress some of our spontaneous reactions. We are also (many of us at least) impatient to settle disputes in which we are engaged, and keen to avoid trouble, so that stubborn and vocal opposition on several fronts, such as the number of international forums often makes possible, may have a wearing-down effect. And we value visible success in endeavours in which we are ourselves involved. If we have taken part, however unenthusiastically at the beginning, in setting up a meeting that has particular aims in view, these aims tend to become important to us personally. If the aims entail resolution of some disagreement, that objective readily becomes our own, and delay in reaching it can be unsettling to us.

These human characteristics, present more or less among international negotiators, play out on a stage which, over the twentieth century and into the twenty-first, has become full of international forums, official and unofficial. Heads of government and corresponding ministers and officials have plenty of opportunities for communicating with each other, even of meeting face-to-face. They may also repeatedly come across certain insistent and capable lobbyists, for interests or for causes.

And it is possible for new forums to be set up, with unimpeachable objectives ('international tax co-operation', for example, or 'the Millennium Project'). If such forums are furnished with high-level staff, there will be a force released for serious pursuit of the objectives, a force that can add its weight to those of other parties with similar aims. Even though most of the participating governments may initially regard any possible progress on the issue as entailing too much trouble to be worth the effort – because they cannot envisage easy compliance on the part of other countries, say, or because of the technical complexity of the issues, or because of contrary lobbyists or vocal legislators on their own domestic scenes – they may be presented in international forums with appeals to sympathy or justice; expressed or implied promises or threats; evidence; arguments over cause and effect; specific options; or possible sequences of action, which they will at least feel obliged to find plausible reasons for ignoring or rejecting. If, in addition, there is an effective campaigning NGO or NGO alliance – seeking interviews, submitting memos, briefing the press, possibly organizing demonstrations – all perhaps in support of the ostensible objectives of the forum, then, from the point of view of the delegations of major governments, this may serve to tip the balance of potential trouble-making between the sides, tilting it in favour of progress as against immobility (Chasek and Rajamani 2003).

Of the four types of movement that may be needed to remove political obstacles to a course of action – in attitudes, understanding, focus and process – it is possible to see how a co-ordinated alliance (potentially governments, firms and NGOs) may produce shifts in all four, even in the absence of explicit menace or of the offer of concrete concessions, and it is clear why, in the process concentrating expertise, imagination and ingenuity – besides any potential weapons of promises and threats – in the appropriate forum or forums may well be crucial. Providing the forum with the resources of a well-staffed international organization – one directed by its founding brief at the recognized public good sought (freer trade, sovereign-debt sustainability, the MDGs) – will bring obvious advantages to the cause of movement in the direction of that public good.

Can these insights be relevant to the cause of additional development finance? In contrast, admittedly, to some other questions, such as those relating to trade or direct investment, the global volume and terms of development finance have *not* generally been a matter of negotiation between richer countries and poorer countries collectively other than through the replenishment negotiations for the International Development Association (IDA). This is no doubt partly because there is no institution linking together the amounts of 'bilateral' (government-to-government) financial aid coming from the various donor countries. Global targets for amounts and 'quality' of aid from rich countries have been declared, but they have been no more than aspirations. In part, it may be because, to a much greater degree than with the relationships of trade and direct investment, the bilateral donor–recipient relationship in aid seems to be asymmetrical: the recipient has nothing intrinsic to the relationship with which it can bargain.

However, some modification of this situation may be achieved if negotiations can consider questions of aid together with other objectives, some of them of interest to the countries that would be predominantly donors of aid. If an alliance such as the (Cancún) Group of Twenty could be united enough to entrust a small subset of its members to negotiate on its behalf with, say, a similar subset from the G8, a number of issues might be put on the table together. For good reasons, the conventional wisdom on negotiation is that the likelihood of an outcome acceptable to all parties is enhanced if several more-or-less connected issues can be considered at the same time so that they can be traded-off against each other. Possible examples are considered in the next subsection entitled 'Bargains'.

Moreover, the idea of development finance as a bounty rather than a responsibility or obligation on the part of potential donors is a matter of prevailing values, which may be altered. There are vocal NGOs and highly-respected world personalities pointedly challenging these values. Those who mistrust their own and others' engaged politicians and officials may well pay attention to statements by Oxfam or Nelson Mandela. Negotiation over the total volume and quality of external development finance is thus not necessarily off the agenda for ever.

Bargains

In the context of financial aid, we may picture aid-receiving countries as offering some concessions to aid-givers, explicitly or implicitly, as a *quid pro quo* (Cassen and Associates 1994). There are matters over which organized public opinion seems to be more exercised on the whole in rich countries than in poor ones: such as the general observance of human rights, or the need for environmental restraints with global implications. Rich-country governments are also likely to value security for their citizens' investments abroad, security that need not be against the interests of the host countries. There might be possibilities of financial aid in exchange for conformity on the part of its potential recipients to conventions that both sides might recognize as good in themselves, or that neither side might see as significantly harmful to its interests.

One case of this sort over which, it would seem, a bargain might have been made, and may still be made, is global warming. With quotas of emissions ('assigned amounts') worked out for individual countries more or less on the basis of previous emission levels alone, as they were for the purposes of the Kyoto Protocol, there was not the slightest possibility that quotas would be adopted by most of the less-affluent, low-emitting countries; and little enough chance that they would sign up for *any* serviceable and efficient system of quotas unless there was some pay-off for themselves. In fact, it is quite possible to conceive of an efficient and arguably equitable system of quotas, with financial incentives for observing them, that at the same time is likely to involve transfers from high-income high-emitters to lower-income lower-emitters (Clunies-Ross 2000). If the countries in the latter category had come to Kyoto with such a scheme, clearly worked out and argued, behind which they were prepared to stand, it is still doubtful that they would have prevailed. But, as public opinion in the affluent countries and the world at large becomes more serious about the question and about the increasingly important gap in any arrangements that do not involve co-operation by low- and middle-income countries, a genuine opportunity along these lines may well arise. Yet it is unlikely to bear fruit without active co-operation among major developing countries, possibly in alliance with environmental NGOs, and broadly the kinds of tactics foreshadowed under 'Alliances', above.

Double-dividend devices

On the face of it, the case for aid might be enhanced by any device that plausibly tied its provision to the simultaneous pursuit of some other widely-approved objective. A possibility sometimes discussed is the collection for development-aid purposes of a universal tax on carbon emissions. This is a tempting idea, because a levy of trivial dimensions, such as the equivalent of 5 US cents per US gallon of gasoline, would (on the assumption of very little resulting change in demand) raise worldwide such a large sum: on figures from the mid-1990s already of the order of US$130 billion a year. (The fact that there probably would be very little resulting fall in demand does, of course, greatly dilute the double-dividend case.) However, as with other suggestions invoking the same principle, consideration of the means by which this would need to be done makes its political appeal dubious. It would have to be collected by each country individually, under authorization achieved through its own fiscal processes, and, if this happened, there would be no obvious moral or pragmatic reason why the proceeds of this tax, rather than of any other, should be directed internationally. In fact, on grounds of equity, it might be considered an unsatisfactory tax for assignment to international use, since the level of carbon-emission is related only very loosely to national income, and the tax, if collected at a constant rate per physical unit, would take much larger shares of income from some countries than from others, and indeed larger shares from some developing, rather than from some affluent, countries. The worst of the inequity might be avoided, however, if only those carbon-tax proceeds raised from affluent countries were to be applied to international purposes.

Similar practical difficulties from a political standpoint, complicated by questions of international equity, arise with other suggested methods of raising global revenue – such as air travel or airline fuel taxes – that involve each national authority in separately authorizing and collecting the tax within its jurisdiction and then (so it is hoped) remitting the proceeds internationally.

One rather different suggestion, still perhaps to be fully investigated, is that of a tiny levy on emails, which might have the public-good effect of reducing 'spam', and would probably have to be enforced through voluntary agreement among internet service providers (ISPs). The robustness of the agreement might depend on whether the public was prepared to pay a small amount for the benefit of reducing spam. This cannot necessarily be ruled out, but a worldwide levy collected by voluntary agreement among commercial enterprises would be a first of its kind.

Shift from explicit, apparent or concentrated burdens to implicit, concealed or diffuse burdens

Where aid has to be voted through national budgetary processes, each unit of its funding is competing with other public purposes. Even if public opinion within the country concerned is broadly favourable, the temptation for a government, faced with the choice, to prefer other spending items is always likely to be great. Spending an extra 0.5 per cent, say, of national income on aid will probably benefit no one within the country directly; only the grubbers among figures are likely to be aware of whether it has or has not happened, and among them only a subsection are likely to recognize what its significance may be. But a similar amount diverted to domestic purposes can make tangible differences. Perhaps ways of transferring resources that avoid national budgetary processes and are not so explicitly competitive with domestic purposes may yet be discovered. It will be said that the burden of surrendering the resources must fall upon someone, and generally that is likely to be true. However, if the burden-bearers were, in spite of quite open procedures and practices, to be largely unaware of the burden, and the humanitarian grounds for imposing it were good and widely approved, it might be both politically acceptable and morally justified.

One of the politically attractive features of a possible currency transaction tax (CTT), at the minuscule rates usually discussed, is that its burden, though undoubtedly real and probably touching in some degree most of the world's people, would be highly diffused and very hard to detect except perhaps by high-level workers for firms in parts of the financial sector (firms whose shareholders would probably in fact carry a differentially large part of the burden: more, that is, than the average for groups of people of similar income, though still a very small fraction of the total). This advantage would not depend on any secrecy or deceit about what we could know or reasonably guess about the tax and its impact. It is simply that the burden would be spread so widely, and would not be apparent in any tangible way to the overwhelming majority of those carrying it.

Segregation of global-public-good elements from other purposes within the processes of allocating 'development finance'

To formulate the tactic in this way implies, of course, a narrower definition of global public goods than that used above. The term is confined to goods in which each state can recognize a concrete benefit to its own people, rather than encompassing ideals such as social justice and mutual responsibility. Inge Kaul and colleagues in several publications (for example, Kaul *et al.* 2002: 19–23) have argued that national outlays for global public goods should be separated from aid outlays, a reform in presentation envisaged as going hand-in-hand with a transfer of responsibility for global public goods from overseas-aid ministries to those concerned with the particular subject-matter involved: for example, transfer of responsibility for contributions toward international infectious-disease control to the national health ministry. The pragmatic argument for this change seems to be that this will result in more adequate cover of global public goods, in that contributions to them will be recognized as self-interested rather than charitable, and that it will also work to the benefit of aid proper, whose slender dimensions will be made manifest when contributions to global public goods are stripped out.

The case has been made only recently, and time may be needed to see whether governments will take up the proposal. Doing so would disturb existing departmental empires, and that is always likely to face opposition. It is probably too technical a reform to motivate NGO agitation. Moreover, there is an intrinsic difficulty in that the dividing lines between global-public-good and aid outlays are not always easy to draw. This is exemplified by considering a national contribution to the Global Fund to Fight AIDS, Tuberculosis and Malaria (GFATM). It may be argued that the process of eliminating tuberculosis anywhere in the world (like the process of eliminating smallpox) is clearly in the material interest of every nation individually. The present gaps may be mainly in poorer countries, but everyone has a stake in their elimination. The same is not so obvious in the case of malaria. It is now almost entirely a tropical disease. Most of the temperate rich world is touched by it only when its residents travel or live temporarily in the tropics, in which case reasonable protection can be obtained at prices that simply have to be costed in to the expense of the travel or stay. For many of us, large outlays against malaria are contributions for the benefit of others. The case is even clearer with more localized tropical diseases such as schistosomiasis.

Similar questions could arise over UN peacekeeping. In some places, its benefits are purely local; while in others, they have world implications. Considered as an undivided whole, it is a global public good, even within the narrow definition. But many of its particular operations may not have obvious spillovers elsewhere. Unless we adopted the wider definition of the concept of global public goods, which would include the mutual-responsibility and social-justice ideals, and would hence cover all well-motivated and well-judged aid, UN peacekeeping would count in part as a global public good and in part not.

Moreover, it is not obvious that in all cases transferring the funding of the global public good to the related domestic ministry would be likely to increase spending on it. The domestic health ministry might reasonably be expected by habit to rate various projects on their surplus of benefits over costs for the country's own residents. Reducing the incidence of tuberculosis across the world, or contributing to eliminating through vaccination remaining pockets of smallpox in, say, West Africa, might well be regarded as being of *some* domestic value in Finland or Austria. But there is still the intrinsic problem of adequately funding public goods when the parties are attending independently to their own interests. On the strict criterion of domestic value, the health ministry in Finland would be evaluating the returns on an outlay of, say, a million dollars devoted to smallpox vaccination in Niger against its value not to Niger or to the world, but to the very small part of the world that is Finland: that is, on the value of the expected reduction that it would generate of smallpox infection in Finland (which has probably not seen a smallpox case for decades) through the contribution it would make to eliminating smallpox finally from the world – *other things being equal*, the other things including the outlays expected from other countries. By that standard, the outlay might appear to be less well-spent than if it were devoted to, say, training additional nurses in Finland – despite its potential for relatively large human benefits in Niger and (in the context of an international programme to eliminate the disease) some additional expected benefits to the rest of the world.

Of course, the health ministries of the rich world might covenant together to complete the elimination of the disease with an agreed scale of contributions, and they might fight their respective treasuries and cabinets to realize these outlays. There are various favourable *mights*. And indeed health ministries may very well combine for these purposes whether or not their aid ministries are instructed *not* to concern themselves with diseases whose elimination can be regarded as global public goods. Kaul and colleagues indeed propose additional devices or practices that might facilitate the outcomes desired: such as requiring relevant sector ministries to provide separate accounts for their domestic and international outlays, and to co-ordinate with aid ministries. But still, transferring the potential responsibility for programmes of vaccination in Niger and the like from Finland's aid ministry to its health ministry might seem to provide no strong presumption of increased attention to such goods, or of increases in other elements of aid.

Segregation of directly humanitarian outlays

For the purpose of providing a relatively incontestable case for expansion of 'development finance' in at least certain directions, a fund or funds might be set up for certain purposes that are likely to be regarded as clearly and indisputably humanitarian. These might include, say, emergency relief, including the maintenance of global food stocks against famine; the combating of contagious diseases and provision of basic facilities and supplies required for primary health care; plant, training and running expenses for primary and secondary schooling; accessible clean water and sanitation; and UN peacekeeping. The line could be drawn wherever it was necessary to ensure the purposes remained uncontroversial. It would be an advantage if the methods to be promoted were to be largely technical or routine, and the outputs concrete and readily monitored. Grounds for assurance that the funds would be used effectively would add to their uncontroversial character.

Two approaches are possible. One, pursued already, is the multi-stakeholder global fund for a particular area of activity, such as the combating of AIDS, tuberculosis and malaria, or the vaccination of children: the UN Children's Fund may be regarded as a somewhat more general version of the same principle. These funds have the further advantage of being set up in forms in which they are open to contributions, and in some cases to influence and expertise, from outside the public sector. The other possibility is a more general fund, whose uncontroversial humanitarian purposes might be held by enough of the world's public to justify drawing on a source of revenue that was otherwise untapped, or that could in some way be regarded as international – such as a tax on (international, or all) air fares, airline fuel or currency exchanges. The third section of this chapter (see page 111) explores how such a fund (whether closely confined in its purposes as suggested here or not), with its sources regarded as being of global provenance or devoted by agreement to global purposes, might be set up and managed.

Perhaps the idea of segregation of purposes might, with advantage, be carried further: several funds, each with a particular class of purposes that could readily be explained, might be created, and each possibly fed by a particular source of global revenue. It may be that the idea of undifferentiated 'aid' is not a good marketing device.

Appropriate public-relations activity

Professional, and at the same time scrupulously honest, public-relations material might be presented. Ideally, this might itself be financed by a specific donation from outside the public sector. Its task would be easier if each exercise of the kind was confined to the support of the uses of a particular fund with a limited range of purposes – for example, one of the multi-stakeholder funds concerned with particular health needs, or a more general humanitarian fund as mooted in the subsection on segregation, above. If allocations from the fund concerned were targeted on relatively well-governed recipient countries, as proposed in the Sachs report, or there were other devices to prevent waste and misappropriation, this could be emphasized. These possibilities point to the advantage of having *international* funds of large enough scale, either already in operation or at least as frameworks awaiting activation. This would mean that the same publicity material, with minor necessary variations such as to the language in which it was produced, could be presented across those countries that were predominantly donors, without the need to tailor it to the peculiarities of each country's ODA programme. At the same time, we might expect some halo effect to operate in favour of aid in general.

Means of manifestly circumventing 'governance' deficiencies in recipient countries

Among the genuine doubts about the value of aid and the pretexts for opposing it is the belief, justified in a number of cases, that aid has been wasted through governance failures in recipient countries, principally corrupt misappropriation. Removing as far as possible the fact and the perception of misappropriation is likely to reduce one obstacle on the donor side, quite apart from its value in the country receiving the aid. There are two possible approaches. One is that proposed in the Sachs report (UN 2005), as mentioned below. This is to concentrate aid explicitly on a smallish number of comparatively well-governed countries deemed capable of using large amounts of additional aid effectively. The second approach, necessary where trust in the recipient government is inadequate, is to provide checks and scrutiny, not only through international monitoring but also through agents within the recipient country that appear likely to be independent of government. It was reported, for example, that aid to Chad had recently been channelled through an ad-hoc body composed of respected people and organizations separate from the executive government.

Targets, explicit and quantified

Because development finance is a matter of more or less, negotiations to increase it may lack a point unless a quantified target, with some plausible basis for it, is propounded. This has been half-recognized in the Finance for Development process of 2000–2, by the publication on the part of the World Bank of attempted best estimates of external public-sector finance needed on the part of the developing and transition countries in order to fulfil the MDGs (Devarajan *et al.* 2002). These, roughly US$50–60 billion a year, were accepted informally after the 2002 Monterrey summit during debate about additional finance. But somewhat more ambitious external-finance targets were later put forward in connection with the UN's Millennium Project (UN 2005), as mentioned above.

The ten tactics or strategies discussed above are by no means mutually exclusive. They form a quiverful of possible weapons. Some are much more general in their application than others. The approach outlined in the subsection 'Alliance and concentration...' (see page 77) will probably be both relevant and needed in most cases, while others are designed to make use of particular opportunities.

A further point is worth making, following in part from the subsections on 'Segregation' and 'Public relations activity' above (see page 86). There is a positive advantage in tapping global-provenance funds, rather than simply concentrating on expanding nationally-budgeted ODA – an advantage that may at least be set against the drawback that the whole idea of international co-operation in the revenue field has been inclined in recent years to induce apoplexy among the legislators of one important donor country. The advantage is that they must be allocated and administered internationally. If a broadly accepted way of doing this can be found (a task we attempt to consider in the next section) and the funds are substantial, then it may be possible to follow something akin to a strategy for meeting poverty-reduction targets, such as the MDGs. Pursuit of a poverty-reduction strategy is difficult so long as most of the world's aid comes in the form of national votes of ODA, each allocated at the donor government's discretion. It is notorious that, in the Cold War period, much aid was given for the sake of political allegiance, with little attempt being made to monitor whether it served any 'development' purpose rather than simply enriching the Mobutus, Suhartos and Mengistus and their hangers-on. In spite of deliberate attempts more recently to channel aid to where it can usefully be 'absorbed' – for example, in the rigorous rules applying to the US's post-Monterrey Millennium Challenge Account (MCA) – political-diplomatic objectives, worthy or not, are difficult to eradicate from bilateral ODA, as is evident in the large concentration of US aid still being given to Israel and Egypt. The International Finance Facility (IFF) proposal from the UK involves an aspiration, among other things, to co-ordinate bilateral aid, but without much to guarantee that this will happen.

The ten 'key recommendations' of the Sachs report (UN 2005) suppose a capacity on the part of the world community to pursue a strategy, with priorities over the objects on which aid would be spent (a high priority for certain 'quick-win actions', for example, such as free mass distribution of bednets and anti-malaria medicines, or ending fees for primary schools); and discrimination among recipient countries in favour of a dozen well-governed 'fast-track' countries with the capacity to absorb rapid increases in ODA. Propounding such priorities as an ideal for all aid may have *some* impact on how individual donor governments allocate what they give. But it is much more likely to influence what actually happens if a large part of total aid can be allocated by acceptable global processes. And, for practical purposes, this *must* happen with funds of unquestionable global provenance, such as proceeds from a CTT or from SDRs. As suggested above, these two sources also have other 'political' advantages. They would not need to go through any government's budget. Any costs of either would be highly diffused and not easily identified. And the use of SDRs for increasing development finance, which would, of course, necessitate reviving their issue, would on those grounds contribute significantly to the global good of increased economic stability, and on balance (issue and 'recycling' together) would arguably approach the status of a win–win improvement for all the nations affected.

There is a further political or marketing point. If the proceeds of certain sources of funds are being blatantly, exclusively and demonstrably devoted to following such a strategy, with aid going for purposes that ordinary people can easily understand *and* doing so either under strict international monitoring or through governments that can be given a fairly clean bill of health as administrators, the operation of tapping those sources should be easy to 'sell'. The presentational tactics mooted in the subsections on 'Segregation' and 'Public-relations activity' (page 86) could readily be followed.

Obstacles to additional development finance

Several factors – depending on either objective interest or some other determinant of attitude – that constitute political obstacles to additional development finance will be considered here. In several cases, there will be suggestions on how any of the devices listed in the previous section may be used to surmount the obstacle concerned.

A common complaint among those who favour increasing development finance is lack of political will among the governments that would have to authorize it. Where these are governments in democracies there may well be a misperception or underestimation of the extent of support for ODA among voters (see the next section, entitled 'Potential support for...' on page 95). Yet certain expressed, intellectual grounds for opposition doubtless seep into popular consciousness and have a bearing on the general climate of opinion. Some of the opposition to additional development finance applies to all forms of concessional assistance, and some to one or other of the innovative forms of fund-raising now being proposed. Among the opponents to *any* increase in aid are people who consider that developing countries do not need external assistance, and others who are sceptical about the effectiveness of ODA.

The view that aid is unnecessary

Some observers argue that developing countries have sufficient capacity to raise any additional funds they need from domestic sources, while foreign direct investment (FDI), together with borrowing for economically viable projects, could provide all the external funding required, and the investment and loans would be forthcoming if only those countries' governments would adopt appropriate policies.

It is not our business here to contest that set of beliefs, which may or may not be influential. Knockdown arguments against it are not easily found, because its differences from our own view, or indeed from prevailing officially proclaimed views, are based not entirely on different beliefs about facts and social mechanisms but at least in part on different values: differences in *attitudes* and not simply differences in *understanding*. If this outlook can be shifted, it may have to be through a combination of facts such as those about national incomes, budgets and costs of various facilities, and the extent of developed-country contributions, together with the opportunity to enter imaginatively into the real situations faced by individuals, households, entrepreneurs and officials in low-income countries.

How can those who do see the potential value of additional aid manipulate the arrangements so that such underlying counter-aid orientations lose some of their political potency? This question will be considered below in answer to the same challenge raised in the subsection 'Alliance and concentration' on page 77.

Doubt about the effectiveness with which aid is used

A second source of scepticism about external financing relates to uncertainty about the effectiveness of concessional external finance in contributing to economic and social development. Critics of this are opposed to the growth of ODA, arguing that experience shows that increases will not stimulate economic growth efficiently. They argue that much of it will be mis-applied or otherwise wasted; it will encourage tendencies within government to private rent-seeking; and what is available for public purposes will discourage local effort, saving, and economic reform. It is not that extra resources are not needed: simply that this method of attempting to provide them will be worthless or even counter-productive.

There is now considerable solid research ammunition against a comprehensive dismissal of this sort. For example, McGillivray (2005) has surveyed the literature on aid and growth, and concludes that 'the overwhelming majority of recent empirical studies find that aid increases growth, despite many valid criticisms of aid delivery'. Aid increases public expenditure, including expenditure that aims to improve services for the poor. Donors now tend to focus more actively on policies that assist development than in the past, when the objectives of aid were more diffuse. In a widely-read World Bank study, Burnside and Dollar (2000) concluded that aid works when allocated to well-governed countries. However, others have reached more nuanced conclusions: that aid generally benefits growth, but the benefits are greatest in countries with well-judged policies. A further paper, by McGillivray and others (2006) reviews a number of empirical studies since the late 1990s with diverse findings about the conditions in which aid appears to contribute to growth, but almost all of them implying that it does so *under certain conditions*.

This empirical evidence at least raises questions for the ideological opponents of aid, many of whom simply mistrust public expenditure and public-
sector activity in general, and it should also serve to reassure those who are
fearful that aid creates dependence or reduces the motivation of receiving
countries for improving the collection of national revenue or engaging in
other economic reforms.

Partly because of its intrinsic character, this set of objections to aid is thus
easier to contest than the first of those outlined on page 89 (subsection 'View
that aid is unnecessary'). The trouble, from a political viewpoint, with the
counter-evidence is that it is likely to percolate to only a small section even of
the economics profession, let alone become the stuff of public-house assever-
ations. It provides ammunition for arguments with politicians and officials,
and a good licence for wording-up serious journalists and endorsing serious
marketing in the cause of aid. It may help gradually to shift the climate
of opinion. But a politically potent answer both to this objection and to
that expressed under the first heading may require not only some professional and transparently honest public relations (combining the visual and
personal perhaps with a few significant statistics) but also some segregation
of different forms of aid, so that the case for each can be clarified without
confusion.

A controlling consideration in determining the actual criteria used should
be the likely perception of the public. For transparency and public-relations
purposes, there might be a threefold division. There is emergency aid; there is
aid which, while not geared to any unusual disaster, is directly and manifestly
humanitarian in immediate purpose; and there is aid that is predominantly
directed towards economic growth.

The first of this trio – disaster relief – is easy enough for people in donor
countries to appreciate once they see on television, as most of them probably
now do – the startling effects of famines and floods, earthquakes and hur-
ricanes, and, of course, warfare. The response to the Indian Ocean tsunami
in December 2004 suggests that, once people recognize, through repeated
exposure, a really serious need that clearly demands funds for its mitigation,
they can be generous and expect their governments to be generous too.

But it will be good to separate emergency relief in people's minds from
the clearly and immediately humanitarian improvement that must continue
year on year when nothing of striking journalistic interest is happening. This
too is easy enough to understand, but there is less to see. Some deliberate educational or public-relations work is probably needed if enough people are to
become its active supporters. The knowledge that a fund specifically for this
class of activity is proposed may help to gain support for tapping whatever
sources are under consideration for the purpose. The fund might hope to
acquire the sanctified status of the UN Children's Fund, and to this end it
might be endowed (perhaps from a separate source, such as a single very rich
individual or foundation) with a budget that would allow it to do a certain

amount of public relations. Vivid ways might be found of showing that for, say, Uganda or Ethiopia, in spite of moderately effective governance, to provide from its own fiscal resources ARV drugs *and* impregnated bednets and antimalarials *and* vaccination against tuberculosis *and* free primary schooling and school meals, to all who could be regarded as needing these things, would require an inordinate proportion of the country's budget, or indeed its national income. And these are requirements that most people can readily see as being essential.

The third segment, which might for marketing purposes be called a 'self-help fund', could cover the rest: not only infrastructure and training but all the relatively quick-acting growth-increasing outlays, including such unglamorous but sometimes necessary elements as budget support, debt-reduction, port improvement, and feeder roads. Again, it may not be difficult to make a convincing public case for these forms of help. After all, the debt-reduction campaign since the mid-1990s has generated wide support that seems to have borne fruit. But, once more, relevant marketing will be needed, and the case is not the same as for the other two categories. Publicity for the second and third funds might stress the extent to which their proceeds would be concentrated on countries with appropriate governance, as the Sachs report proposes, and might possibly also stress the extent to which methods of aid administration would be used that might enable the effects of bad governance to be circumvented, as suggested in the subsection above entitled 'Means of manifestly...' (see page 87).

There might be sense in proposing to divide the proceeds of any big new ('innovative') sources of finance sought between three funds specified in this way. There are good and easily explained reasons for all three, but the presentation of outlays of the three different classes together as 'aid' may confuse the cases for them. And it may make (political) sense to propose the assignment of one new, arguably global, source of funds to each.

Suppose a group of rich and not-so-rich countries such as the France–Brazil quadrilateral (and perhaps also a number of others that assented to the New York Declaration of September 2004) were to agree with a number of effective campaigning NGOs that they would back, say, an air-ticket or aircraft-fuel or email tax to supplement resources available for emergencies, a CTT for other humanitarian purposes (possibly including peacekeeping), and recycled SDRs (plus something else to pay the interest for the poorer supplicants) for infrastructure and training and other high-return growth outlays: could this, or support for any one of the funds individually, grow into a concerted campaign such as the Jubilee campaign over debt?

This type of 'assignment' of particular revenue sources to particular purposes can be criticized on grounds of inflexibility, and hence inefficiency (the usual objection to earmarked taxes), but it could sharpen a campaign for seriously supplementing the funds that are already available, which is all that is proposed here. The proposals in the next section (see page 111) for institutions to allocate global-provenance funds could be applied whether or not the uses of the funds were separated according to source.

Hostility to globally networked governance

A third obstacle is the movement of donor countries into unilateralism, as happened in the US during the first George W. Bush administration. How far unilateralism will continue after the end of the second administration remains to be seen. American unilateralism has already constrained international organizations working collaboratively for development. The US has since 2001 opposed the creation of international forums for the promotion of common economic and environmental purposes, as, for example, on tax co-operation. Longer-running Congressional hostility to global governance has weakened the UN system and its finances, and constrained international initiatives that would have served common goals – through either new institutions or new instruments within existing institutions – such as the International Criminal Court, and proposals for the review of various aspects of the international economic and financial system suggested for consideration at the Monterrey summit in 2002.

The obvious remedy here, though not necessarily an easy one, is to prove to any major country inclined to unilateralism that this orientation does not pay. In other words, there may need to be an effective alliance of developing countries prepared to bargain with the power inclining to unilateralism and prepared if necessary to withhold concessions within their collective gift that it would value.

Power of adverse vested interests against

The huge inequalities of power between and within states give some of the people who would be affected most adversely by the various proposals for innovative sources of finance a great capacity to resist them. Global corporations and business associations can be particularly influential in blocking measures that they find commercially unwelcome.

So each of the innovative-finance proposals is likely to receive criticisms particular to it above. Banks (which are major dealers in foreign exchange) and oil companies, both especially powerful types of corporation, tend, for example, to be resistant to the proposals, respectively, for a CTT and for a carbon tax. Improved international tax co-operation was opposed by the US for a time, motivated by the opposition of corporations that had been minimizing tax through the use of tax havens. Fortunately, that US opposition has been withdrawn, in order for action against money laundering by terrorists to be strengthened. In fact, the US has also come to oppose tax havens unambiguously.

The failure of OECD countries to act together to tax unrepatriated income earned abroad by their multinationals, a failure largely prompted by influential multinationals from certain countries, has been blamed (Littlewood

2004: 425-7, 454-7) for a loophole concerning this element of income in the tax regimes of most rich countries. This loophole also damagingly leaves incentives for the countries in which the investments are located to reduce taxes competitively on inward foreign direct investment. Vested interests in tax loopholes may well have a bearing on the refusal of the George W. Bush administration even to discuss the formation of a global institution for the promotion of tax co-operation.

The wide departure from the population principle over the allocation of voting power within the Bretton Woods institutions, in which developing countries' peoples are severely under-represented, is another arrangement with implications for proposals on innovative finance for development. So the opposition of just a few members has been enough to prevent new issues of SDRs since 1981. (On the single occasion in the mid-1990s when the US administration spearheaded a proposal for an SDR allocation that in the circumstances required amendment of the IMF's Articles of Agreement, and had the whole package approved by the necessary majorities in the IMF, the project was stopped by the failure of the US Congress to ratify the amendment.) The opponents' ostensible reasons have bordered on the national or ideological. Thus new SDR issues have been opposed by the US Treasury for much of the intervening period, apparently because its officers dislike the idea of a further competitor to the dollar as an international reserve currency. They have been opposed over a similar period by Germany, probably on the grounds of the inflationary impact that additional international currency might be supposed to have. Yet it is not impossible that interests of a sectoral character, such as that of financial enterprises within the major economic powers, have played a part in their governments' resistance on these grounds, resistance which the countries' own voting-power within the IMF has made conclusive.

The general cast of the remedy here is probably to make clear that the vested interests concerned conflict with the national interests of the countries whose policies they influence. In other words, of the four requirements listed earlier, it is primarily *information* that is needed: making clear that, from the viewpoint of nations, we may even in some cases be considering what are more or less win–win improvements that respect for vested interests is leading governments to reject.

Ideological opposition to aid or to particular measures for financing it

There are philosophical and ideological opponents to several of the specific 'innovative' proposals for aid – in addition to the general scepticism on the part of market fundamentalists over any suggestion for increasing public revenue and expenditure.

There has, for example, been intense opposition to a CTT from within the US Congress, which passed an Act in 1996 requiring that, before the US paid any assessed or voluntary contribution to the UN or its agencies, the president must certify that the receiving agency has 'not engaged in any effort to develop, advocate, promote, or publicize any proposal concerning taxation or fees on United States persons in order to raise revenue for the United Nations' (Raffer 1998). Opposition from Congress is an expression of habitual hostility to any proposal that would affect national sovereignty. However, the particular animus in this case seems to have been based, at least in part, on a misunderstanding. Often the CTT in the form discussed is misrepresented as a UN tax. Yet this is quite impossible: only governments can tax; the UN does not have that power. Without big institutional developments, any so-called international tax could only be the result of international agreement and would still have to be collected by national authorities.

The more doctrinaire neo-classical economists are sceptical of any idea that would involve intervening in markets, arguing that this would distort competition and reduce efficiency; and most taxes do in fact have some potentially 'distorting' effect in this sense. The saving grace is that these extreme views are, of course, not held universally by officials of rich-country treasuries and finance ministries, or of the Bretton Woods Institutions and the OECD, even where they may appear to represent the prevailing view. Their political masters and mistresses are, if anything, even less likely to be monolithically doctrinaire. Successful democratic politicians are rarely ideological extremists. So there may be opportunities for developing-country governments, sufficiently well-briefed and united on particular issues – and perhaps supported by non-official allies – to wear down ideological opposition. Both *attitudes* and *understanding* may need to be modified, but even where the opposition at first seems obdurate, there may well be openings that can be exploited.

There are also strong *advocates* of aid, and specifically of innovative sources of finance, as will been seen in the next section. The questions are whether they or the opponents are likely to have greater weight in the various arenas where a contest can be played out; if the latter, whether there are potentially effective actions that could change the balance; and, in view of judgements on these matters, which arenas are worth entering for the advocates of more development finance. These questions are considered below, in the section 'Ways of overcoming...' (see page 99).

Potential support for additional development finance

Two events at the beginning of 2005 suggested a strengthening of support for aid to impoverished countries. By far the more important was the global outpouring of contributions to disaster relief for the survivors of the Indian Ocean tsunami, which also shamed governments into increasing their aid. The swift global response to the disaster showed that the human instinct to help others in desperate need continues to be strong in many people, and that this can bear fruit when they are aware vividly enough of the need. The enormity of the disaster evoked substantial giving and mobilized external physical assistance from many countries. The level and extent of contributions to the appeal for tsunami victims is one of many reasons for thinking that there could be sufficient depth and breadth of concern for poverty internationally to motivate support for new and demonstrably effective ways of mobilizing funds.

The second basis for encouragement was the vote at the World Economic Forum at Davos endorsing a motion that tackling poverty was the most important global issue. Bono remarked that 'something significant is emerging, and I have the feeling this is one of those moments we will look back on and say it marked a turning point'. There was reported to be an erosion of confidence in the military campaign against terrorism; a recognition that much more needed to be done in the non-military dimension; and that business has a vital interest in contributing to this (Kitney 2005: 53). The G8, meeting against a background of unusually public and co-ordinated campaigning on aid, trade and debt questions at their summit in July 2005, agreed to double aid to Africa by 2010, implying ostensibly an additional US$25 billion a year (*Financial Times* leading article, 9 July 2005). The World Social Forums, most of which were held at Porto Alegre, have demonstrated repeatedly some of the breadth and depth of concern for global social justice. What, then, are the forces on the side of increasing aid?

Popular support for aid

Within donor countries there has always been substantial support for ODA, the strength of which naturally varies between societies and over time. In the US, the highly industrialized country that gives the lowest amount of aid as a proportion of income, a study of public attitudes found that most Americans supported the principle of aiding developing countries, but that they over-estimated the amount given by the US, by between ten and twenty times or more. That is, the median estimate of the proportion of the US budget given as foreign aid was between 10 per cent and 20 per cent in various surveys. In fact, it is much less than 1 per cent. When those questioned were asked what proportion they thought it should be, the median response was 5 per cent, more than five times as high as the actual level (Kull and Destler 1999). Readily available, accurate information is a necessary condition for public support for aid. This evidence suggests that much greater generosity may prevail if people are given enough accurate and relevant information.

According to the Landau Report (France 2004a: 61), surveys have shown that 92 per cent of the public in Germany supported development aid in principle, and the percentages for other countries are: 79 per cent in the US; 78 per cent in the UK; and 74 per cent in both France and Japan. Support for increased ODA was expressed by 83 per cent in Germany, 81 per cent in the

US, 72 per cent in the UK, 68 per cent in Japan, and 96 per cent in France. While these results may exaggerate the support that aid would receive if its opportunity-costs had to be taken into account, and the implied support in the US for *increasing* aid seems much greater than would be consistent with the Kull and Destler findings mentioned above, they at least suggest a potential that might be realized if ruling politicians were so minded.

Increasing support among developing-country governments for innovative sources of finance

Potential beneficiaries are becoming increasingly strong supporters of innovative methods of financial assistance. For example, there was uncertainty among the G77 (developing countries) about supporting a CTT and other innovative sources of funding during the negotiations about the content of the declaration to be issued by the special session of the UN General Assembly on social development, held in Geneva in June 2000. Yet by September 2004, over 100 countries accepted the invitation of Brazil, France, Chile and Spain to attend a summit meeting in order to discuss ending poverty and hunger. The meeting considered a report by a Technical Group of experts on innovative sources of financing: the so-called Quadripartite Report (France 2004b) issued by those four governments, which took up the agenda studied by the French government's Landau Report (France 2004a). Eventually, 113 countries supported the New York Declaration (Brazilian Mission to the UN 2004), which includes a paragraph on the innovative proposals (emphasis added):

> In addition to the need to raise and improve assistance levels, we acknowledge that it is also appropriate and timely to give further attention to *innovative mechanisms* of financing – public and private, compulsory and voluntary, or universal or limited membership – in order to raise funds needed to help meet the MDGs and to complement and ensure long-term stability and predictability to foreign aid. In this respect, we urge the international community to give careful consideration to the report that has been prepared by the Technical Group.

This report (France 2004b) explores ways to find new resources for development, on a sound economic basis and at a significant level.

The Declaration was supported not only by developing countries; many European countries also signed. Many national representatives were explicit in their expression of support for the Technical Report, which included analysis and positive comments about a CTT, taxation of the arms trade, the International Financing Facility (IFF), issuing SDRs, and improved international tax co-operation. This meeting was the first at which most of these issues were placed explicitly on the inter-governmental agenda. Developing-country governments have been catching up with many of their parliamentarians, academics, some of their business people, and their civil-society organizations, who have long been advocates.

Support from non-governmental organizations in the rich world

Many scholars, development NGOs, and faith-based, professional and social-democratic and liberal organizations from developed countries have been advocates of innovative methods of financing since the early 1990s. Universities often have a conceptual interest and at the same time receive financial benefits from the fees of international students, the number of whom increases with the growth of income. Private foundations are sometimes involved in philanthropy for developing countries but want dependence on their assistance to fall, and so are interested in alternative funding mechanisms as well as the pace of economic growth. Anti-globalization protesters have also advocated internationally agreed taxes. The political norms of international discourse include international justice and so incline towards support. Similarly, the staffs of international organizations, including the IMF and the World Bank, and UN agencies such as the ILO and UNDP, are generally, though not uniformly, supportive.

Several international civil-society and professional-development networks linking concerned organizations have been active for some years in supporting the tapping of innovative sources of finance. They include both international development organizations and specialist study and advocacy groups. Potent examples include the international Catholic development network, CIDSE; the French-based, but now more widely spread, ATTAC; War on Want in the UK; New Rules in the US; and the Halifax Group in Canada. They have major achievements to their credit. A recent development that must be encouraging for these networks, and possibly demonstrates their effectiveness, is the call by President Chirac of France at Davos on 26 January 2005 for various innovative ways of financing development; and the support of the French and German governments, announced in February 2005, for a pilot IFF project on immunization, and for a tax on air travel (tickets rather than fuel being the base favoured just before the July 2005 G8 summit) 'which would finance health programmes in the poorest countries, especially for AIDS' (France 2005a). One of the sets of illustrative rates cited for the air-ticket tax was estimated to yield, with full participation, 10 billion euros a year (France 2005b). Another encouraging development for the campaigners is the passage through the Belgian parliament of statutory support for a CTT.

Support from multinational businesses

Many multinational corporations with interests in developing countries – through production, trade, financial intermediation, international consultancy or tourism – have also been supporters of increased aid, and might well become advocates for any methods of financing that would add to aid flows without cost to their own activities.

Increasing recognition of the importance and range of global public goods

The imperatives of globalization highlight the necessity for improvements in the provision and extension of global public-goods as well as the demands of equity, and this is becoming increasingly widely recognized.

Ways of overcoming or circumventing the obstacles

Main ideas and inferences from the previous two sections

Four main points emerge from the last two subsections as guides about what is likely to be useful in breaking down barriers to additional development finance, and in particular barriers to 'innovative methods', some of which may lead most naturally to funds administered and allocated globally.

One is that professional but transparently honest public-relations work, involving not only key relevant facts in a widely digestible form but also some immersion (through, say, television) in the visible and personal realities of world poverty, may be necessary to realize the potential for public support that is latent in rich countries.

A second is the possible value, for reasons of public relations, and indeed public understanding, of some segregation of funds – especially perhaps those raised by innovative methods and allocated internationally – according to two or three broad purposes, such as 'emergency', 'humanitarian', and 'self-help or growth-generating' (which could include transport and energy infrastructure, and possibly most forms of training). For practical purposes, this may make one degree clearer what 'aid' truly means. (The Landau Report puts the case for possible earmarking of the proceeds of an international tax: France 2004a: 25–6.)

A third is the special opportunities provided by funds of genuinely global provenance, partly because they make it relatively easy to introduce the greater transparency following from the kind of arrangement just mentioned, fortified by devices adopted to neutralize the effects of weaknesses of governance among some recipient countries; partly because they permit a definable strategy to be adopted over a significant part of world development aid (which will itself have public-relations advantages); and partly because they enable the political hurdles and hazards of national budgetary processes to be circumvented. (The last of these advantages arises in part because the costs of the aid can be diffused widely; and hence, in spite of complete openness, may not be readily noticeable by those that bear the burdens, and may sometimes be zero or even negative on balance, or at least of dubious sign.)

A fourth is the need, and the great potential, for mobilization of the numerous forces – governmental, commercial and humanitarian – favouring additional development finance. Not simply pleas and protests, but hard-headed negotiation will be needed; and this is unlikely to happen unless developing-country governments are prepared to play an assertive and co-ordinated leading role.

Conditions for mobilization

If the forces are to be mobilized, then, governments of some major developing countries must be prepared to take the lead – with or without the support of sympathetic affluent countries. It will be most valuable and effective if alliances, or *an* alliance, can be formed *over a range of issues* relating to poverty and development, a range that goes beyond additional finance. This will provide a richer field for negotiation, which is always more likely to realize benefits for both sides if several issues are on the table together. However, it is likely to require the various parties on the developing-country side to make some concessions over their particular concerns for the purpose of being able to act together. To be most effective, the lead governments (i) will need to be authorized by a number of others to act together on their behalf; (ii) will equip themselves with a high-powered secretariat to concentrate the intellectual and research resources of the alliance; and (iii) will be prepared to interact with NGOs and other potential allies. The task will be facilitated if the campaigning NGOs that are generally sympathetic to development and anti-poverty aims are prepared to behave to some extent tactically, and to concentrate their immediate demands on targets that have a reasonable chance of being achieved (rather than, as sometimes happens, weakening their message by appearing to make common cause with every movement of protest against the world as it is).

Yet, while a steady alliance over a range of issues represents the ideal, solutions that appear to be second-best may have to be accepted because they are available. A limited ad-hoc coalition of developing countries can achieve significant victories, as demonstrated powerfully by the (new) G20 led by Brazil, China, India and South Africa during the 2003 Cancún trade negotiations. The formation of this group suggested a redistribution of power resulting from changed attitudes rather than from changes in weight. The Summit in New York called by Brazil, France, Chile and Spain in September 2004, as mentioned above, is an example of another species: a core alliance between countries across the 'North–South' divide – even though there are widely different interests within the group about agricultural trade. Its members may continue to act together in order to promote the study of innovative finance, and perhaps, as suggested above, campaign together for the innovative sources that they judge most feasible politically.

Innovative sources: aiming at soft targets

The public-relations activity suggested above may have favourable effects on the amount of *national* ODA provided. But, together with the 'segregation' of funds by major purpose, it fits most easily with sources of finance that can be globally allocated, as explained above (see page 89, paragraph before the subsection heading: 'Obstacles to additional...'). Some of the 'innovative' methods *must* by their nature be treated as global: others may be. In any case, the more intrinsically global of the innovative methods avoid the need to be subject to national budgeting. And it seems likely that any big increase in funding in the near future, an increase of the order foreseen in the Sachs report as being necessary to meet the MDGs, will have to rely extensively on innovative methods. So the remarks in this section refer mainly to innovative sources.

A sensible rule for groups of governments wanting the world to tap new sources of development finance may be to pick those that seem for the time being to represent relatively 'soft targets' politically; to reach understandings with sympathetic NGOs that they will embody these explicitly and prominently in their campaigns; and to do what they can to form governmental alliances that will be prepared to negotiate the targeted approaches against objectives valued by the major economic powers that will have to be brought on-side.

What makes targets 'soft' may be (i) the absence of serious and objective national, as distinct from sectoral, interests against; (ii) gains of a common or fairly widespread 'public-good' character across nations from tapping them (gains that may be incidental to the financial proceeds); (iii) clear paths to implementation, requiring a minimum of active administrative co-operation and co-ordination among governments; (iv) the absence of clear and striking inequity in the distribution of any burden; and (v) the absence of intense ideological fervour on the other side.

Which innovative sources best fit these requirements at any time will be a matter of judgement. We consider now how some of the candidates meet these tests.

Tax co-operation.   As pointed out earlier, some important objects of tax co-operation can be expected to give fiscal gains (or, at worst, no losses) to all the large sovereign parties, rich and poor. These ought to be the star examples of soft targets for advocacy and negotiation. If a number of prominent developing-country governments that would be major beneficiaries of a particular measure of this character (such as a uniform withholding tax on all interest income flows to non-residents as a means of eliminating the tax-evasion obtainable through capital flight) could combine to press for it (and/or for an international body likely to further its realization) – enlisting for the purpose campaigning NGOs and rich-country governments they could muster in support, and drawing in the highest level of intellectual ammunition – there would seem to be good a priori reasons why they should prevail, even if no concessions on other matters of primary interest to some rich countries were simultaneously on the table for negotiation. Though the US has recently set its face firmly against an international tax organization of the kind advocated by some of those eager for reforms, the UN agreed in 2004 to upgrade international tax co-operation by establishing a strengthened Committee of Experts on International Cooperation on Tax Matters. Both the OECD generally and the EU have moved in the direction of eliminating the capital-flight abuse among their members, and the OECD has engaged in continuing activity against tax havens (Avi-Yonah 2000: 1654–62; OECD 2002; France 2004a: 52–4). This is at least a half-open door.

'Increasing remittances' benefits'. The Quadripartite Report (France 2004b) uses this expression to cover measures (which, in general, it supports) to preserve and enhance the value of migrant workers' remittances to their (usually poorer) home countries. A particular mode of doing this has been suggested (Clunies-Ross 2004, largely drawing on Addison and Chowdhury 2004, and Solimano 2004) under which the only cost or pain would be to certain (largely informal) financial intermediaries, and the gain would be not only enhancement and increased security for the migrant funds but also, incidentally, some addition to funds available at any given time for lending at non-concessional rates by the World Bank. This, again, should be a very soft target politically, requiring only some co-ordinated assertion by the governments of beneficiary countries with a carefully worked-out scheme to propose. (As if to emphasize the relatively easy path likely to be open to this and the preceding method for increasing development finance, the Quadripartite Report places them under the heading 'Political Co-ordination'.)

International finance facility (IFF). This (for some time from early 2003 the 'innovative method' championed most consistently by the UK government) would depend on an agreement among major donor countries to commit a certain part of their ODA (specifically, the extra they had promised during and after the Monterrey Summit in early 2002) to the servicing of loans that would be raised in the markets. The borrowing would be done in order roughly to double the disbursements that could be made as aid to developing countries in the years leading up to the MDG deadline of 2015. To achieve this, the participants would need to commit themselves initially not only to honour their Monterrey offers but also to increase them in real terms at 4 per cent a year for at least fifteen years, with rolling commitments that would need to extend for a further fifteen years if the increased rate of disbursements were to be maintained until 2015. But the additional aid disbursements provided would be essentially bilateral, in that the donor countries would each decide individually the projects or programmes for which the funds raised by virtue of its guarantees of servicing payments would be spent. Any joint organization would be a purely financial intermediary, with no allocative function. It would issue bonds in the commercial markets, and would service them from the funds provided by the donor countries. At the same time, it was intended that a certain degree of co-ordination of allocation among the donors would be achieved, and a number of specific rules of good aid practice observed. The laudable aim was thus to gain substantial benefits for 'development' without the normal political costs: to improve the quality and co-ordination of aid while not requiring donors to vote funds to international institutions; to increase greatly the quantity (immediately) disbursed to recipient countries without increasing greatly the amount (immediately) voted by the donors.

However, there would be inevitable doubts over how far the legislators of donor countries could bind their successors far into the future to meet the obligations required – and how far the markets would believe them if they purported to do so. As security against default, the projections suppose that only 80 per cent of the funds committed in advance by donors would be necessary to meet servicing costs: a sensible precaution, but one that implies that the commitments by the donors could not be assumed to have a cast-iron character. There were also misgivings expressed from the first over the projected pattern of cash flows to recipients in the form of aid, which would fall sharply after 2015. The Landau and Quadripartite Reports (France 2004a: 24–6; 2004b: 46) suggest that some other new source such as a tax might need to come, or to have come, on stream at that time in order to avoid such a fall. An apparent advantage over some other proposed innovative sources was that the scheme could work, if necessary, with a small number of donor participants.

The fact that donors participating would need to commit their countries (eventually for thirty years if the full programme with safety margin were to be completed by 2015) to increase the post-Monterrey segment of their annual aid appropriations by 4 per cent in real terms each year, would mean that the segment would have risen by about 224 per cent (that is, to over three times its initial real value) by the end of the thirty-year period. As time went on, this segment might well come to represent a very large part of their total annual aid appropriations, and even in the early 2030s they would have no discretion over how it would be applied: it would be committed to servicing debts already incurred.

In early 2004, it appeared that only France and the UK among potential donors were committed to the IFF. By early 2005, at the Davos meeting, France and Germany were not ruling it out, though they were mainly backing other innovative methods. Yet, as mentioned above, a pilot IFF scheme for immunization supported by Germany and France was put on the agenda of the July 2005 G8 Summit and is now under way.

Agreements among governments that each should impose a tax for global use on some negative externality or untapped base (such as carbon emissions, arms sales, airline fuel, air tickets).   Some or all of these are considered to be attractive because they are held to offer the (armchair) advantage of 'double dividends': charging for a negative 'externality' as well as raising revenue.

Though these various possible bases have their own differing advantages and difficulties, they also have certain problems in common. None of these tax bases may be regarded as *intrinsically* global: a considerable amount of revenue can probably be raised from each of them by individual governments without international co-operation. In addition, each government will need to apply the tax individually if the base is to be covered adequately across the world. (In both of these respects they differ from a CTT.)

Anything resembling a consistent global tax on any of the bases will require legislation and the relevant administrative arrangements on the part of nearly two hundred separate states. Any lack of confidence among the world's governments that the cover will be substantially complete may affect their willingness to take part: the doubts will tend to be self-fulfilling.

There is another awkwardness: there is no natural link between imposing the tax and directing its proceeds to global purposes. A government that imposes the tax within its jurisdiction may see no powerful reason why it should not keep the revenue for itself. The distribution of the tax burden in relation to income across countries from a constant *ad valorem* or specific tax on any of these bases is also not likely to be progressive in relation to income. In fact, a uniform carbon tax would be highly regressive across certain rich–poor pairs of countries (such as China–Japan, India–USA). Or the incentive effect of the tax may bear especially heavily on particular groups of poorish countries, as an air-travel tax is likely to do on small island-states specializing as tourist destinations. In summary, considered as world taxes, levies on these bases are unlikely to be equitable. If it is good to impose them for the sake of charging for negative externalities, there is still no good reason why the proceeds of *those* taxes, rather than graded income-based levies on the various states, should be devoted to global purposes. It would be surprising if the anomalies of any such proposed arrangement did not assume political importance.

It would also be only by very good luck that the two elements of the 'dividend' could be made simultaneously significant, while also satisfying the requirement that the tax should not be so severe as to put it outside the realm of political feasibility: a total of three demands upon it. It is not difficult, for example, to think up a rate of additional carbon tax small enough not greatly to annoy consumers and at the same time large enough to make a substantial contribution to global funds, even if levied only within rich countries, but such a rate would have little impact on carbon use.

Though, as noted above, Germany and France are actively supporting the use of a tax on air tickets, the Quadripartite Report (France 2004b: 36–41) considers from among this group only *taxes on arms sales* – sales in general, not simply exports – and the device supposed seems to be in effect a uniform tax on value-added in armaments, which is equivalent to a uniform tax on final price. The Report treats the possibility as important, but its own discussion suggests that implementation would be riddled with difficulties. On that point we can only agree. An underlying anomaly is that the governments, the taxing authorities, would also be the main users of the taxed articles. They would be taxing themselves and each other, ostensibly to discourage themselves from activities that they consider nationally important. The arms-sales tax sounds politically attractive as a disembodied idea.

The closer we come to envisaging it in practice, however, the less compelling the attractive features seem.

A co-ordinated *tax on aircraft fuel* would certainly raise fewer practical problems. And its global assignment would be more acceptable on equity grounds than either an arms-sales tax or a general carbon tax. By a strange anomaly, aircraft fuel has long been free of duty under international agreements. For the most rudimentary reasons, it is inefficient that aircraft fuel should be tax-free while fuels for competing modes of transport are taxed, as they largely are in rich countries. This is quite apart from the important negative externality involved in all hydrocarbon burning, because of its contribution to climate change.

There are good grounds for scrapping the exemptions; for taxing aircraft fuel; and for doing so uniformly. To agree on that would be an achievement. But it would be another big step politically to devote the proceeds to global purposes. Cheap tourist destinations might suffer differentially. But the welfare case for the tax itself could be presented so that it would be difficult to gainsay through any intellectual argument. And, if the international purpose for which it would be used could also be presented effectively to the relevant publics, its global assignment might even on balance be popular. If the fuel were to be taxed everywhere at rates similar to the highest rate applied to petrol for road vehicles in Western Europe, the contribution that the proceeds could make to filling the Sachs Report gaps could be significant.

An alternative, with broadly similar advantages and drawbacks, would be a uniform *tax on all air fares*, a proposal that France and at least eighteen other governments have moved towards introducing at the time of writing (2007). However, the case for it is less strong, because the lack of a tax on aircraft fuel can readily be presented as an anomaly. Moreover, on environmental grounds, it is far more efficient to tax the particular polluting input rather than the output.

Regular issues of SDRs, and their recycling. Despite the almost consistent opposition on the part of the US, Japan, Germany and the UK during most of the period since the early 1980s, the regular creation of SDRs would appear to have virtually all the characteristics listed above for qualifying as a soft target.

First, while some firms in the financial sector may consider that they have interests against it, the only arguable national interests against are those of the countries, mainly the US, that are able to continue accruing short-term debts as foreign holdings of their currencies expand. Foreign holdings of these currencies, even official foreign holdings taken alone, will continue to grow in the face of the annual amounts of SDR creation generally discussed – and, in fact, to grow by larger absolute amounts than the stock of SDRs. In any case, it is dubious whether adding to these holdings without limit is an unalloyed boon to the countries issuing the currencies held – let alone something that they can consider a right.

Second, SDR creation would make a contribution to the world public-good of economic stability. The issue of SDRs not only increases the real income of most developing countries by reducing the costs they incur for holding reserves, but also, in so far as it leads them to increase their reserve holdings, contributes to the stability of their currencies, failings in which, as the East Asian crisis of 1997–8 showed, might have important implications for the world economy. (The contribution to world macroeconomic stability could, on the face of it, be increased considerably if, as the Quadripartite Report (France 2004b: 48–9) suggests, the issue and withdrawal of SDRs could in part be managed counter-cyclically; but this would require alterations in the IMF's working rules and possibly also in its Articles of Agreement; and there would undoubtedly be knee-jerk reactions against it.)

Third, the 'path to implementation' for regular 'allocations' of SDRs could hardly be clearer or simpler. IMF staff, moreover, have often been favourably inclined.

Fourth, in spite of the fact that the conservative US Congresses of the late 1990s chose to frustrate the attempt of the Clinton administration, backed by most of the rest of the world, to increase the stock of SDRs significantly, and to make their cumulative distribution more equitable, the issue can hardly be said to have generated ideological fervour.

Several of the same advantages can be predicated for the proposed 'recycling' of the 60 per cent or so of each allocation of SDRs that would pass to rich countries, which have no use for them. Recycled SDRs would be most obviously 'global-provenance funds', necessarily available for international use. Making them the basis of low-interest loans for global purposes – more or less as proposed by Soros (2002), and endorsed by the Quadripartite Report (France 2004b: 48) – would appear to have no readily detectable costs for any 'nation'. It could be used, to take one example, as an effectively no-cost way of reducing the burden of the deadweight debt of certain poorish countries, with advantages not confined to those countries alone. There would, admittedly, be institutional paths to be worked out, but they do not seem intrinsically difficult. Allocation of the recycled SDRs might be managed by the mechanism to be outlined in Part B. Countervailing fervour seems unlikely to be serious.

Altogether, the ramparts against the regular issue of SDRs and their recycling seem intrinsically weak. But nothing is likely to happen in the near future unless the major developing countries take the issue on board as a matter for serious and assertive negotiation.

E-mail levy.   A tiny levy on e-mails, administered by the ISPs, and having the public-good impact of reducing 'spam', is an attractive idea, but perhaps needs further exploration. Part of its political attraction is that it would not need to involve governments. But that emphasizes the major ground of doubt about its practicality: that it would depend on the voluntary co-operation of a number of private firms – on their readiness both to make and to observe an agreement for imposing the levy, and to remit its proceeds to some world body for allocation. However, the history of the internet has displayed some striking examples of apparently disinterested behaviour. And perhaps some arrangement could be found – some system of charging senders and/or recipients – whereby those ISPs that failed to charge would lose customers through failure to discourage the sending of 'spam'. Devoting the proceeds of the levy to global use would be a further step. But perhaps, if the use could be segregated in such a way as to have enough moral/emotional appeal, that too could have a commercial advantage, or at least no significant disadvantage, for the ISP. Again, appropriate segregation of funds by class of use may be crucial.

Deep-sea mineral rents.   Though this is not an issue at present, it is important that campaigning NGOs, developing-country governments, and all those concerned about either development or rudimentary justice, make clear that they will be adamant in support of the arrangements approved under the 1978 International Law of the Sea Convention for treating any economic rents of these deposits as a world resource. There will be vested interests keen on upsetting these arrangements for their own benefit. But it is a case in which international law, natural justice, and the purposes covered by 'development', all point in the same direction, and there is no coherent ideological position on the other side. Attempts to nullify the exercise of the world interest in these resources can readily be, and must be, exposed as simple plunder.

Currency-transaction tax (CTT).   Given the way its implementation can now be envisaged, a general CTT as a source of global funds has a number of intrinsic political advantages. Its costs, though real and concentrated to some extent on the financial sector, will otherwise be highly diffused, nationally and individually, and, because of that concentration on the financial sector, will on the whole be mildly progressive across nations. It appears now that it could be imposed almost universally on the kinds of transaction it would target given only the active co-operation of four monetary authorities, though ideally with a few others ready to co-operate if need be. This is all that will be required if the method adopted for imposing the tax is to collect it on settlements of transactions within banking systems (Schmidt 1999, 2001). And it now seems that this is the method by which a CTT could be implemented most securely. This mode of imposition appears to be accepted as a possibility within the IMF staff (Ter-Minassian 2003), and it is presented in the Quadripartite Report (France 2004b: 32) as probably the most reliable method. Emotive stereotypes aside, the political odds would appear to be fairly heavily in favour of a CTT. It might look prima facie quite like a soft target.

We have argued for the advantages springing from the fact that a source of funds is of 'global provenance', which means in effect that it must be allocated under global authority. A CTT (most clearly, if it is collected at the point of settlement) has to be so regarded. Those authorities collecting it cannot be deemed to own it. The world will be asking them to collect the tax on its behalf. Their own peoples will bear only part of its burden, and the administrative costs of collection by the settlement method will be small. If they were to keep for themselves more than a tiny fraction of the revenue they had collected, this would simply be theft.

Yet, until recently, there have been two difficulties: one technical, the other political. The technical difficulty was that previously there has been no approach to certainty on how activity in the currency markets, and hence the revenue collected, will respond to different rates of tax. This might be overcome by starting with a tax at an extremely low rate and raising it gradually and experimentally. But this, however rational in principle, would probably seem a strange proceeding, readily open to contumely from interested opponents. However, by late 2007, systematic empirical estimation of the elasticity of activity in the markets with respect to the width of price 'spread', to which a tax would contribute, suggests that a tax rate of 0.005 per cent – chosen, because of its small size in relation to the recent variation in the spread, as highly unlikely to disturb the market fundamentally – could be expected, on recent market figures, to raise over US$30 billion a year, provided the US, the European Central Bank, Japan and Britain co-operated in collecting the tax (Schmidt, 2007).

The strictly political difficulty is this: the co-operation of the US will be highly important politically, even though, without it, the other three authorities working together might still technically be able to raise over US$20 billion a year (ibid.). Yet the fact that in 1995–6 the UN Secretary-General, Boutros Boutros Ghali, had merely mentioned the possibility of a CTT, and that a UN Specialized Agency had run a conference to discuss the idea, and published the papers and debate covering a variety of views, led to the violent reaction, mentioned above, in the US Congress. This response probably drew on fairly deeply-rooted attitudes in a number of the members of the very conservative 104th Congress, and the fact that it took flight depended partly on ideology, and partly on ignorance. Greater clarity and consensus on how the tax would actually be imposed and what its impact on the markets was likely to be may eventually enable a more rational debate to take place. But time may be needed before that clarity and consensus can be reached. Until recently, there may have been no great advantage in trying to negotiate it – in spite of considerable support in a number of rich countries – given that US Congressional approval will be so important, at least politically. The CTT is possibly not yet (in late 2007) a soft target, but may well become so quite soon.

So a revenue-directed CTT, possibly the most promising of all the innovative methods examined on a longer perspective – not least for what may eventually prove political advantages – will probably have increasingly good prospects as more clarity and agreement appears in sympathetic circles on its mode of administration; and when the aftershocks of the ill-informed hysteria attaching to its 1996 exposure have had more time to subside.

Conclusions on eligible sources and tactics

Two sorts of conclusion arise from this discussion: on which devices for increasing funds appear politically within range and, given their other advantages, justify concentrated assault; and on which strategies or tactics are particularly likely to help.

Eligible devices for targeting

The most eligible immediate targets seem to be those that approach win–win (Pareto-type) improvements, at least as far as they concern the various nations taken as a whole. A prospective gain all round may sometimes result from the fact that the method for enhancing development resources also serves to advance some (other) global public good. On these grounds, we should aim at:

- International tax co-operation toward certain ends: in particular, blocking paths to the evasion (and, incidentally, concealment for other purposes) achieved through capital flight and the use of tax havens; closing the channels to avoidance that exist when a single firm's tax liability is split between two or more independently operating revenue authorities; and removing the incentives from host countries for competitive reduction of business taxes for the purposes of attracting foreign investment.
- Measures to maintain the value of migrants' remittances.
- Regular issue of SDRs, and recycling of those that are 'surplus'.

Among the various suggestions for co-ordinated taxes across the world on certain untapped bases or negative externalities, the most promising politically and administratively of those mooted seem to be:

- A universal and equal duty on aircraft fuel; with a tax on all air fares a possible substitute: one that is less environmentally efficient but has recently received more political support.

From the same category, we were highly dubious about a universal tax on arms sales for both administrative and political reasons.

- A further possibility discussed, with prima facie political appeal, is a uniform additional carbon tax, which could in principle realize large amounts of revenue from fairly trivial rates of levy, even if only the rich countries complied. (It would, in fact, raise problems of inequity *unless* it was confined to rich countries.) Administration within each complying state would not be difficult, but, as with the rest of this class of tax proposals, getting sufficient agreement to tax *and* to devote the proceeds to global use might be daunting.

- An e-mail tax, administered entirely by ISPs on a voluntary basis, might be worth investigating, to see whether incentives, reinforcing goodwill, could be devised to discourage free-riding.
- On current evidence, we doubt that the IFF, as a widely supported scheme channelling a large share of the ODA from most donor countries, has enough political attractions – for enough of those groups/countries that would have to finance it – to compensate for the demands it would make upon them, and its other arguable drawbacks. Support for the proposed pilot on immunization, however, might demonstrate further possibilities.
- A CTT, perhaps the most promising of the innovative methods in the somewhat longer term, seems eminently worth further work now, so that agreement might be reached on its mode of imposition, and greater certainty over its revenue possibilities and impact on the markets. But active attempts by interested governments to bring it into being might best wait for, say, four or five years, in order to give these developments in knowledge and thought time to mature, and to give hostile knee-jerk reflexes in the US Congress time to die down.

Elements of strategy and tactics

Four elements have been emphasized, all obvious enough when enumerated but, we suggest, too little considered so far in the context of increasing and improving aid. The cases for the first three are interconnected, and the argument for each would be strengthened by the presence of the other two. These are:

- Professional, but scrupulously honest and accurate, public-relations material, financed if possible by private sources, combining a few hard, quantified facts with personal and grassroots stories and pictures.
- Special attention to those 'innovative' sources of finance that must (or can) be allocated globally, so facilitating both a coherent anti-poverty strategy and coherent presentation of its elements.
- Segregation of globally allocated finance into two or more funds according to the uses to which they will be put, with the possible assignment of particular innovative sources to each.
- Mobilization, as far as possible under the leadership of major developing-country governments, of both official and non-official support for additional development finance, and in particular for the tapping of

innovative sources, with a solid source of research and intellectual back-up and a readiness for assertive negotiation in which development finance is considered together with other objectives valued by poor or rich countries, or both.

A global allocating mechanism

The first part of this chapter argued that it was desirable, and implied that it was not necessarily impossible, to obtain funds for development finance whose collection or generation depended on international co-operation, or whose burden fell significantly and necessarily on the residents of a number of countries, or both (what we called *global-provenance funds*): funds which, for either or both of those reasons, could not be regarded as the property of any particular state. And there might be other funds which, though their realization did not in fact *require* international co-ordination, various countries might agree to collect under agreed terms for international use. In fact, ways of obtaining such funds were under consideration on the part of a number of governments in late 2004 and early 2005, when this chapter was being drafted, as evidenced by the Quadripartite Report put forward by two major developing, and two major developed countries' governments, and the New York Declaration (Brazilian Mission to the UN 2004) on the part of 113 governments that it inspired. It would seem necessary, before a decision were to be made over mobilizing these funds for global use, to agree on a way in which they could be allocated through international institutions.

Suppose, for example, that a method were to be agreed for raising, by intrinsically international action, some part of the additional US$50–75 billion or so a year (from sources outside developing countries) that the Sachs report (UN 2005; see above) considers necessary over the years between 2006 and 2015 to achieve the Millennium Development Goals by 2015, and is unlikely to be provided by additional ODA. One or more of the mechanisms discussed above for raising the funds might be applied.

These sums might be accessible in the form of grants, or low-interest loans. (Recycled SDRs would probably have to be available as loans at the SDR rate.) The question here is how these funds, considered a global possession, might be allocated. Even if it had been agreed that they were to be administered by various global institutions, there would at the very least need to be one procedure for deciding *which* international bodies should have the disposition of the funds, and in what amounts.

Indeed, the possibility that such sums could be raised might very well depend on a reasonably clear idea of the purposes for which, and the mechanism *by* which, they would be allocated. A popular groundswell in favour, comparable to the Jubilee movement over debt – or serious consideration by governments – might well have to await coherent and realistic agreement on these two questions.

There are many ways, in principle, by which these questions might be answered. We believe it would be helpful in the debate about additional sources of finance to have at least one plausible and reasonably thought-out answer. Any answer propounded for this purpose should not pretend to be the only possible one, or necessarily the best, let alone the one (if any) that would ultimately be adopted. But, to make a good case for saying that there is a (politically as well as administratively) plausible answer (*at least one*) would remove one debating-point against any of these methods of funding and would enhance the credibility of all of them.

What we offer here is a sketch of what might be a plausible method for defining the purposes for which the funds would be allocated and specifying any other limitations on their use, and for actually allocating them.

Political issues in the choice of institutions of allocation

In order to be plausible, any scheme must have a reasonable prospect of being generally acceptable, especially to the governments of those countries that would see themselves, on balance, as donors. To be acceptable, it must combine trust, legitimacy, and a reasonable prospect of efficiency. Preferably too it should involve no unnecessary leap into the dark.

Trust means that the institution making the allocative decisions is seen as being likely to have reliable procedures in place that meet acceptable standards of transparency and integrity, and that it will not depend on values or views of how the world works widely different from the values and assumptions of those that need to approve it. There might be difficulties in establishing the necessary degree of trust on the part of the US, and possibly of some other countries on the donor side, if the procedure were left to certain institutions in the UN system. And, on the other hand, there might be mistrust on the part of some developing countries, and of campaigning NGOs whose pressure might have some importance in advocacy, if it were entirely in the hands of the Washington multilaterals.

Legitimacy would require that the decisions should be in the hands of a body generally regarded as properly authorized to act on the world's behalf.

Efficiency would, again, require regular and transparent procedures not likely to be subject to corruption or favouritism; adequate sources of information and experience in assessing funding applications and possibilities; and no more than the necessary minimum of additional bureaucratic infrastructure.

Stating the requirements in this way narrows the possibilities. In the solution proposed below, it is intended that the demand for trust and legitimacy should be met in part by dividing the critical decisions – in a consistent way, with a definite rationale – between the UN system and the Washington multilaterals. Other aspects of the demand for trust, and at the same time the demand for efficiency, would be met by putting the operative management of the allocation in the hands of an existing institution with considerable relevant expertise, knowledge and experience upon which to draw.

Choices to be made about the uses of the funds: policy limits and guidelines

We refer in what follows to three levels on which decision would be required: (a) on essentials of the understanding on which the mechanism is set up, the *'initial bargain'*; (b) on general *policy and rules* over allocation of the funds, as determined under the mechanism; and (c) on *specific allocations*. To put it another way, there would be constitutional, policy and management decisions. Policy questions – over the potential uses of the funds (which sectors of activity should be eligible); over the forms (loans or grants) in which they should be released; and over the kinds of institution that should be eligible recipients – might, however, be decided either as part of the initial bargain or under the arrangements set up by that bargain.

For what purposes?   One way or another, a decision would have to be made over the eligible purposes of the funds: should they be available to be devoted, for example, at the discretion of the body actually managing the allocation, to any of the functions commonly covered by 'development assistance' in the broadest sense? These would include the three categories proposed above: (a) emergency humanitarian help in the wake of wars, famines, or natural disasters; (b) medical, general education, water, sanitation and similar needs of the highest consumer value but for the most part having only a longish-term impact on productive power; and (c) power and transport infrastructure, technical training, technical consultancy, and similar inputs to production, with relatively speedy dividends in output and income – investments and functions, moreover, of which a number might potentially be financially self-supporting. Or should only a subset of these be included – for example, only those with an immediate and obvious humanitarian purpose, or only those with no chance of being acceptably self-supporting: probably on either criterion those in the first two of the categories mentioned? (Most of the MDGs refer in fact to the purposes included in the second category.)

It is also not out of the question that some purposes not normally included in 'development' but with high immediate humanitarian importance, such as UN peacekeeping, might be included. This might perhaps enable the UN to engage in forms of peacekeeping or peace-enforcement more ambitious than has been possible in the past. (Peacekeeping, alternatively, might be excluded on the ground that including it might lessen the sense of responsibility for it on the part of governments; or because balancing its demands against 'development' needs would be unfamiliar territory to any allocative body whose expertise was in assessing only the more familiar claims on a development agency; or because of the urgency of the peacekeeping demands when they arise, and at the same time the long-term commitments they often involve.)

Or the fund might be agreed to be potentially available for debt mitigation or debt forgiveness – or for environmental outlays beyond those attending to immediate need, such as domestic water-supply and sanitation: flood control, or forest conservation, for example. Cases could be made for or against the inclusion of a number of these elements. Or, as suggested in the first section (from page 72), two or more separate funds might, for presentational reasons, be set up, each possibly assigned a particular source of finance, but all administered by the one set of machinery.

Such limitations on the uses of the funds might be part of the initial bargain; for example, if there were strong views among major potential participants that some possibility should be excluded or included. Or they might be imposed by the policy-making body set up under the initial bargain. Which categories were excluded or included as part of the initial bargain would probably depend in part on the range that the initial negotiators considered would command sufficient support among the populations that would have to bear the burden of any measures for raising the funds.

In what form?   A further question that would arise, either in the making of the initial bargain or as a matter of policy subsequently, would be whether the funds should be disbursed wholly as loans, wholly as grants, or in principle as either, with the decision between them being purely one of management. Inclusion of 'surplus' SDRs as a source of funds under present arrangements would make it almost inevitable that some of the finance should come in the form of low-interest loans, so that their proceeds would probably have to be allocated in the form of loans. (World Bank thinking – no doubt inspired in part by the difficulties bequeathed by official loans to a number of poor countries – appears latterly to favour a greater use of grants, which at present are not allowed to be provided by the World Bank Group except to certain countries poor enough to qualify for IDA terms.)

To or through whom?   Should the immediate recipients of the funds be confined to governments, as has been the case with the IBRD, IDA, the regional development banks, IMF and UNDP? Or should other possibilities be admitted? Might the first-level administrator of the funds (inevitably a multilateral institution itself) be allowed to channel them through other multilaterals; through multi-stakeholder global funds (such as the GFATM); through other multinational networks; through subnational and local governments; through NGOs; through research institutes; or through private firms? (For the sake of transparency and preventing misappropriation, it might in fact be increasingly recognized as necessary in certain cases to give an entity in the recipient country other than the national government some involvement in the disposal of the funds: somewhere in a range from rights of scrutiny to executive control.) If the range of permitted direct recipients went beyond national governments, should a government have a veto over any allocation made within its jurisdiction? Again, this could be either part of the initial bargain or be left as a policy decision to be made under the machinery set up.

It has been represented to us that the IMF would demand control of the allocation of any funds generated though the recycling of SDRs – with the implication that this demand would be irresistible. Within the politics of international agencies, this might turn out to be so. But any claim of *right* on the part of the IMF (in effect, of IMF staff) to control the allocation of these funds – on the grounds presumably that they (the IMF staff) created the SDRs by their own efforts – is surely ludicrous. It is comparable to arguing that foreign-exchange dealers should control the allocation of the proceeds of any CTT. This could be regarded as a claim over allocation of resources that even went beyond 'producer choice': allocation in the interests of the producers rather than of the consumers of goods. Current IMF staff would not have produced SDRs through their own labour and sacrifice.

The IMF and World Bank are almost exactly parallel in their main governing structures and the shares of the various governments of the world in their control. Relevant differences are between their respective staffs' particular expertise – and probably also their prevailing outlook – because of the differences in the tasks that they perform. In assigning the allocation of certain funds (generated as a by-product of world arrangements for economic stabilization) to one of the two organizations rather than the other, the world would *not* be making a decision in favour of the views of one group of governments over another – merely between cadres of staff with differing expertise, and coincidentally perhaps with a difference in outlook that follows from this. The decision ought surely to be determined according to which body of expertise is more relevant rather than according to the supposed rights of one or another set of officials.

Constitutional matters: essentials of the 'initial bargain'

Constitutional questions would need to be settled in the 'initial bargain'. What is supposed by that term is a set of arrangements for establishing the fund. These arrangements would need the agreement of the organizations that would be required to play a part in implementation. In the scheme foreshadowed below, these would include the UN General Assembly and the World Bank. The arrangements might in principle be proposed to the General Assembly by one or more of its members. But, in order to have a realistic expectation of acceptance, a major proposal such as this would need to come with prior consensus in principle among the major players: presumably the members of the G8 and at least a group of developing countries such as those that have played a leading role on 'North–South' issues recently, such as China, India, Brazil and South Africa. This agreement might be worked out extensively behind the scenes, or in part within one of the various forums available, such as the original (1999) Group of Twenty, which comprises the G8 and twelve developing countries.

Whatever the means by which the proposal is derived, it would then come with support in principle from a group of countries that would have agreed to further it in its essentials within the UN and, where relevant, within the Washington multilaterals. The proposal as envisaged here would probably entail the General Assembly inviting the World Bank (and possibly also the IMF) to play a role in the working of the fund. The arrangements projected would doubtless be scrutinized (for practicalities, legalities and conformity to existing policies and practice) by the UN Secretariat, and the World Bank and IMF staffs, and might be referred to the Economic and Social Council (ECOSOC). Under the constitutional scheme mooted below, not only the General Assembly but also the Executive Board of the World Bank would need to assent.

For the content of the constitutional arrangement, we propose the following division of functions. In order to meet the requirements set out above for trust, legitimacy and efficiency, we propose that, of the broad policy questions – about the purposes and limits of the uses to which the funds might be put, and the forms in which, and the immediate recipients to whom they might be disbursed – any that are not embodied in the initial bargain should be decided by the UN General Assembly on a recommendation from an inter-agency drafting group of professionals representative of the UN Secretariat, the World Bank Group and the IMF. The General Assembly might either accept the recommendation or return it, with advice on its own preferences, for reformulation. A mechanism similar to this was used in the preparation of Secretary-General's report to the International Conference on Finance for Development held at Monterrey in 2002, and the draft of the Monterrey Consensus.

Approval by the General Assembly would, in the view of many, set the best available seal of legitimacy on any policy adopted. But, because of the nature of the General Assembly, with nearly 200 members – among whom the vote of Equatorial Guinea or the Solomon Islands counts formally as highly as that of India or Germany, and with small, poor countries carrying between them a weight proportionately far ahead of their share of population, let alone of economic size – trust and efficiency may require additional safeguards.

The use of an inter-agency drafting group of professionals was judged to have been effective in the Finance for Development process. Not only was it held to increase mutual understanding among the staffs of the organizations, it was also said to have produced greater coherence in the international economic policies of the individual member countries. Whereas a country's foreign ministry that instructed its Permanent Representative to the UN might have in the past taken a different position from its finance ministry or central bank that had the responsibility for its World Bank and IMF representation, the fact that the three organizations were deliberating together on given questions obliged the country to decide on a consistent position.

But the main purposes of the arrangement here would be, first, to ensure that whatever package went to the General Assembly for consideration would have been vetted seriously on grounds of practicality; and, second, to reassure those who set more trust in Washington multilaterals than in the UN Secretariat that policy recommendations were likely to be acceptable to both sides.

At the same time, we propose that the agency making the allocation decisions from day to day should be a component of the World Bank Group – either the IDA with a modified mandate or a new function or arm of the Bank comparable within the organization to the IBRD, IFC or IDA. The constitutional form of the allocating agency as a subsidiary or operative function within the World Bank could be decided by agreement between the World Bank and the General Assembly on the basis of a draft from the same inter-agency drafting group.

The argument for siting the executive/administrative process of allocation within the World Bank is this. First, it is better – on grounds of economy and to avoid a leap in the dark – to use an existing institution than to create one afresh. Second, among the existing institutions that might be considered, the World Bank has overwhelmingly the most professional resources relevant to the task. Third, it is necessary to satisfy, above all, the major net-'donor' governments and their constituencies that the executive body is sound; the World Bank seems the most likely of the relevant organizations to meet this test.

Yet the World Bank also arouses its share of suspicion and hostility among developing-country governments, and among some NGOs and students of development in both rich and poor countries. It would be good to be able to show that the big decisions – relating to limits and guidelines over allocation – would not be made within the World Bank: that it would play, through its staff, a part, but not an exclusive or ultimately decisive part, in these decisions.

It is appropriate that 'the world' should set the guidelines over how funds raised by, and for, the world are to be spent. The General Assembly, on the one hand, and the World Bank and IMF on the other, can each claim to represent the world, though with vastly different voting weights and different functions that have led them to build up cadres of staff with different cultures and outlooks, all of which may easily lead them to give different verdicts on important questions. The method suggested makes the General Assembly the ultimate arbiter over these guidelines. But the method allows it to make a positive decision only on the basis of an agreed recommendation from a committee of professionals from various multilateral institutions, and otherwise (in its instructions to this professional committee) only to express its preferences in fairly general terms; second, it will be clear where the major donor countries stand over any motion contemplated, and it is very likely that the drafting group will refrain from any recommendation, and the General Assembly will avoid any decision, that seems likely to alienate these members. So the method probably gets the best of General Assembly participation, but without its risks.

Auditing of the allocating agency might best be undertaken through the World Bank's own processes. Monitoring (from outside the World Bank) of the executive agency seems desirable. A monitoring committee, representing the General Assembly, might be formed to express an outside view on the executive/administrative process of allocation and its results, and to verify that any policy rules and guidelines laid down were being observed. It would need full access to all the activities of the allocating agency.

Objections that the World Bank, through its constitution, is dominated by the industrialized countries, can perhaps be met, first, by the provisions proposed above for determining the rules and policies under which allocations would be made; second, by the monitoring process outlined above; and third, by the plausible prospect that, in response to much recent critical discussion of the constitution of the BWIs, governance in the World Bank may before long be modified to give more weight to the positions and views of developing and transitional countries, and to be more susceptible to consultation with other international bodies.

Should the allocating agency operate, partly or exclusively, by financing other multilaterals? This would be a new departure, but seems a not-impossible arrangement. Furnished with sums of the order that we are contemplating, the allocating agency would have very great bargaining power. It would be able to exercise considerable influence over what was done by any receiving multilateral with the funds allocated. And restricting it to dealing directly *only* with other multilaterals could be supported on the grounds of economy: duplication of appraisals, monitoring and the like would be reduced; in addition, the other multilaterals would become the agency's clients, having incentives for co-operation with it, rather than being competitors in the same game. Indeed, confining the allocations made directly by the agency to other multilaterals could well be desirable if it tended to reduce duplication of effort and inter-agency rivalry.

However, one of the attractive features of the possibility of substantial global-provenance funds is that they make possible a coherent international strategy for delivering targets such as the MDGs. Equipped with considerable resources, and insulated from the particular diplomatic and other motives not directly related to development and welfare with which national governments are often burdened, the operating agency could concentrate its allocations at points where they were likely to be used effectively, and could focus on filling critical gaps or providing incentives for them to be filled. This would be a heavy responsibility for the agency but also an opportunity that should not be squandered lightly. To meet the challenge, the agency would need to be aware of political constraints, but as far as possible insulated from political pressures that might operate improperly in favour of, or against, particular potential beneficiaries. On the whole, these considerations are largely in favour of the World Bank. At least, there is no obvious candidate that would fit the requirements better. Providing it with funds that could be used as grants, rather than only as loans, would greatly extend the Bank's capacity to support areas of activity such as many aspects of health and education that cannot be, or are best not left to be, financially self-supporting.

Detailed guidelines as matters of policy? Whether, on balance, it would be good or not for the guidelines to extend beyond the broad decisions outlined above on purposes, forms and immediate recipients of the allocations, the possibility that the General Assembly might want to extend them in this way could presumably not be excluded by the initial bargain. Yet it might well be difficult for guidelines of this sort to be tight enough to be operationally meaningful without the risk of distorting decisions away from what would appear to be the optimum in particular cases. Perhaps the best compromise might be an expressed understanding in the initial bargain that the General Assembly might propound objectives for the use of the funds in rather general terms, and otherwise rely for scrutiny and criticism on the proposed monitoring committee. That committee would represent the General Assembly, and, with or without participation by some other bodies, it could at least lay the policy and practice of the allocating agency open to debate.

Summary of elements in the proposed arrangement

1 An 'initial bargain', probably agreed in broad principle among major high-income and developing countries before its submission to the UN and other multilaterals, would embody the main constitutional elements that follow, together possibly with some main policy rules; and those making the bargain would undertake to pursue agreement to these provisions in the UN General Assembly and in the World Bank Executive Board and Board of Governors.

2 The UN General Assembly would be the body ultimately responsible for setting limits to the powers of the executive body, including the purposes for which, the forms in which, and the recipients through which it should be authorized to allocate funds; giving it any guidelines for allocation; and, in agreement with the World Bank, fixing its constitutional form.

3 A subsidiary or operative arm developed for the purpose within the World Bank Group – or possibly the IDA with a modified brief – would be the agency with executive responsibility for the allocation of funds.

4 An inter-agency drafting group of professionals from the UN Secretariat, the IMF and the World Bank would be responsible for formulating proposals to the General Assembly under item 2 above. The General Assembly

would either accept the draft presented or return it with a general direction on how it should be amended.

5 A monitoring committee, representing the UN General Assembly, would scrutinize, and report on, the procedures and decisions of the executive agency.

Conclusion

The overall message

The message of this chapter is predominantly one of hopefulness for those who, like the authors, believe that there should be a large and reliable increase in the funds made available internationally for development and welfare in low-income and middle-income countries, and who look, moreover, for an effective international strategy within which the funds can be applied.

The need to pursue a strategy argues strongly for a significantly large source of funds to be available for global disposal, and this in turn is likely to depend on so-called 'innovative' sources of finance, especially what we have called finance of 'global provenance'. There are a number of possible ways around the obstacles to these outcomes. They would draw more or less on the forces we have identified that support increases in aid. Several of the possible ways of surmounting the obstacles seem to be potentially highly relevant, with some especially relevant to sources of funds for global disposal.

Much depends on the readiness of the developing-country governments to build effective alliances: alliances prepared to make use of support from campaigning NGOs and to draw on the expertise, ingenuity and other relevant resources of international secretariats, and of potentially sympathetic research institutions and charitable foundations. To be effective, the alliances will need to be sufficiently institutionalized to be able to negotiate forcefully and rationally over sources of development finance, together with other objectives of interest to various groups of rich and poor countries. It will help if an alliance has a fairly high-level secretariat of its own.

The campaigning, development-orientated NGOs also have a role: in ensuring that as far as possible they throw their weight in a concentrated fashion behind objectives that are coherent and realistic. Identifying what are politically soft targets is important for both governments and NGOs. It will be useful if they can make common cause over certain objectives rather than operate at cross-purposes. And there is a variety of possible tactics that may circumvent some of the obstacles.

To the objection that there is no machinery by which the world could administer a large excess of funds available for global purposes, we have suggested one plausible way in which the machinery could acceptably be set up.

Since early 2005, a debate has been taking place between the leaders of some large European economies over the methods to be adopted for releasing considerable additional funds in order to help finance a co-ordinated attack on the extremes of world poverty through pursuit of the MDGs. The main alternatives on the table in early 2005 were the IFF and forms of internationally agreed taxes, though with some recognition that the first of these would need to be complemented by the second. As mentioned above, some middle-income countries have played a leading role in this debate, and there has been an unusual degree of consensus between the European powers promoting the moves and major developing-country governments. Devices that had seemed visionary only three years earlier, at the time of the Monterrey summit, had come to be debated for their relative advantages. And the champions of each method (as at the Davos meeting in January 2005) were prepared to accept combinations of their favoured solutions with others.

That is one change. A second one tending to reinforce it is the increasing interest on the part of governments of developing countries in tapping innovative sources of development finance, combined with an increasing readiness of certain major developing countries to play an active and concerted role in international negotiation.

For these reasons, and also because of technical economic work that has been undertaken since 2005, the possibility of substantial additional finance in the form of global-provenance funds, or of other funds that might be used under international agreement for global purposes, seems to have come closer.

References

Addison, T. and A. R. Chowdhury (2004) 'A Global Lottery and a Global Premium Bond', in A. B. Atkinson (ed.), *New Sources of Development Finance*, Oxford: Oxford University Press for UNU-WIDER.

Atkinson, A. B. (ed.) (2004) *New Sources of Development Finance*, Oxford: Oxford University Press for UNU-WIDER.

Avi-Yonah, R. (2000) 'Globalization, Tax Competition, and the Fiscal Crisis of the Welfare State', *Harvard Law Review*, 113: 1575–676.

Boughton, J. (2001) *Silent Revolution: The International Monetary Fund 1979–1989*, Washington, DC: IMF.

Braithwaite, J. (2004) 'Methods of Power for Development: Weapons of the Weak, Weapons of the Strong', *Michigan Journal of International Law*, 26(1): 297–330.

Braithwaite, J. and P. Drahos (2000) *Global Business Regulation*, Cambridge: Cambridge University Press.

Brazilian Mission to the UN (2004) *The New York Declaration*, 20 September. Available at: www.mre.gov.br/ingles/politica_externa/temas_agenda/acfp/final.declaration_doc.

Burnside, C. and D. Dollar (2000) 'Aid, Policies and Growth', *American Economic Review*, 90(4): 847–68.

Cassen, R. and Associates (1994) *Does Aid Work?*, Oxford: Clarendon Press.

Clark, P. B. and J. J. Polak (2002) 'International Liquidity and the Role of the SDR in the International Monetary System', IMF Working Paper 02/217, Washington, DC: IMF.

Chasek, P. and L. Rajamani (2003) 'Steps Toward Enhanced Parity: Negotiating Capacity and Strategies of Developing Countries,' in I. Kaul, P. Conceição, K. Le Goulven and R. U. Mendoza (eds), *Providing Global Public Goods: Managing Globalization*, New York: Oxford University Press: 246–62.

Clunies-Ross, A. I. (2000) 'Untying the Knots of International Environmental Agreements', *Journal of Economic Studies*, 27(1/2): 75–93.

Clunies-Ross, A. I. (2004) 'Development Finance: Beyond Budgetary "Official Development Assistance"', *Michigan Journal of International Law*, 26(1): 389–410.

Devarajan, S., M. Miller and E. Swanson (2002) 'Goals for Development: History, Prospects and Costs', World Bank Policy Research Working Paper 2819, Washington, DC: World Bank.

Financial Times (2005) Lead article, 9 July.

France (Government of) (2004a) *Rapport à Monsieur Jacques Chirac, Président de la République*, English version, Groupe de Travail sur les Nouvelles Contributions Financières Internationales (the Landau Report), Paris, December.

France (Government of, with the Governments of Brazil, Chile and Spain) (2004b) *Action Against Hunger and Poverty*, Report of the Technical Group on Innovative Financing Mechanisms (the Quadripartite Report), Paris, September.

France (Government of) (2005a) Embassy of France in the US, Daily Press Briefing, 15 February, Available at http://www.ambafrance-us.org/news/briefing/us15025.asp. Downloaded 18 February 2005.

France (Government of) (2005b) 'A Solidarity Contribution on Airplane Tickets', internet release. Available at: www.elysee.fr

Kaul, I., K. Le Goulven and M. Schnupf (eds) (2002) *Global Public Goods Financing: New Tools for New Challenges A Policy Dialogue*, New York: UNDP, Office of Development Studies.

Kitney, G. (2005) 'Rich Put Poverty on Global Agenda', *Australian Financial Review*, 31 January: 53.

Kull, S. and I. M. Destler (1999) *Misreading the Public: The Myth of a New Isolationism*, Washington, DC: Brookings Institution Press.

Littlewood, M. (2004) 'Tax Competition: Harmful to Whom?', *Michigan Journal of International Law*, 26(1): 411–88.

McGillivray, M. (2005) 'Is Aid Effective?', Mimeo, UNU-WIDER: Helsinki.

McGillivray, M., S. Feeny, N. Hermes and R. Lensink (2006) 'Controversies Over the Inpact of Development Aid: It Works; It Doesn't; It Can, but That Depends. . .', *Journal of International Development*, 18: 1031–50.

Mussa, M. (1996) 'Is There a Case for Allocation under the Present Articles?', in M. Mussa *et al.*, *Exchange Rate Regimes in an Increasingly Integrated World Economy*, IMF Occasional Paper 193, Washington DC: IMF; cited in Clark and Polak (2002).

OECD (2002) 'Proposed Legal Framework for Exchange of Information'. Available at: www.oecd.org/daf/ctpa; cited in J. Owens, 'The OECD Work on Tax Havens', Paper for the Friedrich Ebert Foundation Conference, New York, 8–9 July, on 'Money Laundering and Tax Havens – the Hidden Billions for Development', typescript, Friedrich-Ebert-Stiftung, New York.

Raffer, K. (1998) 'The Tobin Tax: Reviving a Discussion', *World Development*, 26(3): 532.

Schmidt, R. (1999) *A Feasible Foreign Exchange Transaction Tax*, Ottawa: North–South Institute.

Schmidt, R. (2001) 'Efficient Capital Controls', *Journal of Economic Studies*, 28(3) 199–212.

Schmidt, R. (2007) *The Currency Transaction Tax: Rate and Revenue Estimates*, Ottawa: North–South Institute, October.

Solimano, A. (2004) 'Remittances by Emigrants: Issues and Evidence', in A. B. Atkinson (ed.), *New Sources of Development Finance*, Oxford: Oxford University Press for UNU-WIDER.

Soros, G. (2002) *On Globalization*, Oxford: Public Affairs Ltd.

Tanzi, V. (1995) *Taxation in an Integrating World*, Washington, DC: Brookings Institution.

Ter-Minassian, T. (2003) 'Comments on the UNU-WIDER Project on Innovative Sources for Development Finance', Paper prepared for the UNU-WIDER conference on 'Sharing Global Prosperity', Helsinki, 6–7 September.

UN (2001a) Report to the Secretary-General of the High-level Panel on Financing for Development (the Zedillo Report), New York, 25 June.

UN (2001b) General Assembly, Preparatory Committee for the International Conference on Financing for Development, Note by the Secretary General, 'Technical Note 3: Existing proposals for innovative sources of finance', A/AC.257/27/Add. 3, 20 September.

UN (2005) *Investing in Development* (the Sachs Report), New York: United Nations Millennium Project, January.

5
Financing Global and Regional Public Goods through ODA: Analysis and Evidence from the OECD Creditor Reporting System

Helmut Reisen, Marcelo Soto and Thomas Weithöner

Introduction

Since the late 1990s, the UNDP Office of Development Studies has raised awareness among the development and donor communities that the enhanced provision of international public goods will be of critical importance to achieving the Millennium Development Goals (MDGs),[1] notably the objectives of reducing poverty (Kaul *et al.* 1999). The UN conference on Financing for Development held in Monterrey, Mexico, in March 2002 has challenged the donor community to put in place the means and the structures required to mobilize the finance needed to support these goals, which, among others, stipulate the reduction of world poverty by half by the year 2015. Available evidence (Dyer and Beynon 2003) suggests that the impact of investing in international public goods can be high and is important for achieving the MDGs. For example, the cost of lifting one person out of income poverty through agricultural research and global trade expansion is estimated to be much lower than the cost of the same impact through aid to poor countries.

The Zedillo Report, by a panel established by the UN Secretary-General in 2000 and chaired by the former President of Mexico, Ernesto Zedillo, estimated that at least US$20 billion per year – four times the current spending level – would be required to begin addressing the need for global public goods in a more satisfactory manner. Some donors have documented the concern that international public goods (IPGs) remain severely under-supplied. Sweden's Ministry of Foreign Affairs has produced a wide-ranging book with a discussion of the concepts, financing and mechanisms of provision (Sagasti and Bezanson 2001). The International Task Force on Global Public Goods was created by an agreement between France and Sweden signed on 9 April 2003. The task force's mandate is to assess and clarify the notion of international public goods, global and regional, and to make recommendations to policy-makers and other stakeholders on how to provide and finance these.

This policy background raises the importance of defining, analysing and determining the allocation of official development assistance (ODA) between traditional development projects and international public goods, given donors' budget constraints. To date, global actions and funding have tended to occur on an ad hoc basis, in response to highly visible emergencies (such as HIV) or as a result of catalytic actions by philanthropic organizations. The UK Department for International Development (DFID) has recently undertaken a strategic review of resource allocation priorities, including its future commitments to international public-good expenditure.[2] This choice was explicitly introduced and emphasized as a new element of aid allocation at a joint OECD-DAC Development Centre Experts' Seminar ('Aid Effectiveness and Selectivity: Integrating Multiple Objectives into Aid Allocations'), held in Paris on 10 March 2003 (OECD 2003). It was recognized at the seminar that the analytical work done so far on this issue is 'limited and preliminary'. The summary record to that seminar concluded for the provision and financing of global public goods that 'more policy analysis and related work is required, including on appropriate incentives and financing mechanisms'. The seminar chairperson stated that the discussion on aid allocation, including that for global public goods, was likely to become a more central part of the DAC agenda in the future, as a result of the DAC/Centre seminar, of DFID's strategic review analysis and of the Swedish–French task force on global public goods.

This chapter aims at providing help for thinking through at least six important issues. First, it will (re)define the concept of international, global and regional public goods on the basis of taxonomy elaborated in the theory of public finance. Sharp definitions are necessary to avoid confusion about the actual allocation of ODA between traditional development objectives and the provision of international public goods; they are a prerequisite for establishing sound evidence on possible aid diversion, where ODA would be diverted to fund global public goods (GPGs) that do not benefit predominantly developing countries.

Second, based on the definitions, data from the OECD Creditor Reporting System (CRS) will be used to attribute ODA to the provision of global public goods, regional public goods (RPGs), and traditional aid for the five most recent years of data availability – 1997–2001. This section will then present a descriptive set of graphs for this recent observation period, in order to show the evolution of ODA allocation between the three broad categories; for DAC donors, the respective percentage shares have averaged around 15 per cent (GPGs), 15 per cent (RPGs) and 70 per cent (other aid) during that observation period.

Third, the chapter presents a highly stylized, standard model of public goods, adapted to the special donor–recipient relationship. The model highlights the trade-offs between free and earmarked donations, and hence the underlying tensions between deleting the under-provision of international public goods (where a maximum effect per ODA dollar is reached by earmarking) and recipient countries' 'ownership' (where free transfers maximize the utility of the ODA dollar for the poor).

Fourth, the model is estimated with CRS data in order to quantify the donors' interest in the provision of international public goods. The estimation shows clearly the strong association between the provision of international public goods and donors' income and budget balances.

Fifth, the chapter deals with a special concern of the donor community, namely that the provision of international public goods might discriminate against ODA allocated to the poorest countries. Such concern has arguably reigned in ODA spending on international public goods. While the hypothesis of extreme crowding-out is strongly rejected, the *average offset coefficient* between GPG-related ODA and traditional aid is also significantly greater than zero, namely 25 per cent. However, the data presented here cannot support the concern that an increase in ODA spending allocated to international public goods is associated significantly with a bias toward lower (or higher) per capita income levels of the recipient countries.

Finally, the chapter concludes by showing that its results favour the separation of traditional ODA and spending on the provision of international public goods, both to maximize 'ownership' by ODA partner countries, and to provide international public goods.

Defining global public goods: international, regional and global

A definition as sharp as possible of what constitute international public goods is necessary, for several important reasons:

- The definition is a precondition to establish evidence on the current sources of financing global public goods and, in particular, the extent of ODA spent on the provision of international public goods; estimates currently available on CRS basis range from 3.7 per cent (Anand 2002) to 25 per cent (Raffer 1999) for the share of ODA spent on GPGs, with such an extreme range of estimates being largely explained by differences in definitions.
- Governments in general, and donors specifically, are in need of clear concepts to separate finance for humanitarian and technical assistance from finance for global public goods if severe under-funding in either of these categories is to be avoided – under-funding that would be likely to threaten the realization of the MDGs.
- Public goods (which generally are not provided by the market) are often not sufficiently distinguished from merit goods (such as education,

provided by the market but where the social benefits exceed the private benefits); the lack of distinction implies a virtual boundless assignment of policy problems to the public sector, impedes organizational responsibilities and accountabilities, and hinders the search for cost-efficient policy solutions.

The necessity of finding a proper definition of GPGs has been recognized by many authors. Morrissey *et al.* (2002) classify GPGs into those that yield direct utility, those that help to reduce risks, and those that enhance capacity. However, when it comes to matters of provision and finance, this distinction is not very helpful. The approach of Sandler (2001), who focuses on the question of how beneficial a particular GPG is to a particular generation, group of people, or groups of countries, seems more fertile. We take this concept as a starting point, although restricting attention to goods that serve some agents and do not harm any other agent.

A proper definition of GPGs should be based on classical public finance conventions, especially the concepts of non-rivalry between users and non-exclusion from use. Non-rivalry implies that a good can be used by more than one user simultaneously, or more than once. Non-exclusion means that the good is available to more than one user at no (or at a negligible) extra cost. Public goods are not (or insufficiently) provided by the market – where marginal utility must equal marginal cost for the provision to be efficient – because of the free-rider problem among potential users. Users are not willing to reveal their preferences and pay accordingly. The incentive problem is aggravated by the fact that public goods are rarely 'pure', and measures that are beneficial on a global scale may at the same time be harmful to a particular group of agents, or vice versa.

Contrary to the view expressed in Anand (2002), it appears to be indispensable to include future generations in the definition of GPGs. Otherwise, the notion of development becomes almost meaningless, since most development activities are deemed to serve, at least partly, future generations.[3] Given the long lags in the production of GPGs (witness climate change), the financing of GPGs at the time of writing amounts in effect to a resource transfer to future generations. And as current generations in poor countries live in great poverty, they may prefer to consume and to grow now rather than to provide global public goods with their limited resources (Schelling 2002)

A definition of GPGs should also be confined to considerations of allocation; that is, leave out issues of distribution. This implies that, if intergenerational concerns are to be accounted for, then this must be based on future utility estimations. Allocative efficiency requires that the sum of the marginal utilities of all present and future users and every country equals the marginal cost of the GPG. In the light of these considerations, the chapter approaches the definition of GPGs in a recursive, four-step manner, as follows.

Definition 1

A *public good* is a commodity, measure, fact or service

- which can be consumed by one person without diminishing the amount available for consumption by another person (non-rivalry);
- which is available at zero or negligible marginal cost to a large or unlimited number of consumers (non-exclusiveness); and
- which does not bring about disutility to any consumer now or in the future (sustainability).

The degree of non-exclusiveness determines the public good's degree of purity.

Definition 2

An *international public good* (IPG) is a public good which provides benefits crossing national borders of the producing country.

Definition 3

A *regional public good* (RPG) is an international public good which displays spillover benefits to countries in the neighbourhood of the producing country, in a region that is smaller than the rest of the world.

Definition 4

A *global public good* (GPG) is an international public good which, although not necessarily to the same extent, benefits consumers all over the world.

Not all of the eight Millennium Development Goals constitute pure global public goods; and in turn, there may be GPGs relevant for development that are not included in the MDGs. In a recent study, DFID identified key development GPGs, on the basis of matching the GPGs with the MDGs (Speight 2002):

- knowledge generation and dissemination;
- communicable disease eradication;
- the global commons;
- a free and open trade system;
- international financial stability.

Other important GPGs are narcotics control and global peace. Drug consumption and its consequences are a major problem for some countries that are not necessarily producers (the US being the best example). In this sense, the fight against drug production may have positive cross-border externalities. Peacekeeping operations create external benefits as they create security, not least for the affected and neighbouring economies. In the light of the definitions given above, the following GPGs were added to the DFID list:

- protection from crime and narcotics;
- global peace.

The concept developed here, similar to the DFID approach, stresses the spatial dimension of spillover. Conversely, the World Bank prefers a classification of GPGs into *core* and *complementary* activities.[4] While this distinction is useful to underline the need of certain conventional aid measures for GPGs to foster development, it is of little help when discussing innovative ways of financing GPGs.[5] Many complementary activities are of national or regional dimension only; and this might even be true for some core activities. To give an example, the World Bank defined post-conflict peacebuilding and reconstruction relief as 'core', although the spatial dimension of this IPG is certainly limited. While global peace as itself is clearly a GPG, any measures aimed at establishing or preserving peace between conflicting parties benefit primarily the citizens of the countries that are involved in a (potential) conflict. Therefore, one should distinguish between institution building that improves global conflict prevention, and concrete (UN) missions. The latter would better fit the definition of RPGs. The same is true for expenditures for land mine clearance and the like.

This example shows that focusing on the spatial dimension of public goods (rather than their functional properties) has the advantage of making the principle of subsidiarity applicable: wherever a nation or region (for example, via a regional development bank) can provide a public good, it should assume the responsibility to do so. GPGs, on the other hand, should be provided on a global scale.

ODA and international public goods: the CRS data set

This empirical analysis makes use of data from the OECD Creditor Reporting System (CRS). The CRS dataset is unique as it is based on common definitions agreed by all DAC donors: this is important for any empirical analysis on the sectoral allocation of aid. Thus, the CRS data are the only source of information available on ODA that provide true comparability across donors. The CRS data cover official development assistance (ODA), official aid (OA), and other lending to developing countries and countries in transition. It is noteworthy, however, that the CRS data show commitments rather than actual spending, that there can be a time lag in reporting, and that some donors tend to report incompletely. In the CRS, data on the sector of destination are recorded using 5-digit purpose codes. The first three digits of the code refer to the corresponding sector or category, each code belonging to one, and only one, category.

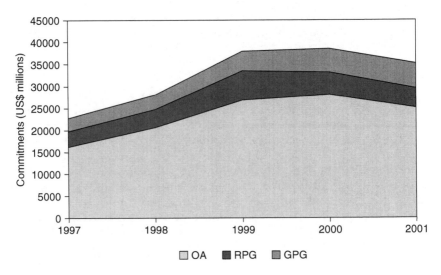

Figure 5.1   Evolution of ODA

The last two digits are sequential and not hierarchical; that is, each code can be selected individually or grouped to create subsectors. Appendix Tables 5.A1 and 5.A2 illustrate the classification of the ODA that is committed to global and regional public goods, as defined in the previous section. The classification is needed for the subsequent empirical analysis of this chapter. The residual ODA is defined as *other aid*.

Before proceeding with the empirical analysis, let us examine briefly the current situation in ODA flows. The observation period selected for the empirical analysis runs from 1997 to 2001, the latest year for which CRS data are currently available. This time frame results from a compromise between the aim of using most recent data and obtaining as many observations as possible. Only grants are considered, and so concessionals have been dropped from the data.

Figure 5.1 shows the evolution of commitments on regional public goods (RPG), on global public goods (GPG) and on other aid, from 1997 to 2001. We can see that while overall ODA was rather volatile, the ODA financing of GPGs has been increasing constantly since 1998. Conversely, spending on RPGs seemed to reach a peak in 1999 and has been decreasing slightly since then. Total ODA spending on international public goods has therefore, remained flat as a percentage share of ODA. The figure also shows that the share of GPG in total aid was fairly stable over the period 1997–6 (around 16 per cent). This result ranges above the earlier World Bank estimate (2001), which, in its 2001 *Report on Global Development Finance* calculated a 12.5 per cent share of ODA (for 1994–8) spent on GPGs. However, as the share of RPGs also oscillated around 15 per cent of ODA during the observation period, donors have spent around 30 per cent of ODA on the provision of international public goods during the observation period 1997–2001.

Figure 5.2 displays the most important contributors to the current provision of GPGs, RPGs and other aid. The United States finances almost half of all DAC donor commitments to GPG provision; this is largely explained by US funding to fight drug production in Latin America. Other important contributors to the provision of global public goods are currently the UK (10 per cent of total DAC commitments for GPGs), Germany (7 per cent) and the Netherlands (6 per cent). The US finances about a fifth of all DAC commitments for the provision of RPGs, and only 30 per cent of other forms of aid. The EC, a multilateral donor, occupies an important role in the provision of RPGs (14 per cent of DAC commitments), while its part of DAC spending on GPGs (5 per cent) and other aid (9 per cent) is relatively modest. Japan is also strongly committed to RPGs (12 per cent of DAC spending) but contributes a minor share of total spending on GPGs.

Figure 5.3 illustrates the repartition of GPG commitments over sectors. We can see that the largest sectors – narcotics control and economic policy and planning – each consume about 15 per cent of total GPG commitments.

Finally, Figure 5.4 presents the main items of aid not classified as global public goods in the chapter as their benefits accrue predominantly to the recipient country. The largest single item is non-food emergency and distress relief, which represents 10 per cent of total aid other than GPG (that is, some US$15 billion over the period 1997–2001).

Modelling the trade-off between ownership and GPG supply

This section presents a highly stylized, standard model of public goods, adapted to the special donor–recipient partnership. The model and its empirical estimation will be useful for gauging the extent of the underlying tensions between deleting the under-provision of global[6] public goods (where a maximum effect per ODA dollar is reached by earmarking) and recipient countries' 'ownership' (where free transfers maximize the utility of the ODA dollar for the poor).

Suppose that both the 'rich' donor country and the 'poor' recipient country draw additively separable utility from a private good x and a (global) public good z, which can only be provided by the poor country (for example, preservation of the rain forest). In addition to the utility derived from the two goods, the (rich) donor country 'cares' about the (poor) recipient country; that is, it is better off when the utility of the poor country increases. Assuming log utility functions for the sake of a closed solution, let us define:

$$U_p = \ln(x_p) + v_p \ln(z) \qquad (5.1)$$

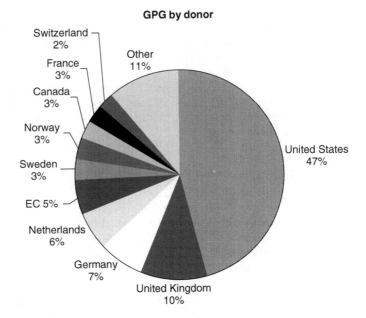

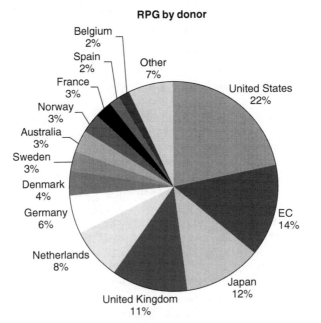

Figure 5.2   GPG, RPG and other aid, by donor

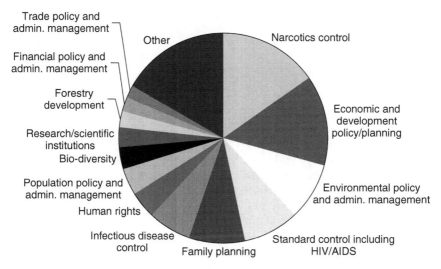

Figure 5.3 GPG commitments, by sector (per cent)
Source: OECD Creditor Reporting System.

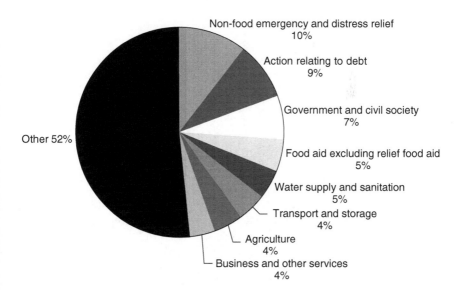

Figure 5.4 Non-GPG commitments, by sector
Source: OECD Creditor Reporting System.

$$U_r = \ln(x_r) + v_r \ln(z) + \alpha U_p \tag{5.2}$$

The parameters $v_r > 0$ and $v_p > 0$ measure the relative importance that the global public goods has on the two countries. The parameter $\alpha \geq 0$ measures how much the rich country 'cares' about the welfare of the poor country.

Free transfers

The analysis starts with the case of traditional development aid. The donor country transfers a certain voluntary amount $t \geq 0$ to the poorer country and lets the latter decide the use of the received funds. In the model's framework, this implies a two-stage game, to be solved with the concept of backward induction. The recipient country decides how much it wants to spend on the public good and maximizes its utility (Equation (5.1)) subject to the budget constraint:

$$\overline{Y}_p + t = x_p + z \tag{5.3}$$

where $\overline{Y}$ denotes the (exogenous) income of a country. Substituting the constraint into Equation (5.1) and optimizing for z yields:

$$z = \frac{v_p(\overline{Y}_p + t)}{1 + v_p} \tag{5.4}$$

The donor country anticipates this rule $z(t)$ and optimizes Equation (5.2) subject to its budget constraint:

$$\overline{Y}_r - t = x_r$$

It finds that the optimal transfer is:

$$t = \gamma \overline{Y}_r - (1 - \gamma)\overline{Y}_p \tag{5.5}$$

where:

$$\gamma = \frac{(v_r + \alpha(1 + v_p))}{1 + v_r + \alpha(1 + v_p)} \quad \text{and} \quad 0 < \gamma < 1$$

This result is quite intuitive. The donor country is prepared to transfer more resources to the poor country if its own income $\overline{Y}_r$ is high, if it 'cares much' (high α), and if the public good yields a high utility relative to the private good (v_r and v_p). Conversely, if the poor country's income rises, the donor country's willingness to transfer resources diminishes.

We can now substitute Equation (5.5) into Equation (5.4) to find the equilibrium supply of the public good when transfers are free:

$$z^{FT} = \frac{v_p(v_r + \alpha(1 + v_p))}{(1 + v_p)(1 + v_r + \alpha(1 + v_p))}(\overline{Y}_p + \overline{Y}_r) \tag{5.6}$$

Using comparative static analysis for the case of free transfers, it is possible to see that the supply of the public good depends positively on both countries' income, on the importance the countries attribute to the public good relative to the consumption of private goods, and on the level of altruism in the rich country with respect to the welfare of the recipient country.

Earmarked transfers

Donors will be inclined to provide funding for global public goods only for earmarked use. From the donor perspective, the model thus groups ODA allocation into funds z that might be spent exclusively on the public good and other aid (OA) (contributions to the poor country's private good). This implies that the recipient country cannot freely allocate the transfer at home. (Since both goods yield positive utility to the poor country, there are no participation concerns to consider.) However, in case the donor country offers too few funds for the public good supply, the recipient country may wish to contribute to the public good out of its own budget, which adds a side condition to the budget constraint in the donors' optimization problem:

$$\max_{z,TA} U_r \quad \text{subject to}$$

$$\overline{Y}_r - OA - z = x_r, \overline{Y}_p + OA = x_p \quad \text{and} \quad z \geq z^{FT} \tag{5.7}$$

From the previous section, we already know how much the recipient country would contribute voluntarily to the public good (z^{FT}), given the transfer t. If it can be shown that the donor country voluntarily transfers no less than t and funds no less than z^{FT} in transfers earmarked for international public goods, the last constraint does not apply.

Combining the two first-order conditions for optimality[7] yields that, in equilibrium, the rich country's marginal utility of spending an extra transfer-dollar on the public good equals its marginal utility of spending it on the private good:

$$\frac{v_r}{z} + \alpha \frac{v_p}{z} = \frac{1}{x_p}$$

Clearly, for any $\alpha < 1$, the public good supply is inefficiently low, since the Lindahl condition is violated – a standard public finance result. The Lindahl equilibrium requires that the sum of the marginal utilities from the public good equal the marginal utility from the private good.

The same first-order conditions, when substituted into each other, yield the equilibrium values for earmarked ODA transfers:

$$z^{ET} = \frac{(v_r + \alpha v_p)}{1 + v_r + \alpha(1 + v_p)} (\overline{Y}_p + \overline{Y}_r) \tag{5.8}$$

$$OA = \frac{\alpha(\overline{Y}_p + \overline{Y}_r)}{1 + v_r + \alpha(1 + v_p)} - \overline{Y}_p \tag{5.9}$$

As before, the supply of the public good increases with the available income of both partner countries and with the degree of relative appreciation of the public good. However, an increase of altruism (α) only leads to more supply of the public good if $v_p > v_r$; that is, if the poor country receives a higher relative utility than the donor country from the provision of the public good, even though a higher α will result in higher donor spending on ODA. The intuition is that, while a higher 'care factor' α implies more willingness for transfers, the extra transfer goes where it benefits the recipient country most. With the relative utility derived from a public good lower in the poor country than in the donor country ($v_p < v_r$), increased altruism (α) makes the donor pay less attention to its own direct interest (v_r) and more to the recipient country's utility (which, under the condition $v_p < v_r$ is dominated by the consumption of its private goods).

Note that the sum of z^{ET} and OA equals exactly the free transfer t. This means that binding the transfers to a certain use in the recipient country does not affect the donor's willingness to transfer resources in the model. This may seem counter-intuitive, as a donor perfectly in control of the use of funds should be willing to provide more aid. Technically speaking, the effect is related to the choice of the utility function (Cobb–Douglas property).

Yet there remains an important difference between the two ways of providing ODA to poor countries. Since one of the two goods is public, the donor country benefits from it in a 'double' way: it not only draws direct utility from it (because of higher consumption of the global public good), but it also benefits from increased welfare in the recipient country (via altruism). This is why the earmarked transfers naturally lead to a higher supply of the public good. To see this, simply compare the equilibrium public good supply in the two regimes, Equations (5.6) and (5.8):

$$z^{ET} - z^{FT} = \frac{v_r(\overline{Y}_p + \overline{Y}_r)}{(1 + v_r)(1 + v_r + \alpha(1 + v_p))} > 0$$

This result implies a clear crowding-out effect. When total transfers remain constant but more is spent on the public good, then this is detrimental to conventional development assistance. On the other hand, the under-provision of the public good is mitigated, which increases efficiency. The less 'ownership' the recipient countries have on the use of the funds, the better the world's provision with international public goods. Summing up, we expect the provision of earmarked transfer to be a function of the model parameters, as follows:

$$z^{ET} = F(\underbrace{v_r, v_p, \overline{Y}_p, \overline{Y}_r}_{+}) \tag{5.10}$$

The impact of α is ambiguous, depending on the importance of v_p relative to v_r when transfers are earmarked. More specifically, if $v_r > v_p$, then z^{ET} increases with α. This is so simply because of a size effect: as α becomes relatively large, the donor gives more aid, part of which will be earmarked if the recipient cares little about the public good; that is, if v_p is small.

Before doing the econometric section and to bring the model closer to the real world, it would be interesting to identify some variables related to two key parameters of the model; namely, the relative preference of donors for public goods, v_r, and their degree of altruism, α. The model states that the higher the value of v_r and α, the higher will be the share of global public goods in total aid, and the ratio of total aid to national income, respectively. Consequently, the chapter compares a number of variables that are thought to be related to the parameters with the GPG/ODA and ODA/GDP ratios. The variables selected correspond to: (i) indicators of the economic openness of rich countries, measured by the ratio of direct investment abroad and exports plus imports to GDP; (ii) the size of the government (measured by share of the government consumption in GDP); (iii) the shares of public spending in education and health in GDP; and (iv) the share of military spending on GDP. The rationale for linking the openness indicators with the parameters is that the openness degree may in part reflect the extent to which donors care about the rest of the world (that is, their altruism). Similarly, the size of government may be related to both the level of altruism and the preference for public goods. This may be so because countries with higher levels of altruism arguably spend more on poor people (through, for example, health and educational programmes). Also, if health and education are thought to have positive externalities, there would be a higher involvement of the public sector in the provision of these goods. Similarly, governments caring about the global public good of 'global peace' need to be prepared to carry out respective actions through relatively higher military spending.

Table 5.1 presents the rank correlations of these indicators with the GPG/ODA and ODA/GDP ratios. The figures are based on the average over the period 1997–2001 for each of the nineteen donor countries in the sample (see below). The two indicators for openness are correlated significantly with the ODA/GDP ratio, which gives support to the hypothesis that economic openness is associated with altruism. Total government consumption is also related to the ODA/GDP ratio, which could also be interpreted as the fact that larger governments are associated with stronger altruism. Of the other indicators selected, only public spending on education is correlated significantly with the share of ODA in GDP. In contrast, the combined spending on health, education and defence is correlated with the share of GPG in total ODA. This supports the hypothesis that the total public spending on education, health and defence *is* associated with the relative preference of donors for public goods.

Table 5.1   Correlation of selected variables with aid

	GPG/ODA	ODA/GDP
FDI outflows/GDP	0.296	0.628[a]
(X + M)/GDP	−0.007	0.570[a]
Government consumption/GDP	0.018	0.495[a]
Public health expenditure/GDP	0.330	0.163
Public expenditure on education/GDP	0.254	0.509[a]
Military expenditure/GDP	0.318	0.054
(Health + education public expenditure)/GDP	0.304	0.398
(Health + education + military expenditure)/GDP	0.460[a]	0.302

Notes: Rank correlations for 19 donors (average over 1997–2001); [a]Correlation is significant at 5 per cent level.

Empirical analysis

The objective of this section is to investigate whether aid in the form of global public goods is crowding out aid to the poorest countries and traditional aid. In order to isolate the impact of ODA related to international public goods, it is first necessary to have a better empirical understanding about the determinants of aid. Equation (5.5) predicts that total aid depends positively on the donor's income and negatively on the recipient's income, in addition to specific parameters of each country. More specifically, total aid by donor i to recipient j in period t can be written as:

$$\text{Total aid}_{ijt} = \pi_{ij} Y_{jt} + c_i + \tau_{it} + e_{ijt} \tag{5.11}$$

where π_{ij} depends on a set of parameters specific to the donor and the recipient country; c_i is a specific effect related to the donor; and τ_{it} is a time dummy. This is introduced in order to account for any time-varying effect (such as the donor's income or any other determinant of aid relevant for the donor but not considered in the model). Equation (5.11) represents the baseline for the regressions reported below. Since the parameter π_i may vary from donor to donor, the estimates are carried out separately for each donor. This approach allows accounting for the specificities of the donors but not those of the recipients, therefore an implicit assumption of the estimates presented below is that recipient countries have similar preferences for global public goods. Note that the model assumes implicitly that there is a single person in each recipient and donor country, which means that income is measured in per capita terms. Consequently, it is necessary to take into account the population of recipient countries. We expect to find that the higher the recipient country's income and the lower its population, the lower the level of aid allocated to that country by each donor. The data correspond to the annual committed grants (concessional loans are not included) donated by each of the nineteen countries and the European Commission, as reported in the OECD Creditor Reporting System. The sample covers the period 1997–2001 (the latest year available), hence roughly the period that has seen a rising awareness of the underprovision of international public goods. Further, the five-year period has been selected to reach a sufficient number of observations for the panel data analysis carried out below.

The results are presented in Appendix Table 5.A3. The table shows that the income of recipient countries explains aid commitments only modestly.[8] Although the average response of donors to recipients' income displays the expected sign, there is great heterogeneity in the coefficients – some of them display the wrong sign – and, most importantly, only few countries display significant coefficients. Therefore, the most important determinants of aid are hidden in the recipient country-specific effects, which in itself is not very informative. By contrast, when recipient country-specific dummies are replaced by regional dummies (see Table 5.A4), it emerges that these dummies are good explanatory variables of aid. More specifically, the table shows that, given the GDP and population levels of recipients, Sub-Saharan countries are favoured by most European donors (and the European Commission). On the other hand, the well-known fact that the US gives higher amounts of aid to countries in the Middle East and North African region is clearly observed in the table. On the other hand, Japan favours the East Asia and Pacific and the South Asia regions.

Another variable that is most likely to play a role in the determination of aid is the budget balance of donors. Although the budget balance is not linked directly to the model of the previous section – since that is a static model, whereas the concept of budget balance is related inherently to the time dimension – common sense would suggest that donors suffering from a tight budgetary situation would tend to be less charitable with recipients of aid. The significance of the budget balance variable is tested in two separate sets of regressions (one for total aid and the other for global public goods). However, a preliminary analysis shows that the effects of the budgetary balance cannot be observed in regressions where each recipient enters as an individual observation. Yet a tight budgetary situation may still have an impact on the overall aid programme of the donor. This may be the case if, for example, under fiscal strain a donor would cut aid more easily to one particular group of countries while keeping aid to other recipients untouched. Under such circumstances, an analysis of the overall aid programme would be more pertinent than considering the effects on each recipient. We do this by examining the impact of the budget balances on the average annual aid given by every donor. The results are presented in Table 5.1.

In the first two columns, the donor's GDP is also included to account for size effects. The budget balance enters with positive and significant coefficients in both total aid and GPG regressions. Taking the point estimates at face value, one percentage point increase in the budget balance of the 'average' donor country would increase total aid to each recipient by a little less than US$8 million, and aid destined for global public goods by some US$2 million.

These results need to be interpreted with caution, since donors with very different characteristics are grouped together; in particular, the size of their economies varies considerably. When the aid variables are scaled by the GDP of donors, the resulting estimates on budget balance are also significant (see the last two columns of Table 5.2). These results confirm that the budgetary situation of donors has an effect on their global aid programmes, but changes in the budget balance do not seem to have a uniform effect on recipients.

The discussion of the constraints imposed by tight budgets leads us to the problem of crowding-out. It has been argued that donor countries may be tempted to substitute spending on global public goods for traditional aid. This could be so because donors could benefit more, though indirectly, from the donation of aid destined for GPGs than from contributions in the form of traditional aid. The concern is that, if global public goods are less beneficial to at least to some poor countries than traditional aid, earmarking aid to global public goods would reduce the utility that developing countries can derive from aid; hence the importance of analysing the eventual crowding-out effect of GPGs on traditional aid. Notice that since there is no information available on earmarked aid, it is assumed that all aid destined for global public goods is earmarked.

There is no straightforward way to test for crowding-out. As a matter of fact, it is first necessary to define what we understand precisely by crowding-out. The chapter will address two different situations that can be thought of as particular examples of crowding-out. The first, which can be called the extreme case, would occur if donors make increases in aid conditional on

Table 5.2 Budget balance and aid (annual observations over 1997–2001 for 19 donors)

Dependent variable	Total aid	GPG	Total aid/GDP	GPG/GDP
GDP (donor)*	0.0066[a]	0.0014[a]	–	–
Budget balance/GDP	76.8[a]	21.3[a]	8.6×10^{-5}[b]	1.2×10^{-5}[a]

Notes: Fixed effects estimation; data are averaged over recipients; all variables are significant at a 1 per cent level; *coefficients on GDP are multiplied by 1000; [a]significant at 1 per cent level; [b]significant at 7 per cent level.

them being fully allocated into GPGs. Under such conditions, the ratio of traditional aid to total aid would fall as total aid increases. We call this case extreme because every additional dollar of aid would be used for the specific use earmarked by the donor.

Table 5.3 reports the results of regressing the ratio of traditional/total aid on total aid. Since the focus is exclusively on the presence of crowding-out, regional variables are replaced by fixed-effect dummies. Notice that these estimates are biased downwards spuriously, since the only explanatory variable, total aid, appears in the denominator of the dependent variable. Thus, by running such regressions, the likelihood of finding a crowding-out effect is increased artificially. However, Table 5.3 shows that the extreme version of crowding-out is not supported by the data. Most of the donor countries display a positive coefficient on total aid, and the few negative coefficients in the table are not significant. While the hypothesis of extreme crowding-out is strongly rejected, the average offset coefficient between GPG-related ODA and traditional aid is also significantly higher than zero, namely 43 per cent.

There may be a second and more subtle form of crowding-out. The model in the previous section shows that the ratio of traditional aid to total aid is independent of the amount of aid, but it falls when the donor has the possibility of earmarking. The model then suggests that crowding-out occurs when countries earmark, but as opposed to the extreme case, increases in aid need not to be fully destined for the specific purposes decided by the donor.

Table 5.3 Crowding-out effect of GPGs (I)

	Coefficient on total aid ($\times 1000$)		Coefficient on total aid ($\times 1000$)
Average	**0.434**		
Australia	0.191	Italy	0.935
Austria	0.801	Japan	0.323
Belgium	2.681[b]	Netherlands	0.240
Canada	−1.316	Norway	3.846[a]
Denmark	0.067	Portugal	0.180
EC	0.472[b]	Spain	0.387
Finland	−1.294	Sweden	1.396
France	0.656[b]	Switzerland	−1.251
Germany	0.092	UK	0.439[b]
Rep. of Ireland	−0.242	USA	0.069

Notes: Fixed effects estimation; [a]significant at 1 per cent level; [b]significant at 7 per cent level; Dependent variable is traditional aid/total aid.

We can thus study whether this less severe form of crowding-out exists in the real world by running a regression of the share of traditional aid in total aid on the aid destined for global public goods. If global public goods are in fact displacing traditional aid, then the share of traditional aid would fall as GPGs increase. Therefore the coefficient on the global public good variable should be negative. Table 5.4 summarizes the main results. All the coefficients but one (Republic of Ireland) are significant and negative. This would suggest that a mild version of crowding-out may be operating. Some caution should be taken, however, for the interpretation of the estimates in Table 5.4. Aid is measured is millions of dollars. This means, taking again the example of Australia, that US$1 million increase in aid destined to global public goods would reduce the traditional/total aid ratio by 1.48 percentage points, at the average aid level given by Australia in the sample. It is important to underline this last point because the estimates are sensitive to the level of

Table 5.4   Crowding-out effect of GPGs (II)

	Coefficient on GPG (×1000)	Average total aid (US$ millions, per recipient and year)	Crowding-out effect of GPG
Average	−54.2	13.5	0.248*
Australia	−14.8	9.3	0.137
Austria	−311.5	3.2	0.990
Belgium	−90.9	4.5	0.412
Canada	−34.7	7.4	0.255
Denmark	−23.9	16.2	0.386
EC	−7.6	22.7	0.173
Finland	−109.5	2.5	0.276
France	−28.0	11.1	0.310
Germany	−10.3	16.1	0.166
Rep. of Ireland	−52.3	3.3	0.175
Italy	−88.6	4.1	0.366
Japan	−43.9	16.9	0.742
Netherlands	−19.7	19.0	0.376
Norway	−35.0	7.7	0.269
Portugal	−55.7	6.0	0.333
Spain	−50.7	5.5	0.280
Sweden	−52.1	9.5	0.494
Switzerland	−48.9	6.5	0.319
UK	−4.7	23.1	0.109
USA	−0.9	75.2	0.070

Notes: All coefficients are significant at a 1 per cent level apart from Rep. of Ireland; *weighted by total aid; Dependent variable is traditional aid/total aid.

aid given be each donor, as can be observed clearly in the table. Therefore, considering that the average amount donated by Australia to each country every year is US$9.3 million, the estimates suggest that each additional dollar donated for global public goods means that traditional aid would increase by around 13.7 cents less than if no crowding-out took place.[9] Of course, this is a purely hypothetical exercise and does not take into account changes in policy: donors may very well decide that future donations in the form of global public goods should not affect others forms of aid, or on the contrary, that every additional dollar donated should be donated for global public goods.

Keeping these caveats in mind, it is possible to see that, as before, the results display considerable heterogeneity across donors. The estimated crowding-out effect is relatively low in the US, whereas it is almost equal to 100 per cent in Austria. The weighted average of the different crowding-out effects is estimated at 24.8 per cent. These results point to the existence of a soft version of crowding-out. It is soft in the sense that the coefficients are globally much lower than one, meaning that donations in the form of GPGs do not appear to be financed only at the expense of traditional aid.

Finally, this study deals with another donor concern, namely that a surge in the provision of global public goods might depress the levels of aid destined to the poorest countries. However, the empirical analysis above has demonstrated that the link between a recipient country's GDP/capita and the per capita level of aid is weak in any case. Indeed, if aid is related only weakly to the income of recipient countries, the provision of global public goods can hardly be systematically reducing aid in the countries with the lowest levels of income. Table 5.5 presents the results obtained in the regressions of total aid and aid spending on GPGs on income, pooling all donors together (all variables are measured in per capita terms). While GDP per capita in the recipient countries is linked negatively with ODA/capita, but positively with GPG-related ODA per capita, in neither regression is the coefficient on income significant. Naturally, it is still possible that a particular recipient has seen the aid it receives reduced because a donor has decided to give more aid in the form of GPG to another, perhaps richer, country. Nevertheless, the

Table 5.5   Crowding-out effect of GPGs (III)

Dependent variable	ODA per capita	GPG per capita
GDP per capita	-1.98×10^{-4}	1.69×10^{-5}
	(2.99×10^{-4})	(2.53×10^{-5})

Notes: Fixed effects estimation; time dummies included; robust standard error in parentheses (no variable significant).

chapter cannot confirm a significant crowding-out of aid in poor countries caused by the provision of global public goods through ODA.

Conclusions

This chapter has applied analysis and created empirical evidence with respect to a growing concern in the donor community in view of the approaching 2015 deadline to fund the Millennium Development Goals: how much of ODA to allocate to the provision of international public goods, and how much to set aside for traditional development projects. This policy concern requires, first and foremost, a proper definition of international public goods, both global and regional, and a correct attribution of CRS categories to international public goods. The chapter has provided such a definition and attribution in view of the MDGs, which in turn has enabled the provision of evidence on recent major trends in ODA spending on international public goods. It has been shown that donors spent around 30 per cent of ODA on international public goods during the last five years for which data are available (1997–2001) – half on global public goods and half on regional public goods. The chapter can confirm allocational trade-offs, as it finds that the average offset coefficient between GPG-related ODA and traditional aid is significantly higher than zero, namely 25 per cent. By contrast, the chapter finds – most importantly for donors who are concerned that increased ODA spending on GPGs might crowd out ODA to the poorest countries – that an increase in GPG spending is not likely to have an adverse effect on the flow of aid transfers to the poorest countries.

Both the formal model and the empirical analysis presented in the preceding sections suggest that the free use of ODA by the poor recipient countries, thought to coincide with 'ownership' of donor and reform projects, is a two-edged sword. On the one hand, more ownership is desirable, because the recipient country feels committed to and has a true interest in the success of a given project. But at the same time, donors who draw 'double' utility from investing in GPGs rather than traditional aid recognize that more 'ownership' means that less will be spent on GPGs, so they are reluctant to give up control on project targeting, planning and execution. In order to overcome this dilemma, a new institutional set-up, with traditional assistance separated from GPG funding, might be helpful.[10] As some determinants of GPG spending – budget balances, the scope of new direct foreign investment (Reisen 2003) – are currently deteriorating in major DAC member countries, earmarking resources for international public goods may be the only practical way to avoid rising under-provision for these goods. In sum, the findings may militate in favour of separating traditional ODA from GPG-related spending, while at the same time such separation may encourage GPG funding where it is appropriate: at the international level.[11]

Appendix

Table 5.A1   ODA and global public goods in the CRS database

GPG	Commitment/expenditure	CRS Code
Knowledge	Educational research	11181
	Medical research	12182
	Statistical capacity building	16362
	Scientific institutions	16381
	Agricultural research	31183
	Livestock research	31184
	Forestry research	31282
	Fisheries research	31382
	Technological research	32181
	Environmental research	41082
	Energy research	23082
Human rights	Human rights	15063
	Women in development	42010
Health	Infectious disease control	12250
	STD control, incl. AIDS	13040
Financial stability and growth	Economic policy	15010
	Financial policy	24010
	Monetary institutions	24020
	Trade policy	33110
Crime control	Narcotics control	16361
	Agricultural alternative	31165
	Non-agricultural alternative	43050
Sustainability	Population policy	13010
	Family planning	13030
	Power generation/renewable	23030
	Hydro plants	23065
	Geothermal energy	23066
	Solar power	23067
	Wind power	23068
	Ocean	23069
	Biomass	23070
	Forestry policy	31210
	Forestry development	31220
	Fuel wood/charcoal	31261
	Fishing policy	31310
	Fisheries development	31320
	Environmental policy	41010
	Biosphere protection	41020
	Bio-diversity	41030
	Site preservation	41040

Source: OECD Creditor Reporting System.

Table 5.A2 ODA and regional public goods in the CRS database

RPG	Commitment/expenditure	CRS Code
Health	Health policy/management	12110
	Medical education/training	12181
	Medical services	12191
	Health education	12281
	Health personnel development	12282
	Personnel development reproductive health	13081
Water	Water policy/management	14010
	Water resources protection	14015
	Supply and sanitation	14020
	River development	14040
	Waste management	14050
	Education/training	14081
Peace	Post-conflict peacebuilding	15061
	Demobilization	15064
	Land mine clearance	15066
	Reconstruction relief	16340
Transport	Policy/management	21010
	Road transport	21020
	Rail transport	21030
	Water transport	21040
	Air transport	21050
	Storage	21061
	Education/training	21081
Communication	Policy/management	22010
	Telecommunications	22020
	Media	22030
Agriculture	Protection and pest control	31192
	Rural regional development	43040
Environment	Flood prevention/control	41050
	Environmental education	41081
Special support	Local aid to refugees	72030
	Support to local/regional NGOs	92930

Source: OECD Creditor Reporting System.

Table 5.A3 Response of aid to GDP and population of recipient countries

	Dependent variable total aid		Dependent variable total aid per capita
	Coefficient on GDP (×1000)	Coefficient on population (×1000)	Coefficient on GDP per capita (×1000)
Average	−0.039	177.8	−0.166
Australia	0.043[b]	134.9	−0.972
Austria	0.005	−58.8[b]	−0.053
Belgium	−0.001	33.8[b]	0.246[a]
Canada	0.000	−178.8[a]	−0.006
Denmark	0.026	−3.6	−1.450[b]
EC	0.012	180.8	−2.054
Finland	−0.002	23.6[a]	−0.205[b]
France	0.046[b]	−115.5	0.220
Germany	0.020	165.7	−0.028
Rep. of Ireland	−0.001[a]	−25.4[a]	−0.085[a]
Italy	0.006	137.6	0.004
Japan	−0.073	40.3	3.053
Netherlands	−0.028	387.5	−6.168[b]
Norway	−0.006[b]	163.2	0.004
Portugal	0.043	26.1	7.282[b]
Spain	−0.007	−8.3	−0.556[b]
Sweden	−0.043	−11.6	−0.016
Switzerland	0.012	−37.0	0.188
UK	−0.055	136.9	−2.464
USA	−0.773	2564.9[a]	−0.256

Note: Fixed-effects estimator; time dummies included; [a]Significant at 1 per cent level;
[b]Significant at 7 per cent level.

Table 5.A4 Response of total aid to GDP, population and region of recipient countries

	GDP (×1000)	Pop. (×1000)	EAP	EUR	LAC	MEA	FAF	SAS	SSA	CAS
Average	**-0.004**	**27.6**	**-5.5**	**-0.7**	**-4.2**	**7.3**	**7.1**	**2.9**	**0.4**	**-7.1**
Australia	-0.021[a]	32.4[a]	19.1[a]	-4.0	-2.9[b]	-3.8	1.7[b]	-2.2	-3.8	-4.0
Austria	-0.007	4.6	-1.6[b]	3.7[b]	1.8	-0.4	-1.9[b]	-2.1[b]	0.7	-0.3[a]
Belgium	-0.006[b]	5.7[a]	1.1[b]	-1.2	0.0[a]	0.0	1.6[a]	-2.2	2.3[a]	-1.6[b]
Canada	0.005	22.2[b]	-0.6[a]	4.8[a]	-1.2[b]	-2.3[a]	-2.5[a]	5.0[a]	0.7[a]	-3.9
Denmark	0.007	-8.0	0.4[b]	-2.4	-3.9[b]	-8.3	7.7	11.4	6.3[b]	-11.2
EC	-0.028[a]	22.4[a]	-6.9[a]	2.0	-2.5	-3.7	-5.0	-7.4[a]	25.1[b]	-1.6
Finland	-0.002	4.0[a]	0.4[a]	0.3	0.0	-0.1	0.3	-1.1	0.9[a]	-0.7[a]
France	0.017[b]	-4.4	-8.1[a]	-3.7[b]	-8.6	-7.7[b]	36.9[a]	-8.9	9.8[a]	-9.6
Germany	0.023	52.8[a]	-8.0	1.6	-6.7[b]	1.1[b]	15.8	1.5	-1.0	-4.3[a]
Rep. of Ireland	-0.003	2.9	-0.8	-0.1[b]	-0.3	0.0	-0.7	-1.1	3.4	-0.4
Italy	0.000	4.9	-1.9	2.7	-0.6[b]	0.4[a]	1.5[a]	-2.7	2.8[b]	-2.1[b]
Japan	-0.022[b]	24.1[a]	8.2[a]	-12.6	-7.6	2.5[b]	-2.1	26.3[a]	-2.3[a]	-12.4[a]
Netherlands	-0.036[b]	57.9[b]	0.5	4.9[b]	0.2[b]	0.3[b]	-3.5	2.5	2.9[a]	-7.6
Norway	-0.004	11.0[b]	-2.1[a]	6.1[b]	-1.7[b]	1.5[b]	-4.7[b]	2.7[b]	2.1[a]	-4.0
Portugal	-0.001	-0.6	-0.7	-0.9	-0.9	-0.9	-1.4	-0.5	8.5[a]	-3.1
Spain	-0.007[a]	7.6[a]	-1.8[a]	-0.9[a]	6.2[a]	-0.8[a]	4.9[a]	-3.7[b]	-1.0[b]	-2.9
Sweden	0.003	-2.8	3.0[a]	-0.1[a]	0.6[a]	-1.6[a]	-5.1	4.2[a]	4.0[a]	-5.0
Switzerland	-0.014[b]	20.7[a]	-3.0[a]	3.0	-0.3	-2.5[b]	-1.3	5.0[b]	-0.1	-0.8[a]
UK	-0.127[b]	284.1[a]	-25.9[a]	-5.4[a]	-1.5[a]	-8.4	-17.5	58.7[a]	13.5[b]	-13.5
USA	0.134[a]	9.9	-82.1[b]	-12.0[b]	-54.2	180.5[a]	116.6[b]	-28.0	-67.0[b]	-53.8[a]

Note: EAP = East Asia and Pacific; EUR = Europe; LAC = Latin America and Caribbean; MEA = Middle East; NAF = North Africa; SAS = South Asia; SSA = Sub-Saharan Africa; CAS = Central Asia; [a]significant at 1 per cent level; [b]significant at 7 per cent level.

Notes

This chapter has been produced as part of Activity 2: Finance for Development within the OECD Development Centre 2003–4 Research Programme. The authors have benefited greatly from co-operation by colleagues of the Development Cooperation Directorate, in particular by Jean-Louis Grolleau. Funding for Thomas Weithöner by the German Bureau for International Organisations (BfIO) is gratefully acknowledged. We would like to acknowledge helpful comments from Daniel Cohen and Helmut Strauss as well as from participants at the UNU-WIDER Conference 'Sharing Global Prosperity' held in Helsinki on 5–7 September 2003.

1 These goals are (i) eradicate extreme poverty and hunger; (ii) achieve universal primary education; (iii) promote gender equality and empower women; (iv) reduce child mortality; (v) improve maternal health; (vi) combat HIV/AIDS, malaria and other diseases; (vii) ensure environmental sustainability; and (viii) develop a global partnership for development. For each of these goals, targets and indicators have been defined. For details, see www.unmillenniumproject.org.

2 Available at www.dfid.gov.uk/Pubs/files/dfid_resource_allocation_main.pdf.

3 Kaul *et al.* (1999: 2–3) also stresses the importance of including future generations in the definition: 'Global public goods must meet two criteria. The first is that their benefits have strong qualities of publicness, i.e. they are marked by non-rivalry in consumption and non-excludability. These features place them in the general category of public goods. The second criterion is that their benefits are quasi-universal in terms of countries (covering more than one group of countries); people (accruing to several, preferably all, population groups), and generations (extending to both current and future generations, or at least future generations). This property makes humanity as a whole the *publicum beneficiary* of global public goods'.

4 See World Bank (2001: 110): 'an important distinction is that between core and complementary activities. Core activities aim to produce international public goods. These activities include global and regional programmes undertaken with a transnational interest in mind, as well as activities that are focused in one country but whose benefits spill over to others. Complementary activities, in turn, prepare countries to consume the international public goods that core activities make available – while at the same time creating valuable national public goods'.

5 This view is shared by Speight (2002): 'Problems in discussions of providing GPGs often arise because this distinction between core and complementary activities does not align itself clearly with the difference between funding and activity at the global and national levels' (2002: 5). She also points to the often misleading use of the term GPG: 'the idea of GPGs being used to gather global funding for areas which ... do not necessarily require global actions or funding but are sometimes described as GPGs (such as education, governance, multilateral agencies or even poverty reduction itself)' (2002: 17, fn 11).

6 The model is less helpful for analysing trade-offs and policy choices pertaining to *regional* public goods as their consumption by the poor partner countries does not enter the utility function of donor countries in the same way that the poor-country consumption of *global* public goods does.

7 Differentiate the donor country's utility (Equation 5.1) with respect to the choice variables z and OA to derive the two first-order conditions for optimality. Then substitute into one another.

8 Berthélemy and Tichit (2002) found that since the 1990s aid allocation has been determined significantly by trade links (in particular, for small donor

countries) and angled towards recipient countries with relatively good economic performance and political governance.

9   This figure is obtained by multiplying the estimated coefficient on the GPG variable by total aid.

10   An additional issue relevant to the organizational arrangement for delivering IPGs is that of *economies of scope* (see Sandler 2001). If the cost of providing two or more IPGs in the same institution is lower than when supplying them through separate institutions, the provision should be concentrated in a regional or global unit.

11   Sagasti and Bezanson (2001: 64–5) see the UN as a suitable institution to define a general framework for the delivery of GPGs because they 'have political legitimacy and are representative of the diversity of national interests'. However, since the authors regard the UN as rather inefficient and bureaucratic, they would like to see bilateral donors and the international financial institutions carry out the funding and delivery of individual projects. But it should be clear that if there are *economies of scope*, then multilateral programmes are more efficient than bilateral ones. Conversely, if subsidiarity is important, then local ownership should be stressed no matter whether the transfer is made bilaterally or multilaterally. Still more important, GPGs yield, by definition, low (if any) private returns, so transfers should be made as grants rather than loans. This implies that the financial institutions (in their traditional form) are not suited to funding GPGs.

References

Anand, P. B. (2002) 'Financing the Provision of Global Public Goods', WIDER Discussion Paper 2002/110, Helsinki: UNU-WIDER.

Berthélemy, J. C. and A. Tichit (2002) 'Bilateral Donors' Aid Allocation Decisions: A Three-Dimensional Panel Analysis', WIDER Discussion Paper 2002/123, Helsinki: UNU-WIDER.

Dyer, N. and J. Beynon (2003) 'Strategic Review of Resource Allocation Priorities', DFID Discussion Paper, London: Department for International Development.

Kaul, I., I. Grunberg and M. A. Stern (eds) (1999) *International Cooperation in the 21st Century*, New York: Oxford University Press.

Morrissey, O., D. te Velde and A. Hewitt (2002) 'Defining International Public Goods: Conceptual Issues', in M. Ferrani and A. Mody (eds), *International Public Goods: Incentives, Measurements, and Financing*, Dordrecht: Kluwer.

OECD (2003) 'Aid Effectiveness and Selectivity: Integrating Multiple Objectives into Aid Allocations', *The DAC Journal*, 4(3). Available at: http://www.oecd.org/dataoecd/4/33/18444948.pdf

Raffer, K. (1999) 'ODA and Global Public Goods: A Trend Analysis of Past and Present Spending Patterns', ODS Background Papers, New York: United Nations.

Reisen, H. (2003) 'Prospects for Emerging-Market Flows amid Investor Concerns about Corporate Governance', in P. K. Cornelius and B. Kogut (eds), *Corporate Governance and Capital Flows in a Global Economy*, New York: Oxford University Press.

Sagasti, F. and K. Bezanson (2001) *Financing and Providing Global Public Goods. Expectations and Prospects*, Prepared for the Ministry for Foreign Affairs of Sweden.

Sandler, T. (2001) 'On Financing Global and International Public Goods', World Bank Working Paper 2638, Washington, DC: World Bank.

Schelling, T. C. (2002) 'What Makes Greenhouse Sense?', *Foreign Affairs*, May/June: 2–9.

Speight, M. (2002) 'How Much Should DFID Allocate to Global Actions and Funding?', London: Department for International Development.

World Bank (2001) *Global Development Finance 2001*, Washington, DC: World Bank.

6
Multi-Actor Global Funds: New Tools to Address Urgent Global Problems

Jeremy Heimans

Introduction

Multi-actor global funds (MGFs), as identified in this study, are emerging as an increasingly popular and important mechanism for the mobilization and distribution of international financial resources. Several such funds already have annual disbursements that exceed the core budgets of major UN agencies, and new funds with even broader mandates are currently being proposed. At first glance, these powerful instruments for globally co-ordinated action represent a departure from traditional forms of multilateral governance because non-state actors share decision-making powers and financing responsibilities with national governments, as in other forms of 'networked', multi-actor governance that are developing at the global level. Yet comparatively little is known about the way these funds operate, whether they are desirable as instruments for financing major international initiatives, and what implications they might have more broadly for global governance. This last question seems especially important, considering that, even though a key principle behind these funds is that they are 'additional' to existing sources of finance, the proliferation of MGFs may come at the expense of established international organizations – both in terms of resource flows and of their prestige in the international system.

The funds described here are different from the official trust funds that have been administered by the World Bank and other international organizations for decades. MGFs are dedicated to a specific issue or policy area of global significance, and they explicitly involve multiple stakeholders. They operate as partnerships between the 'official' sector (governments and intergovernmental organizations at various levels) and business (including private charitable foundations and individual corporations), NGOs of different types and geographies, and other actors, such as education and research institutions. MGFs operate independently of any single institution, and are usually set up either as new entities with their own legal identity or as alliances with legally constituted financing arms.

Table 6.1   GFATM, GEF and GAVI/Vaccine Fund

	GFATM	GEF	GAVI
Current annual disbursements	Estimated at US$700 m in first full year of operations. Expected to grow in Year 2	~US$600 m per year	~US$160 m per year over five years currently committed to 53 eligible countries, expected to grow with further rounds of funding awards
Year established	2002	1991, pilot programme; 1994 restructured GEF	1999
Fiduciary arrangements	World Bank is trustee, sub-trustees at national level. Disbursements to be made directly to governments	World Bank is trustee	UNICEF is trustee

The principal case study in this chapter is the new Global Fund to Fight AIDS, Tuberculosis and Malaria (GFATM). The fund, which has so far collected more than US$2 billion in pledges from governments and the private sector, is a major international enterprise that is likely to set an important precedent for future efforts like it in other areas of global concern.[1] The research presented here is based on a detailed study of the negotiation process to establish the fund, and its subsequent start-up phase, a period that raised many of the difficult technical and political choices involved in establishing MGFs. A second MGF with fairly similar characteristics is the recently established Global Alliance for Vaccines and Immunization (GAVI) and its financial instrument, the Vaccine Fund,[2] whose mission is children's immunization. The Global Environment Facility (GEF), which derives its mandate from multilateral environmental agreements formed in the early 1990s, is a treaty instrument that limits the involvement of non-state actors in its governance arrangements, and in that sense is distinct from GFATM and GAVI. But it has faced a number of similar challenges, and so is included here for comparison. Some basic facts about these funds are outlined in Table 6.1.

This chapter evaluates critically the potential of multi-actor global funds as financing instruments, and, as some see them, pilot programmes for new and improved global governance.[3] MGFs aspire to be innovative and more effective than traditional instruments in a number of areas. First, they are designed to be 'lean', 'non-bureaucratic' and 'quick to act' – qualities that are often seen as being lacking in institutions and financing channels with broader mandates. Second, they promise an aggressive focus on results, to the point of withholding funding from non-performing recipients. Third, by giving non-state actors a major stake in their governance and activities, MGFs seek to realize the benefits of multi-stakeholder collaboration and the principles of 'networked governance', including the harmonization of activities across sectors and leveraging the expertise and knowledge of civil society and the private sector. Finally, because of their comparative advantages compared to other funding sources, and because they can be used to focus attention and create a sense of urgency around a particular issue of global significance, MGFs are seen as magnets to raise additional funds from both public and private sources.

Political context: MGFs and international organizations

Before considering the merits of multi-actor global funds, it is important to understand the political context in which they are currently being created. Multi-actor global funds, with their emphasis on decentralization and rejection of bureaucracy, their orientation towards specific issues and tasks in support of a focus on 'results' and the embrace of the notion of partnership, in which non-state actors are key players and international organizations are seen as stakeholders playing narrower, targeted roles, seem at least in part to be a response to the perceived inadequacies of existing multilateral processes and institutions, and of the United Nations and its agencies in particular. Their popularity also reflects the political implausibility of raising much-needed new funds through the UN. In many respects, however, they remain reliant on the infrastructure and expertise of UN agencies.

The history of the United Nations' involvement with the GFATM reveals a great deal about attitudes towards the UN, in particular among donor governments. Participants in the GFATM negotiating process describe an atmosphere of 'hostility' towards the UN from several key governments during the period of the fund's creation. One of several examples of this was at a meeting to discuss the fund in early June 2001, the UN (and particularly the World Health Organization) was almost forced out of the negotiations because of a perception that it was trying to 'grab the money'.[4] As one US government official put it, 'If we wanted to increase WHO's budget, we would. We don't want [the GFATM] to become part of a UN agency.' Later, during the fund's negotiating process, a lengthy debate ensued about whether the fund should be co-located with the UN technical programmes (WHO and UNAIDS) in Geneva. Despite the potential synergies in terms of shared technical knowledge and the ability of WHO to provide administrative support services, several national delegations resisted this strongly, because they feared it would give the UN too much control over the fund.

In interviews conducted for this chapter, US government officials and private charitable foundations in particular set out a number of criticisms of the UN.[5] First, they regarded the UN as too bureaucratic and administratively unwieldy to manage its own resources efficiently, let alone those of a global financial mechanism. Second, they criticized the UN's corporate governance and political culture as being unsuited to making difficult decisions about the allocation of funds. One US government official argued that because the UN's 'board of directors' and its 'clients' are both drawn from the same group (its member states), it is politically obliged to provide a level of financial support to even undeserving recipient countries. Moreover, the UN's lengthy negotiating procedures were regarded as an impediment to reaching rapid international agreement on the kinds of urgent global problems addressed by MGFs. The organizational design and governance arrangements of the GFATM, discussed below, clearly reflect a desire to avoid the above pitfalls. Third, the UN and its agencies were seen as being more interested in 'capturing' new sources of funding and using them to advance their own institutional objectives (or in conducting turf wars among UN agencies) than in being partners in a collaborative arrangement such as the GFATM. In contrast to their attitude to the UN, the US government and other donor governments were generally more comfortable assigning the World Bank significant responsibility in the GFATM, which is reflected in the decision to name the Bank as the fund's trustee (the Bank also plays a key role in the GEF).[6]

Despite this deep ambivalence about the UN's role, UN agencies will nevertheless play a major role in the GFATM, providing capacity-building and technical assistance both at the country level in the preparation and implementation of project proposals, and providing technical and administrative support to the fund's technical review panel, which has the key task of assessing funding proposals and making recommendations to the board. Moreover, in part because Secretary-General Kofi Annan was a key instigator of the fund, the GFATM remains publicly very closely associated with the UN.

The paradox of UN involvement in MGFs is that even those who are generally suspicious of the UN are forced to acknowledge that, because of their technical and in-country operational expertise, UN agencies are often essential to the success of this kind of enterprise. As a GAVI board member interviewed for this study described it, UNICEF and WHO are the most important partners in GAVI, because the alliance is totally dependent on them for the delivery of core functions. Moreover, as the discussion in the rest of this chapter makes clear, MGFs must answer the same difficult questions about governance, accountability and organizational design that the UN and other international organizations faced in their organizational development, and it is not necessarily easy to come up with a better answer.

Evaluating the potential of MGFs

This section considers the claims of MGFs to innovation in four main areas: their governance arrangements, the introduction of a system of performance-based funding, the notion of multi-stakeholder collaboration, and the potential of MGFs to mobilize significant additional funds to address global problems.

Governance arrangements

The GFATM was instigated with the often-repeated mantra that it not be 'another bureaucracy'. MGFs have been conceptualized as financial instruments, not implementing agencies, so that they themselves do not become large technocratic organizations. The governance structure of the GFATM and the other MGFs profiled in this study (outlined in Table 6.1) partially reflect this – they have relatively small governing boards based on constituency representation and, at least by the standards of most UN agencies, pared-down secretariats consisting of only a small number of professional staff.

The preference for small, constituency-based governing boards is designed to achieve ease of decision-making while trying to represent as many actors as possible through the use of a constituency structure. The representational structure of the pared-down MGF boards has had mixed success. One potential problem is that board members may be either unwilling or unable to act as genuine representatives of their constituency groups. For example, Uganda, the East and Southern Africa representative on the GFATM board, angered other key states in the region, including South Africa, by failing to establish adequate consultation processes with them in the first months of the board's operations. Another risk of such structures is that board members will fail to act collectively in the interests of the fund rather than for their own groups. Participants in the Transitional Working Group (TWG) process through which the GFATM was negotiated characterized it as a highly political contest between different national and regional constituencies: 'Not once did I hear someone make an intervention that put their own interests aside for those of the fund as a whole', one TWG member observed of the meetings. This seems to have been reflected in the final composition of the fund, where key criteria, such as which countries are eligible for funding, were left extremely broad in order to satisfy different national constituencies.

Moreover, the manner in which MGFs select their board members has raised concerns about lack of transparency and, by extension, democratic accountability. Unbound by procedural restrictions, the GFATM board was set up in a fairly ad hoc manner. According to participants in the selection process, board membership was mainly a function of a country's participation in earlier discussions about the fund, and in the case of donor governments, the most powerful states were simply 'there by right'. This enabled the board to be assembled quickly and with some flexibility, both of which were important considering the urgency of the issues to which the fund was responding. However, such methods are also less transparent and potentially less accountable than the formal processes that are used to select the sitting members of key UN committees or the governing entities of international agencies, such as elections or formal rotations.[7]

In creating MGFs, many donors have advocated small secretariats that are run according to modern management principles, in an attempt to avoid the perceived inefficiencies and wastefulness of existing international organizations. The lean secretariat model is the subject of some scepticism, however. GAVI's secretariat for example, is so small in part because it relies on informally constituted task forces to do much of the critical policy and review work that would otherwise be the responsibility of an operational body. These task forces do not have dedicated human and financial resources, and so they rely on ad hoc (and uneven) support from the donor government and multilateral agencies that constitute them. As GAVI's application and implementation workload increases, such a small secretariat may be neither realistic nor appropriate (TWG 2001). The concept of an ultra-lean secretariat for the GFATM may also sit uneasily with the substantial responsibilities that have been assigned to it, including oversight of monitoring, evaluation and proposal review activities, and an active role in advocacy and fundraising. It is almost inevitable that, over time, MGFs will need to develop more formalized rules and procedures relating to many aspects of their governance and processes (see Table 6.2).

Early experience suggests that MGFs will face an ongoing tension between the extent to which they adopt the principles of private-sector management or those of the international public sector. During the GFATM negotiations, some stakeholders also saw the criteria used to recruit secretariat staff as a means of injecting private-sector management practices into the fund. For example, the US pushed (unsuccessfully) for a requirement that the successful candidate for Head of Secretariat should have significant private sector experience. Other constituencies, including some donors and many recipient country governments, were more wary of attempts to run the fund according to private-sector principles and expressed a preference for a candidate who was more integrated into the international public sector.

Another aspect of the governance tensions facing MGFs is the extent to which inclusiveness and consultation is compromised in favour of being seen as 'quick to act' in different aspects of fund operations, such as in administrative decision-making and the disbursement process (in contrast to the way many international organizations are perceived). The GFATM was assembled in a matter of months – a remarkably short period given the size and scope of the task – because Secretary-General Kofi Annan and other key instigators feared a loss of momentum and donor confidence if the fund did not come together quickly. This was judged to be more important than a more lengthy but inclusive negotiating process of the kind usually located at the UN. For similar reasons, the GFATM, taking its lead from GAVI's strategy, moved very quickly, once established, to make its first grants. In the GAVI context, the rapid pace of applications and tight deadlines this entails have been criticized

Table 6.2 Governance arrangements of the GFATM, Vaccine Fund/GAVI and the GEF compared

	GFATM	GEF	Vaccine Fund/GAVI
Board and secretariat structure	Paramount structure is 18-member, constituency-based board plus 4 ex-officio members without voting rights;	Assembly consisting of all member states meets every 3 years to decide on overall direction and mandate of facility;	GAVI: Loosely and informally constituency-based board structure, 11 rotating members and 4 renewable members;
	Secretariat and technical review panels support board;	32-member, constituency-based council is key decision-making structure;	Secretariat, working group and taskforces support board decision-making;
	Partnership Forum advises on fund's strategic direction, conducts advocacy work	Implementing agencies, secretariat, country focal points support board decision-making	Vaccine Fund: 11-member board of eminent persons with primary responsibility for fundraising and advocacy. Board considers recommendations of GAVI board and approves funding disbursements
NGOs on board	Yes, 2 Southern and 2 Northern	No – GEF is a treaty instrument, and board only includes governments	Yes (GAVI) No (Vaccine Fund)
Private sector on board	Yes, one foundation and one industry	No: see above	Yes (GAVI) No (Vaccine Fund)
Research community on board	No	No: see above	Yes (GAVI) No (Vaccine Fund)
Multilateral agencies on board	Yes, ex-officio without voting rights	No: see above	Yes (GAVI) No (Vaccine Fund)
Decision rules	Consensus; when votes necessary, two-thirds of donors and private sector, two-thirds of recipients and NGOs required	Consensus; when votes necessary, 60% of donors, 60% of participants required	GAVI: consensus; simple majority voting Vaccine Fund: consensus, largely ceremonial

for preventing nations from developing adequate funding applications (Shoof and Phillips 2002).

Performance-based funding

The introduction of new forms of programme accountability – and specifically the use of 'performance-based funding' – is emerging as a central element of MGFs' claim to innovation. Performance-based funding explicitly links continued funding with programme outcomes, as measured by performance in meeting agreed targets. This contrasts with more traditional methods of programme accountability employed by many bilateral and multilateral financing channels, which tend to focus on the reporting of programme inputs rather than on programme outcomes. GAVI, which has pioneered this model, uses a system of 'performance-based shares', in which US$10 of funding per child to strengthen health systems is delivered in advance, and an additional US$10 per child is paid as a retrospective reward for meeting targets successfully for the number of children immunized. Rather than imposing detailed guidelines on the use of resources, the fund gives governments the freedom to use the funds in whatever way leads to the achievement of targets (Brugha and Walt 2001). Funding eventually stops completely if countries fail to meet targets. In response to the perceived success of that model, the GFATM chose to develop a similar programme accountability regime.

There are several potential advantages of performance-based funding. First, it is seen as 'donor friendly' by making it easier for donors to demonstrate to their constituents that funds are not being wasted, and to show tangible results from fund activities. Second, aggressively linking funding to performance is said to improve programme outcomes. The incentive to misuse funds or spend them on overheads, rather than directly on programme recipients, is minimized. Rewarding high-performing recipients can also draw more attention to the most successful and innovative programme strategies, which should promote a faster convergence towards good practice. From the fund's perspective, restricting funding to reasonably high-performing recipients may improve the overall outcomes of the fund, even if that success is distributed more unevenly across countries or funding recipients. Third, by giving recipients the autonomy to use funds as they choose as long as they meet targets, performance-based funding should increase country-level ownership of MGF activities. Finally, lower transaction costs for recipients may result when the primary obligation of funding recipients is to report their performance in meeting targets, and not describe in detail how they have managed programme inputs.

For the reasons set out above, performance-based funding is seen as highly politically attractive, especially to donors. However, performance-based funding also carries with it several serious potential disadvantages. First, an aggressive focus on meeting outcomes-based targets may distort recipient decision-making in undesirable ways. In order to satisfy donors, governments will have an incentive to manage their funding through dedicated vertical structures that speed progress towards meeting specific targets, but which might lead to higher transaction costs than if funds were submerged into overall health budgets (Brugha and Walt 2001: 154). There is a further risk that performance-based funding will tend to direct funds to those projects whose results are easily measurable and hence more satisfactory to donors, rather than on projects focused on strengthening capacity, whose results may be slower to emerge or less visible.[8] Recipients of funding might also be tempted to focus their activities on better-off groups, where easier gains can be achieved. Second, performance-based funding may simply reinforce existing gaps between the capacities of different grant recipients, having the circular effect of perpetuating the very factors that made recipients unable to meet their targets in the first place. Third, such a system has the potential to penalize excessively short-term dips in performance. Finally, the metrics used to assess performance may be inappropriate in complex conditions. Performance-based funding regimes may be easier to implement in MGFs with a narrowly-focused organizational mission such as the Vaccine Fund, where immunization coverage rates are a measurable, controllable and relevant metric on which to base funding allocations. For funds like GFATM, whose mission is more complex and diffuse, it would seem to be harder to link performance to a set of targets that recipients can reasonably be expected to control and yet which are also focused on the outcomes or results of fund activities (for example, lower disease burdens and death rates). It may be necessary for MGFs to address the potential problems associated with performance-based funding by implementing remedial and support processes with the aim of ensuring that funding recipients are able to receive additional tranches of funding even if they experience initial problems in meeting their targets.

Multi-stakeholder collaboration

By giving non-state actors a major role in governance arrangements and in other activities, MGFs (and other kinds of global policy networks based on similar principles) seek to harness the benefits of multi-stakeholder collaboration in ways that could not be achieved simply by consulting these groups (Reinicke 1999–2000).[9] Partnership with the private sector and civil society occurs in a number of ways. First, non-government actors may be given a seat alongside governments on the governing boards of MGFs, as GAVI and the GFATM have done. This is a contentious issue. According to one view, shared governance arrangements are a precondition for realizing the benefits of multi-stakeholder collaboration, because the private sector and civil society can only be expected to engage seriously when they are treated as equal partners. Others argue that non-government actors cannot be held accountable for the responsible use of funds in the way that (democratically-elected) national governments can. By this logic, only governments should have the authority to make the kinds of decisions made by a fund such as the GFATM, which have the potential for a major impact on the lives of many people. This tension reflects a much broader debate about the democratic accountability of NGOs and their role in global governance.

Multi-stakeholder collaboration is also built into the structure of MGFs at the country level. GFATM and GAVI have established country co-ordination mechanisms (CCMs) that are the interface between the fund and recipient countries. These mechanisms are usually led by governments, but include other national stakeholders such as NGOs, the private sector and the research community, who jointly prepare consolidated national funding proposals, and who oversee key aspects of the country's relationship with the MGF. In some cases, the existence of such a mechanism is a condition of a country receiving funding. The country co-ordination model contrasts with the typical structure of the donor–recipient relationship in organizations such as the World Bank, focused almost exclusively on national governments, and with the model used by the GEF, where governments develop and implement proposals in co-operation with international organizations, which effectively must approve a project before it is put to the GEF's executive board.

The major benefits of CCMs are their ability to bring all key national stakeholders together. This approach opens channels of communication, allows for co-ordinated action, and may foster innovation because of the very different perspectives represented. However, while it is tempting to regard this kind of national partnership as being unambiguously positive, CCMs, like national governments, may come to be controlled by small groups who do not consult widely or secure broad domestic support. Moreover, while existing national structures may be used or consolidated to serve as CCMs, if an entirely new structure needs to be created this could increase transaction costs significantly for recipients. The very existence of a fund entails more reporting and other administrative requirements for developing countries, which represent an opportunity cost in terms of the time invested by senior government officials in particular.

For some, the CCM concept is also an expression of scepticism about the capacities or intentions of national governments, and the view that NGOs are often better partners at the country level. During the GFATM negotiations, the US government proposed to allow individual NGOs to establish a direct relationship with the fund, so that they could make funding applications directly rather than only through the approved CCM. As a result, provision now exists for NGOs to apply directly to the fund in certain exceptional circumstances, although the decentralized approach has not been adopted generally. In doing so, the US seemed to be signalling that, at least in some countries, it had more faith in NGOs to realize the objectives of the GFATM than it did in governments. Interestingly, this position pitted the US against the World Bank who, as trustee of the GFATM, strongly opposed dealing directly with NGOs.[10]

There are several aspects of multi-stakeholder collaboration that relate specifically to the private sector. For example, corporations may act as a supplier of commodities or other services to MGFs, such as the bulk procurement of vaccines from the private sector that GAVI has undertaken, and that the GFATM is carrying out in order to purchase medicines and other products such as bed nets and condoms. MGFs do this with the aim of securing lower prices from companies than would be attainable if procurement was decentralized.

In the case of GAVI, early evidence suggests that this strategy has been successful. UNICEF has successfully negotiated substantially reduced prices on vaccines from GAVI partners. Moreover, as GAVI's executive director, Tore Godal, puts it, because they are being treated as partners and there is 'real money on the table', the private sector has engaged seriously with the objectives of the alliance and has begun to modify its production activities to meet anticipated new demand through the fund. The existence of GAVI is also expected to increase incentives for the private sector to undertake additional research into new vaccines.

GAVI's approach recognizes what one US government official interviewed for this study argues is key to the success of public–private partnerships – that involvement in these alliances must ultimately be profitable for business. However, as NGO critics, among others, have pointed out, the conditions for industry participation can be onerous. In the GAVI context, demands by the private sector for a tiered pricing system, including safeguards against re-export of products from developing countries to high-priced markets, and a prohibition on compulsory licensing, could outweigh the benefits of reduced prices on commodities procurement (Hardon 2001). With the enmeshment of the private sector in the governance structures of MGFs, there is a risk that policy choices by MGFs will be distorted even when procedures are in place to avoid conflicts of interest between individual partners' interests and board decision-making.[11]

Another major role for the private sector in MGFs is as providers of specialized knowledge or of access to in-country networks. A US government official used the example of the way in which Coca-Cola, a member of the GFATM Transitional Working Group, could bring its in-country distribution expertise to bear on the distribution of bednets and other commodities for funding recipients. Participants in GAVI also spoke positively about the role of the Gates Foundation in encouraging innovation, and for infusing 'business thinking' into its core activities, which were once the exclusive domain of national governments and international organizations. In those cases where private charitable foundations are the principal contributors to MGFs, as is the case with the Gates Foundation and GAVI, these funds may increasingly come to resemble, culturally and operationally, the foundations that support them. Over time, this might inhibit the ability of MGFs to integrate effectively with the international public sector, and in particular to conduct the kind of holistic policy-making that recognizes the implications of fund activities for other global policies and priorities.

MGFs as magnets for additional funding

One of the key expectations underlying the creation of MGFs such as the GFATM is that they will be able to mobilize additional resources that could not be raised through existing national or international financing channels. When Kofi Annan announced in April 2001 that the world needed to raise a further US$7–10 billion a year to fight AIDS, tuberculosis and malaria, the explicit aim was that a global fund would mobilize a substantial portion of those extra funds, from both public and private sources.

There are several reasons why MGFs are seen as magnets for additional funds from national governments. First, because they address specific issues, the creation of MGFs can be used to build momentum and create a sense of urgency around particular global problems, increasing their political visibility and importance. Second, they allow governments to demonstrate publicly their commitment to addressing a high-profile global problem such as the AIDS crisis, as the G8 nations did in 2001 when they announced their contributions to the GFATM. Third, because they are sold as innovative pilot programmes or partnerships, governments find it easier to justify their contribution to domestic constituents. Increasing core funding to an international organization (which may be discredited domestically) or even increasing bilateral aid tends to be much more difficult. Finally, MGFs can argue for additional resources from governments on the basis that they are filling a global 'gap' (or providing a global public good) that would not be provided through their existing bilateral efforts, such as global commodities procurement.[12]

That said, there are several reasons why claims about the ability of MGFs to attract additional public resources may be overstated. First, unlike contributions to membership-based international organizations, contributions to MGFs are usually voluntary, and so governments will only contribute to those funds they find politically attractive, which explains the patchy participation by governments in the GFATM and GAVI.[13] Second, donors tend to be highly conscious of the contributions of other industrialized countries. For example, in the most recent GEF replenishment negotiations, the United States announced that it would hold steady its contribution to the facility in dollar terms. This means effectively that, in order for the GEF's funding to grow over a four-year period, other countries would have to increase their contributions in percentage terms. Japan and France in particular are refusing to do this, taking the view that the US is 'free-riding'. Perhaps most crucially, even if MGFs do succeed in attracting significant resources, it does not follow that these resources will necessarily be genuinely additional to existing bilateral aid and other donor spending. A senior World Bank official interviewed for this study said that he expected the vast majority of funds committed to the GFATM would be substitutive of existing spending.[14]

Beyond public resources, MGFs aim to become magnets for substantial private-sector funding. Indeed, some see the private sector and not national governments as the major source of contributions for MGFs in the longer term. A US government official interviewed for this study argued that if, in five years, the majority of funds for the GFATM are not coming from private sources, the fund will have failed. The long-term future of MGFs, according to this view, is philanthropy by wealthy individuals, usually acting through private charitable foundations – with 57 000 individuals whose fortunes exceed US$30 million, they represent a cumulative wealth of US$8.37 trillion. The Gates Foundation argues that 'given financial incentives and technical support' many of these individuals would be willing to commit substantial resources for global purposes (Stansfield 2002).

The emphasis on attracting funds from the private sector has worried some developing countries and NGOs, who are concerned that donor governments could use this focus on the private sector to distract attention from their core responsibilities (Oxfam 2001). The United States already argues that donations from US foundations and corporations should effectively be considered part of its national contribution to the GFATM. Indeed, foundations themselves sometimes take the philosophical view that certain global activities are mainly the responsibility of governments. Strong reservations have also been expressed about soliciting corporate donations from industries that might have an economic stake in MGF activities through procurement decisions. For this reason, the Vaccine Fund does not accept corporate donations from pharmaceutical companies.

The size of the private sector's potential contribution to MGFs is in any case difficult to gauge. In the funds profiled in this chapter, the GFATM has so far failed to attract major private resources, while the GEF has well-developed co-financing arrangements with the private sector, rather than direct contributions. GAVI is the exception – the US$750 million contribution from the Gates Foundation far exceeds any government contribution. Several factors seem to affect the willingness of private charitable foundations and individual corporations to contribute to MGFs. First, they are more likely to make contributions comparable to those of national governments if they are given a formal stake in the governance of the fund, as the experience of GAVI in particular suggests. Second, they are more likely to support funds that are not perceived as government-driven or, as the director of a major a charitable foundation interviewed for this study described the GFATM, a 'politicians' fund'. Third, private-sector donors want to retain the identity of their contributions. Charitable foundations tend to have specific strategic goals and funding priorities that a broad-based fund such as GFATM may not necessarily be able to accommodate. The implication of this is that, in order to secure higher levels of private contributions to MGFs, foundations and corporations may need to be offered a menu of specific projects with clear and tangible outcomes to fund from which to choose, rather than just being solicited to make general contributions. However, this kind of earmarking of funds for donor purposes can distort resource allocation decisions – in GFATM negotiations, it was generally seen as unacceptable (TWG 2001). For similar reasons, once one major private contribution has been made to an MGF, they may crowd-out other private-sector interest. The Vaccine Fund has found it hard to attract additional private contributions because of the size of the Gates Foundation's contribution as a share of the fund. Some of those interviewed for this study argued that the Gates Foundation would have leveraged its contribution to raise additional funds more effectively by not putting such a substantial sum up-front.[15] Finally, the tax and regulatory environment in different national jurisdictions can have a significant influence on the level of giving, especially by wealthy individuals. Ultimately, if MGFs intend to pursue vigorously private resources, they need a comprehensive and professional fund-raising strategy (Rivers 2001).[16]

In the longer term, one of the greatest challenges for MGFs may be to sustain a predictable level of contributions. Because many funds are created in response to perceived global 'emergencies', and are sold to donors as exceptional responses to deal with exceptional problems, there is a risk that interest fatigue will develop among donors over time as other issues begin to take precedence. Donors may be encouraged to 'issue-shop' between MGFs in response to high-profile emergencies, thus reducing their support to funds that may be dealing with endemic problems (such as the spread of communicable diseases) and not one-off crises. Because contributions to MGFs are voluntary, they are particularly prone to free-rider problems over the longer term. MGFs are also vulnerable to other factors such as loss of donor confidence because of mismanagement of disbursed funds. The consequences of a declining or stagnating funding base for MGFs and their beneficiaries are substantial. For example, MGFs may fund expensive and capital-intensive programmes that cannot then be supported in later years if funding shrinks. MGFs often respond to problems with time horizons of ten or twenty years with financial resources that are committed for just a few years. Moreover, uncertainty about future financial inflows arising from lags between pledging and disbursements, or insecure future funding commitments, can have a disruptive effect on the operations of MGFs, although this is clearly a problem that established international organizations such as the UN also face.

MGFs can undertake a number of measures to improve the sustainability and predictability of their funding bases, including securing multi-year pledges from donors,[17] withholding certain benefits to nations who do not contribute or are in arrears,[18] co-financing arrangements with the private sector in order to reduce the ongoing financial burden for global funds and to increase the impact of funded projects,[19] and funds matching with organizations such as the World Bank to leverage an MGF's funds in order to secure larger disbursements.

Conclusions

If the current experiments with multiactor global funds are seen as successful, they can be expected to proliferate in other areas, and the creation of global funds with even broader mandates is foreseeable. What would a world with many more of such instruments look like? One possibility is that it will make holistic thinking on longer time horizons more difficult. The stratification of financing into issue-based silos risks neglecting the critical synergies between policy-making across issues, leading to more ad hoc policy-making and a less coherent response to global problems. Broad-based international organizations may ultimately be better positioned to make these connections, and to make financing decisions accordingly.[20]

There is considerable debate about whether broad-based international organizations can be held to be sufficiently democratically accountable through the national governments that constitute them.[21] However, lines of accountability would seem to be even weaker for MGFs. Unlike agencies within the UN system, there is no supervisory body or constituency to which MGFs, as corporate entities or the individual actors in them, may be held accountable for fund outcomes or particular decisions. Experience so far suggests that the governance arrangements of MGFs can be ad hoc, and that national participation in them is uneven, making it easier for them to be captured by a few powerful states or, as in other forms of international organization, by unelected policy specialists and experts.[22] Formal inclusion of the private sector and NGOs in governance arrangements creates additional challenges in terms of ensuring accountability and avoiding potential conflicts of interest. Some thought is now being given to ways in which MGFs and similar partnership-based mechanisms might become subject to international monitoring and to certain rules designed to make them more accountable, but it may be difficult to do this while retaining the spirit of independence and experimentalism which is seen as key to their success.[23]

There is also a risk that, in spite of their attempts to reduce bureaucracy and wastefulness, MGFs will merely duplicate existing governance structures. Issue-based funds add to an already crowded landscape of international bodies and financial instruments with overlapping organizational missions. MGFs may also increase transaction costs at the country level by creating a new layer of application and reporting requirements for these countries.

For all of these potential problems, however, the future of MGFs is at least as much about politics as it is about their underlying merits. MGFs such as the GFATM currently have political momentum, the interest of some powerful states and, partly as a result, an ability to generate focus on important global issues that international organizations are struggling to achieve.

If governments and the private sector invest their energies and resources into these instruments because they perceive them to be delivering results, MGFs may indeed be able to mobilize genuinely additional funds for global priorities, which would help in meeting globally agreed objectives such as the Millennium Development Goals. Moreover, MGFs may prove to be a politically viable way of advancing the global public goods agenda because they can be sold as dedicated financial mechanisms to fill specific global gaps.

While this chapter has sought to put the aspirations of MGFs into perspective, these instruments, like other forms of networked governance, also promise a great deal. Certain kinds of multi-stakeholder collaboration, or carefully implemented, performance-based funding systems, for example, may indeed produce success stories that can then be replicated elsewhere in the international system. Multi-actor global funds are at least somewhat less encumbered by the rigidities of more established entities, and so they offer an arena for experimentation and innovation in global governance.

Acknowledgements

This chapter is based on a study commissioned by the United Nations Department of Economic and Social Affairs (UN-DESA) in 2002. The author wishes to thank John Langmore and Johan Scholvink for their support for this research, and Ngaire Woods, Jeffrey Sachs, Sanjeev Khagram, David Simon and Anthony Clunies-Ross for their comments.

Notes

1   This chapter draws on more than thirty-five interviews with participants in the negotiating process to establish the GFATM and with other relevant experts, and on a study of internal documentation and options papers charting the choices facing the fund in its start-up phase.
2   While the Vaccine Fund is a financing and fund-raising instrument, and GAVI is an alliance with no financial mechanism, in this chapter they are considered together. Although they have separate boards and are legally independent of each other for tax and other reasons, in practice GAVI functions as the policy and operational arm of the Vaccine Fund, which disburses funding based on the recommendations of the GAVI board. In the GFATM and the GEF these functions are not separated.
3   The claims made by proponents of MGFs are similar to those made about other forms of 'networked governance' at the global level. These transnational governance mechanisms, which have been referred to as global policy or issues networks, might carry out a number of functions such as placing particular issues on the international agenda, setting standards and international norms, gathering and disseminating valuable knowledge (Reinicke and Deng *et al.* 2000) or, in the case of MGFs, mobilizing and allocating international financial resources. The growing interest in the concept of global public goods is another manifestation of the same trend, especially in terms of the disaggregation of key governance

tasks. Indeed, proponents of a global public goods agenda have cited 'networked governance' as an important means of producing, and in some cases financing, these goods (see, for example, Kaul *et al.* 2003).

4 The United States and Japan are said to have been the countries most hostile towards the UN at that meeting, according to participants interviewed for this study.

5 These reservations were less likely to be expressed by recipient governments, CSOs and even some donor nations, such as France. Indeed, in GFATM negotiations, some delegations such as the CIS countries argued for a greater role for the UN technical agencies in the operation of the fund.

6 In interviews conducted for this study, US government officials and others were more sanguine about the Bank's operational efficiency and decision-making processes, but concerns about institutional 'capture' of the fund by the Bank remained an issue. As one US government official put it, 'the Bank has a reputation for taking over everything it touches'. In pre-fund negotiations, some recipient governments and CSOs were also worried that the Bank's fiduciary role would be overly expansive, and that the Bank's standard operating procedures would be imposed on GFATM disbursements.

7 One way of mitigating the concerns about whether constituency-based structures are sufficiently representative or democratic is to build in a paramount plenary body such as the GEF Assembly (comprising more than 170 countries) that meets every three years to determine the overall direction of the facility, while still leaving most operational decisions to a smaller governing board.

8 Similar risks arise when donors seek to apply to performance management principles to MGFs themselves. In recent years, donors have strongly backed a project led by the GEF Secretariat to develop programmatic indicators in order to quantify the results donors can expect for different levels of funding within the facility's four-year financing periods. According to GEF officials interviewed for this study, this is having the effect of distorting GEF's portfolio in favour of projects with shorter time horizons at the expense of long-term, higher-payoff strategies (such as the development of solar thermal power plants, which are not expected to be profitable for at least ten years).

9 As defined here, MGFs can be seen as one type of 'global public policy network', defined by Reinicke (1999–2000), as 'loose alliances of government agencies, international organizations, corporations and elements of civil society, such as nongovernmental organizations, professional associations or religious groups that join together to achieve what none could accomplish on its own' – using information sharing, joint action and, in this case, joint financing to do this.

10 The Bank, which deals only with governments in its regular funding processes, refused to establish independent accountability relationships with individual NGOs and other country-level funding recipients during GFATM negotiations. The Bank argued that this would increase substantially its transaction costs and those of recipients, many of whom would in any case lack the capacity to report accurately to the Bank. Partly to address these concerns, the GFATM has decided to institute a system of sub-trustees where a bank or other group at country level provides a bridge between the Bank and funding recipients.

11 GFATM and GAVI have taken such measures. GFATM has elected not to place a pharmaceutical company representative on its board, partly out of conflict of interest concerns and in response to the opposition of some key nations including France, NGOs and the UN technical agencies.

12   The UK government, for example, has linked its future support for the GFATM to the fund's ability to fill global gaps in development assistance, such as global commodities procurement, that are not met by existing aid initiatives.

13   Only half of the OECD countries have so far pledged to the GFATM, not including the countries represented by the European Commission contribution. To give one example of the unevenness of national contributions, while the Netherlands has pledged US$120 million to the fund, the highest national contribution as a proportion of GDP, Australia – a country with a comparable GDP – has not pledged any support to the fund.

14   The GEF is mainly financed out of existing ODA flows, rather than being additional (see Kaul *et al.* 2002).

15   Another proposal designed to maintain the identity of individual private-sector contributions is to allow corporations and foundations who meet certain conditions to 'brand' their contributions and activities.

16   Rivers (2001) argues that if the GFATM is to undertake serious fund-raising from foundations, corporations, wealthy individuals and the general public in particular, it will need either a dedicated team within the fund itself or, as the UN Population Fund, UNICEF and GAVI have done, it will have to set up a legally independent NGO or network of NGOs to raise funds and represent its interests.

17   Funding commitments to MGFs to date have tended to be relatively informal. The GEF replenishment process provides a more structured forum for donors to negotiate funding commitments over four-year periods, but, as noted above, this process can be protracted and political.

18   An example of this currently being mooted at the GEF is to place restrictions on procurement by the facility from non-contributing countries or those in arrears (the Asian Development Bank is understood to already have such a policy in place).

19   The GEF has pursued what a recent performance review calls 'modest' attempts at co-financing – for example, with the IFC or national energy authorities, and is looking to do more, especially with the private sector. In the broader sense, the GEF claims that its resources have on average leveraged four or five times as much in local investment and other external contributions (World Bank Group 2001: 115).

20   At a national level, proliferation of issue-based global funds also runs counter to the trend in development practice towards integrated, country-owned plans such as PRSPs, supported by non-earmarked funds. This may limit the flexibility and coherence of national policies.

21   For competing views on whether international organizations can be held to be democratically accountable, and whether this matters, see Dahl (1999) and Keohane (2002).

22   As Ngaire Woods argues, the deeper question – and the one in need of more detailed study – is whose interests these new forms of global governance are furthering (Woods 2002).

23   For proposals along these lines, see, for example, Kaul and Le Goulven (2003) and Benner *et al.* (2003).

References

Benner, T., M. H. Ivanova, C. Streck and J. Martin Witte (2003) 'Moving the Partnership Agenda to the Next Stage', in *Progress or Peril? Partnerships and Networks in Global Environmental Governance. The Post-Johannesburg Agenda*, Berlin: Global Public Policy Institute.

Brugha, R. and G. Walt (2001) 'A Global Health Fund: A Leap of Faith?', *British Medical Journal*, 323 (21 July): 152–4.

Dahl, R. A. (1999) 'Can International Organizations Be Democratic? A Sceptic's View', in I. Shapiro and C. Hacker-Cordón (eds), *Democracy's Edges*, Cambridge: Cambridge University Press: 19–36.

Hardon, A. (2001) 'Immunisation for All?: A Critical Look at the First GAVI Partners Meeting', *HAI Europe*, 6(1): 2–9.

Kaul, I., P. Conceição, K. Le Goulven and R. U. Mendoza (eds) (2003) *Providing Global Public Goods: Managing Globalization*, Oxford: Oxford University Press.

Kaul, I. and K. Le Goulven (2003) 'Institutional Options for Producing Global Public Goods', in I. Kaul, P. Conceição, K. Le Goulven and R. U. Mendoza (eds), *Providing Global Public Goods: Managing Globalization*, Oxford: Oxford University Press.

Kaul, I., K. Le Goulven and M. Schnupf (2002) 'Financing Global Public Goods: Policy Experience and Future Challenges', in I. Kaul, K. Le Goulven and M. Schnupf (eds), *Global Public Goods Financing: New Tools for New Challenges*, New York: UNDP Office of Development Studies: 10–24.

Keohane, R. O. (2002) 'Global Governance and Democratic Accountability', Miliband Lecture, London: London School of Economics.

Oxfam (2001) 'Global HIV/AIDS and Health Fund: Foundation for Action or Fig Leaf?', Mimeo, Oxfam: Oxford.

Reinicke, W. (1999–2000) 'The Other World Wide Web: Global Public Policy Networks', *Foreign Affairs*, Winter: 44–57.

Reinicke, W. H. and F. Deng with J. Martin Witte, T. Benner, B. Whitaker and J. Gershman (2000) *Critical Choices: The United Nations, Networks, and the Future of Global Governance*, Berlin: Global Public Policy Institute.

Rivers, B. (2001) 'Risk and Opportunity Factors for the Global Fund during its First Year of Operation', Mimeo, Aidspan: New York.

Shoof, M. and M. W. Phillips (2002) 'Global Disease Fund to Be Strict for Better Chance to Get Results', *Wall Street Journal* (13 February).

Stansfield, A. (2002) 'Philanthrophy and Alliances for Global Health', in I. Kaul, K. Le Goulven and M. Schnupf (eds), *Global Public Goods Financing: New Tools for New Challenges*, New York: UNDP Office of Development Studies: 94–101.

Transitional Working Group (TWG) (2001) 'Paper on Governance', November, Brussels: The Global Fund.

Woods, N. (2002) 'Global Governance and the Role of Institutions', in D. Held and A. McGrew (eds), *Governing Globalization*, Cambridge: Polity Press.

World Bank (2001) 'Effective Use of Development Finance for International Public Goods', in *Global Development Finance 2001*, Washington, DC: World Bank Group: 115–35.

7
The Transition from Official Aid to Private Capital Flows: Implications for a Developing Country

Renu Kohli

Introduction

Since the mid-1990s there has been a tremendous increase in the mobility of international capital. Cross-country trends in capital flows reveal that private capital flows now dominate, with official capital flows being reduced to a trickle. Until the early 1990s, the main source of external financing across the developing world was official development assistance (ODA) provided by the governments of high-income countries. Consisting mainly of grants, concessional loans and contributions from multilateral institutions, dissatisfaction with some of ODA's attributes led to a questioning of 'aid' by both recipients and donors. Among the most important of these have been the 'tying' of aid, whereby conditionalities were imposed on recipient countries, ranging from mandatory purchases from the donor country to provision of market access, and sometimes surrender of ownership of national economic policies. Other factors precipitating the disillusionment with 'aid' have been the misappropriation of aid receipts, corruption at various points, and lack of a visible, positive relationship between 'aid' and poverty or economic growth.

This process was complemented by the simultaneous evolution of factors encouraging the flow of private capital across the globe. Briefly, these were: the industrialized countries' shift to floating exchange rate regimes following the collapse of the Bretton Woods arrangement; the dismantling of capital controls to further facilitate free trade in goods among these countries, and the development of financial markets in these countries as a consequence; the rise of the institutional investor with an appetite to diversify across the globe in search of higher returns; and, last but not least, the push of the World Bank–IMF combine to facilitate payments and settlements in foreign exchange in an effort to encourage free trade in goods. Concurrent with these trends has been the move towards globalization that began in the late twentieth century, and the market-orientated reforms instituted in many countries that have liberalized access to financial markets. These trends suggest that the shift towards private capital transfers as a means of financing development is perhaps permanent and irreversible.

Irreversible though it may seem, this transition is also accompanied by heightened risks, which may require countries to adopt more dynamic and more responsible policies. To elaborate, countries now have to compete with each other to attract private capital flows, a feature that requires putting in place elements and policies that serve to attract the right levels and types of private capital. The latter is critical; in the 1990s, the rise in portfolio capital has tilted the composition of international capital flows towards short-term investments, exposing individual countries to enhanced volatility and sudden withdrawal risks.

These developments have stimulated a keen interest in understanding the nature and economic effects of capital flows as well as the appropriate policy responses to safeguard against financial instability that appears to be associated with the global movement of private capital. While the impact of 'aid' flows has been relatively well researched and understood, the impact of private capital flows is still ambiguous and controversial. For example, the type of capital inflow, direct or portfolio investment, appears to make a critical difference in impact. Foreign direct investment has been proved to have well-known positive effects through technology spillovers and stable investments tied to plant and equipment, but portfolio capital is associated more closely with volatility and its capacity to be triggered by both domestic as well as exogenous factors, thus making it extremely difficult to manage and control. Moreover, the impact of private capital flows varies vastly across countries, time, the stage that financial and economic development as well as economic policies has reached, thus underlining the need for individual country studies to enable comparisons and stylized representations.

Capital flows affect a wide range of economic variables such as exchange rates, interest rates, foreign exchange reserves, domestic monetary conditions and the financial system. Some commonly observed effects of capital inflows that have been documented in recent studies[1] include real exchange rate appreciation, stock market and real estate boom, reserve accumulation, and monetary expansion, as well as effects on production and consumption.[2]

These issues are significant for India, which witnessed a swing from official aid flows towards private capital flows in the early 1990s. Both the international trend towards private resource transfers and the changing profile of India's capital account merit a close examination of the implications of this transition. This context motivates the aim of this chapter. It attempts three things. First, it documents trends in movement and composition of capital flows into India in an international perspective, using the countries in the Asia and Pacific regions as comparators. Two, it examines the impact of these flows on the key macroeconomic variables and the domestic financial sector. Finally, it dwells on the implications of the transition for economic policy.

The following sections characterize briefly the changes in India's capital account from the mid-1980s, assess the macroeconomic impact of these flows, and examine the impact upon the financial sector. The last section discusses the policy implications and concludes.

The changing profile of India's capital account

World capital flows in the 1990s displayed a steep decline in official (aid) flows and a rise in private capital movements; India, as part of the developing world, was not immune to this change. From the late 1980s, official transfers into the country reveal a steady decline, while private transfers show a rise. The reasons for this shift are manifold. Apart from being part of the worldwide trend in declining official assistance following disillusionment with aid, India also embarked on an economic reform programme aimed at transforming the controlled economy into a market-driven one.

Following its balance of payments crisis in 1991, India gradually began to dismantle capital controls as part of its broader financial liberalization strategy. Changes in exchange rate regime as well as trade and investment policy reform prompted an increase in capital flows into the country between 1992/3 and 1997/8. Though the magnitude of these flows is relatively insignificant from a cross-country perspective, the pattern and composition of the flows conform to trends observed in other emerging markets. India also shares some attributes with these emerging economies, a fact that enables comparative assessment. For example, like many Asian and Latin-American countries – which were at various stages of macroeconomic stabilization and/or financial liberalization when capital started flowing into these economies – India is a liberalizing economy too. Notable differences persist. For example, India exhibits far less openness than these countries and still retains strict capital controls, specifically on outflows.

These trends are clearly visible in Table 7.1, which profiles the changing composition of India's capital account. The substantial contribution of aid towards the capital account in the 1980s dwindled steadily by the 1990s and was replaced by private flows. The two spikes in 1991 and 1992 are explained by the IMF loan for stabilization, adjustment and restructuring. A sharp increase in foreign investment, direct and portfolio, can be observed after 1992. Commercial borrowing abroad dropped during the crisis years, and resumed afterwards. Migrants' remittances, a major source of capital transfers from abroad, continue to be buoyant after a short dip in 1993–4.

Portfolio investment flows exceeded foreign direct investment (FDI) in the early years of liberalization. FDI caught up later, peaked in 1995, fell after that and recovered only in 2001. A departure from the APEC region's experience is the excess of portfolio over FDI inflows in the initial years after liberalization. In the former region, foreign capital was dominated by FDI after the opening

Table 7.1 The changing composition of India's capital account (percentage to total [net] capital flows)

	Foreign investment		NRI deposits	External assistance	Commercial borrowings	Net capital account (% GDP)
	FDI	Portfolio				
1986	4.3	0	16.3	30.3	21.1	1.85
1989	5.9	0	34.4	26.5	25.4	2.39
1990	1.3	0.1	21.4	30.7	31.3	2.27
1991	3.4	0.1	10.6	77.7	40.0	1.46
1992	8.1	6.3	51.3	48.4	−9.2	1.59
1993	6.0	36.8	12.4	19.6	6.3	3.54
1994	14.4	41.8	1.9	16.7	11.3	2.84
1995	46.0	58.9	24.5	21.5	29.2	1.31
1996	24.7	29.0	29.4	9.9	24.7	2.96
1997	35.1	18.0	11.5	9.2	38.9	2.47
1998	29.0	−0.6	11.3	9.9	51.8	2.04
1999	20.7	28.9	14.8	8.6	3.2	2.32
2000	25.7	30.3	25.4	5.8	45.3	1.91
2001	40.8	21.0	28.7	11.8	−11.8	–

Sources: Author's calculations based on figures from Reserve Bank of India (*Report on Currency and Finance*, various issues) and Reserve Bank of India (*RBI Bulletin*, July 2001).

of markets. This is partly explained by global trends in the early 1990s, when portfolio capital flows registered a sharp increase.

The process of liberalization in India also explains this, as most FDI approvals remained discretionary; comparatively, a one-off, entry-point registration for portfolio investments in financial markets made it faster and simpler. This might have tilted the composition of flows in favour of portfolio investments.

How do these features relate to other countries in the Asian and Pacific regions? Figure 7.1 plots the trends in net capital inflows (sum of FDI, portfolio, loans and resident Indian deposits) into India between 1985 and 2001. The plot shows a recovery of net capital inflows that had begun to decline in the late 1980s and bottomed out in the 1991 crisis.

As mentioned earlier, following the liberalization of direct investment and portfolio flows there was an increase in capital inflows between 1992–5 and 1996–7, an experience similar to the Asian and Latin-American economies (see Figure 7.2). The magnitude of capital flows into India is, however, much smaller. The peak level for India is 3.5 per cent of GDP in 1993–4, whereas the peak levels are more than 20 per cent for Malaysia, 13 per cent for Thailand, 10 per cent for the Philippines, and almost 10 per cent for Singapore between 1990 and 1993 (Glick 1998: 4–5). But the swing in the capital account observed in the case of other emerging economies is not apparent for India. Khan and Reinhart (1995) estimate a change in the capital

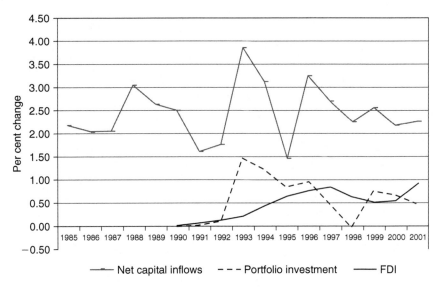

Figure 7.1 Private net resource flows to India, 1985–2001
Source: World Bank (various issues) *Global Development Finance*.

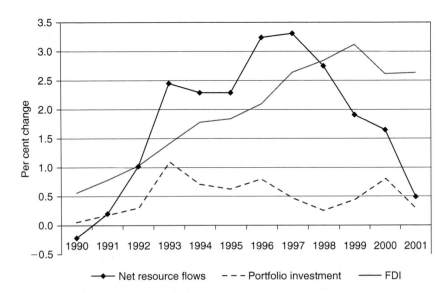

Figure 7.2 Private net resource flows to Asia and Pacific region, 1990–2001
Source: World Bank (various issues) *Global Development Finance*.

account from −2.4 per cent (GDP) on average between 1984–9 to 1.6 per cent (1990–3) for ten Latin American countries, and from 1.6 per cent (1984–8) to 3.2 per cent (1989–93) (GDP) for eight Asian ones. Comparative figures for India are 2.3 per cent (1985–9) and 2.6 per cent (1993–2001)[3] of GDP, indicating only a marginal increase. This is explained by India's relatively late start in financial liberalization, by which time the competition for international capital had already stiffened. Over the next two sections, we examine the impact of these flows.

Capital flows and effects on macroeconomic aggregates

How has this transition affected the Indian economy? Capital inflows impact on a range of economic variables and, unlike aid flows, these also have an immediate macroeconomic impact, with possible adverse implications if not tackled properly. The considerations surrounding these flows are therefore, different, with greater emphasis on economic management and policy response.

Several authors (Calvo *et al.* 1992; Corbo and Hernandez 1994; and Khan and Reinhart 1995, among others) have documented the effects of capital inflows for Latin America and East Asia, and this section draws on these studies in analysing India's experience. Some commonly observed effects of capital inflows are exchange rate appreciation, monetary expansion, rise in bank lending if the flows are intermediated through the banking system, and effects on savings and investment. This section considers the effects of capital flows on the exchange rate, foreign exchange reserves and money supply.

Exchange rate appreciation

In theory, an inflow of foreign capital will raise the level of domestic expenditure in the economy, raising the demand for non-tradable goods that results in an appreciation of the real exchange rate. The price-adjustment process then leads to a reallocation of resources from tradable to non-tradable goods, and a switching of expenditures in favour of non-tradables. The rise in aggregate expenditure also increases the demand for tradables, leading to a rise in imports and a widening of the trade deficit. The transmission channel of the real exchange rate appreciation will, however, depend on the exchange rate regime. With a floating exchange rate and no central bank intervention, the appreciation will take place through a nominal appreciation, but in a fixed exchange rate regime, the appreciation will work through an expansion in the domestic money supply, aggregate demand and the prices of non-tradables. How has this process worked for India?

The real and nominal, effective exchange rates (bilateral, rupee–dollar) over three decades are plotted in Figure 7.3. While both series depreciated after 1985, the nominal depreciation persisted at the time of regime switch in 1993 but the real exchange rate became mean-reverting. Two real appreciation

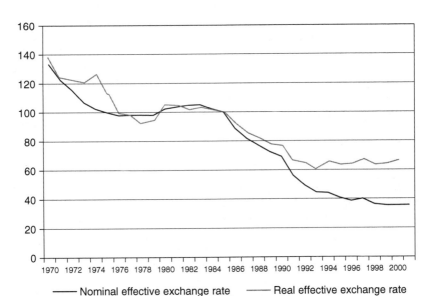

Figure 7.3   Nominal and real effective exchange rates (1985 = 100)
Source: Reserve Bank of India (2001).

episodes are visible after 1993, coinciding with the capital surge in 1992–5 and 1996–7, when the real exchange rate appreciated by 10.7 per cent (August 1995) and 14 per cent (August 1997), respectively, over its March 1993 level.

The policy response of the authorities was to avert a nominal appreciation (Acharya 1999), preferring an adjustment through gradual increases in domestic inflation. Part of the policy response was directed towards encouraging capital outflows through the early servicing of external debt. The timing of these inflows also facilitated India's external adjustment as they coincided with trade reform, convertibility of the current account and liberalization of overseas investments by Indian firms, measures that were financed partly by net increase in capital assets during this period.

Both real exchange rate behaviour and policy response in India bear a closer similarity to East Asian economies than do those in Latin America. The former mainly limited adjustment of their currencies *vis-à-vis* the US dollar, while the latter allowed much more exchange rate flexibility. The extent of real exchange rate appreciation in the Asian region was far less than in the Latin American countries, because of differences in policy response.[4] Circumstances indicate that policy response was undoubtedly a major factor in thwarting appreciation pressures on the real exchange rate.[5]

The behaviour of the real exchange rate in response to capital inflows has been an important area of concern for researchers. Calvo *et al.* (1992) and

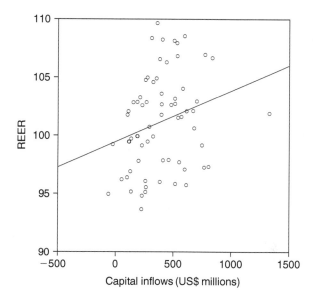

Figure 7.4   REER versus capital inflows
Source: Reserve Bank of India (2000).

Edwards (1999) explored the association between capital inflows and real exchange rates for a set of Latin-American countries. They found substantial evidence that capital inflows contributed both to real exchange rate appreciation and the accumulation of reserves in these countries. Is there any such evidence for India? We attempt a tentative exploration of this hypothesis in this chapter.

The time-series properties of the two series show both net capital account and the real effective exchange rate (REER) to be stationary, I(0), processes at a monthly frequency between 1993–2001.[6,7] Both series are also cointegrated.[8] The simple correlation coefficient between the two series is 0.24, which is comparable to estimates for seven Latin-American economies, which range between 0.14 and 0.72 (Edwards 1999). The bivariate relationship between net capital inflows and the real effective exchange rate is plotted in Figure 7.4. Granger causality tests show that the hypothesis that net capital inflows do not cause real exchange rates can be rejected 96 per cent of the time. Reverse causality – that is, real exchange rates do not Granger-cause net capital inflows – is, however, accepted.

An impulse response function from the vector error-correction model (VECM) estimation between the two series in Figure 7.5 is constructed to illustrate the impact of capital inflows on real exchange rates. The response function indicates that a one-standard-deviation surprise shock to net capital

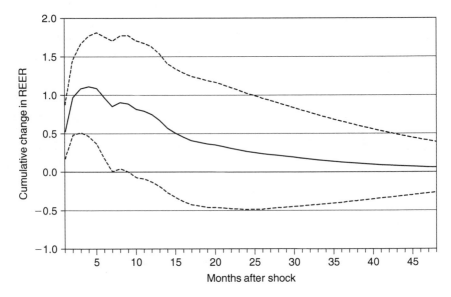

Figure 7.5   Response of REER to innovations in net capital inflows
Source: Reserve Bank of India (2000).

inflows – that is, a net inflow of US$246 million in the first period – caused the real exchange rate to appreciate by 1.0 per cent in the third month, followed by oscillations around this value for the next six months, and then a return to its original value. This is then accompanied by a cumulative appreciation of 0.9 per cent, which then wears out over 24 months; that is, two years.

The impulse response simulations reveal a permanent effect of unanticipated capital account shocks on the real effective exchange rate. The VECM representation also shows a significant adjustment response of the real exchange rate to past disequilibrium, the size of the adjustment coefficient being 0.007.[9] Finally, the net capital account does not move significantly to restore equilibrium, as indicated by the insignificant adjustment coefficient on the capital account equation in the system.

Preliminary evidence for India therefore corresponds to individual as well as cross-country evidence on this issue. However, this needs to be examined within a well-specified context as fluctuations in real exchange rates can also be affected by changes in the terms of trade, government spending, and monetary as well as exchange rate policies. This is an importance area of research for future work as a significant implication of this result is that a rise in inward capital flows into the economy may lead to losses in international competitiveness via real exchange rate appreciation, which has implications for exchange rate policy.

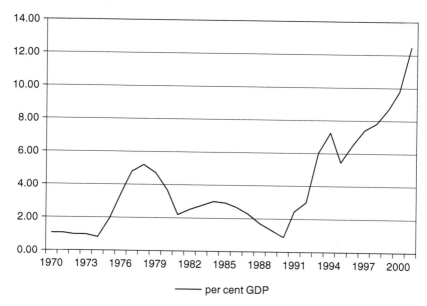

Figure 7.6   Foreign exchange reserves (excluding SDRs and gold)
Source: Reserve Bank of India (2000).

Reserve accumulation

Depending on the exchange rate regime, capital inflows can be traced to either international reserves' accumulation or a current account deficit. If there is no intervention by the central bank – that is, the exchange rate regime is a pure float – the net increase in capital assets via capital inflows would be associated with a similar increase in imports, and therefore a widening current account deficit. Alternately, if the exchange rate regime is fixed and the central bank intervenes to counter appreciation pressures, then capital inflows would be visible in increases in foreign exchange reserves. Since the two extremes are rarely observed in practice, the choice of intervention, or its size, narrows down to the degree of exchange rate flexibility desirable by the authorities and is, in essence, a policy choice.

Figures 7.6 and 7.7 plot foreign exchange reserves and the current account deficit (per cent of GDP) for India over the period 1970–2001. The current account deficit is seen to be narrowing after touching 3.2 per cent in 1991, the year of crisis, and recently turning into a surplus in 2000–1. The steep increase in foreign exchange reserves (Figure 7.6) is concomitant with this decline, indicating absorption of foreign currency inflows by the central bank. In 1993, the first year of the capital surge, almost all of the net capital inflows were absorbed as foreign exchange reserves. In 1994, almost a third of net

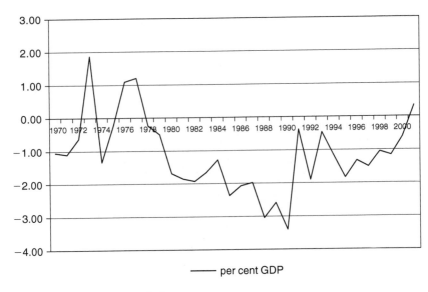

— per cent GDP

Figure 7.7   Current account balance
Source: Reserve Bank of India (2000).

capital inflows were utilized in this way; from 1996 onwards, the Reserve Bank has typically absorbed 50 per cent of net capital inflows into international reserves (Kohli 2000a, 2000b). The stock of international reserves in 2001–2 (US$54.1 billion) represents an increase of nearly 486.83 per cent over the 1991 level. Between 1991 and 2001, the rate of growth of foreign exchange reserves in India averaged 25.2 per cent against a negative average of 7.06 per cent for 1985–90.[10]

The buildup of reserves following a surge in capital inflows mirrors the reserve accumulation patterns of countries in Asian and Latin-American regions, all of which augmented their foreign exchange reserves in a similar way. In fact, Figure 7.6 mimics the trend in international reserves observed for a group of Asian and Latin-American countries in Figures 7.8 and 7.9.

Impact on monetary conditions and sterilization

Capital inflows affect domestic money supply through the accumulation of net foreign currency assets with the central bank. If the central bank intervenes to maintain a fixed exchange rate, then an accumulation of international reserves represents an increase in the net foreign exchange assets of the central bank and has a direct effect on the monetary base. In contrast, if the exchange rate is allowed to float without intervention, there is no impact on domestic money supply. What has been the impact of capital inflows on

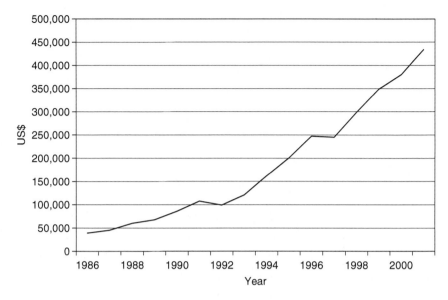

Figure 7.8   Official reserves, East Asia and Pacific
Source: Reserve Bank of India (2000).

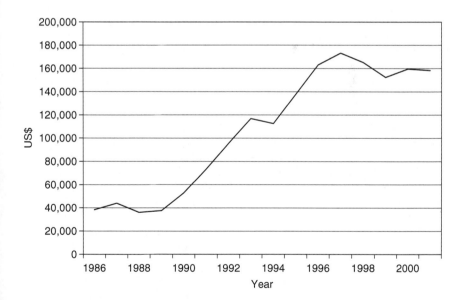

Figure 7.9   Official reserves, Latin America and Caribbean
Source: Reserve Bank of India (2000).

Table 7.2   Movements in the monetary base (reserve money) (percentage to change in reserve money)

	ΔRBICG	ΔRBICC	ΔNFA	ΔGCL	ΔNMLL	ΔRM
1984/85–1989/90*	105.5	13.6	7.6	2.0	28.7	100
1991–2	44.0	−34.0	92.5	0.7	3.4	100
1992–3	38.8	32.7	33.3	0.8	5.6	100
1993–4	3.1	−14.9	103.9	0.5	−7.3	100
1994–5	7.1	26.3	76.1	1.4	10.8	100
1995–6	79.3	34.9	−2.5	0.03	11.7	100
1996–7	50.1	−275.4	366.9	9.4	51.0	100
1997–8	41.8	7.7	80.3	0.8	30.6	100
1998–9	52.4	30.8	66.6	2.2	52.0	100
1999–2000	−20.2	31.0	131.8	3.5	46.1	100
2000–1	24.7	−25.5	137.5	3.4	40.1	100
2001–2	1.7	−27.7	193.5	2.5	70.0	100

Notes: RBICG: RBI credit to government; RBICC: RBI credit to commercial sector, including commercial banks; NFA: RBI's net foreign exchange assets; GCL: Government currency liabilities to the public; NMLL: Net non-monetary liabilities of the RBI; RM: Reserve money (RM = RBICG + RBICC + NFA + GCL − NMLL).
Sources: *Pre-1990 figures from Joshi and Little (1994: 253). Author's calculations for the rest of the table.

domestic money supply in India, and how has monetary policy responded to these inflows?

Table 7.2 presents a profile of monetary indicators and offers a perspective via movements in the monetary base. Some stylized facts can be established about changes in the movements of monetary aggregates after the shift to private capital flows. First, net foreign exchange assets of the central bank accounted for most of the increase in the monetary base (reserve money) in the 1990s. As a percentage share of M3, the monetary aggregate targeted by the central bank, net foreign exchange assets have grown from an average of 3.7 per cent in the 1980s to 12.1 per cent in 1990s. Second, while the fiscal-policy-induced increases in money supply have declined somewhat in the post-liberalization period, it still remains an important exogenous source of monetary expansion. Third, private-sector credit appears to be the only policy variable that is manipulated by the central bank via interest rate and reserve requirement changes to adhere to monetary targets. Offsetting squeezes on private domestic credit correspond closely to accretions in net foreign currency assets. Private-sector absorption thus adjusts during heavy capital inflow.

The monetary impact of the accumulation of reserves cannot only be inflationary, but also affects the domestic financial sector. This impact will be determined by the channels through which the inflows are intermediated within the domestic economy as well as the policy response of the monetary authorities to expansion in monetary base as a result of accumulation of foreign currency assets. The following section discusses the process of financial intermediation and its impact on the domestic financial sector.

Capital flows and the financial sector

There are two channels through which inward capital can be intermediated: the stock market or the banking system. The level of intermediation through either channel will depend on the relative size of the two sectors, the pattern of liberalization and the policy response. For example, if restrictions on inflows and outflows of the banks remain, then the impact on the banking sector will be limited. Similarly, if policy is targeted towards insulating intermediation through the banks, then the expansionary effects on their balance sheets will be limited.

The structure of intermediation within the Indian financial system reveals that the banking sector occupies a central place, with a 52 per cent share in the total financial assets of the economy. The capital market, with a steadily rising share in intermediation (31 per cent) is also an important segment of the financial system. Both components are therefore important as far as intermediation of capital inflows is concerned.

Impact on the banking sector

In theory, if there is no policy intervention, a capital inflow will have an impact on the banks' balance sheets through an expansion in foreign liabilities, exposing the banks to new risks linked to interest rates, currency, country, maturity as well as asset-liability mismatches. Secondary effects of inflows could have an impact on the banking system through a rise in the growth of private domestic credit, lending boom and risky loans. However, policy intervention could either offset or limit the extent of intermediation through the banking system. First, a net inflow could be offset by running a matching current-account deficit, in which case capital outflow would balance the inflow, resulting in no permanent effect on the banks' balance sheets. Alternatively, the central bank could sterilize the inflows deposited within the banking system, which would curb the exposure of banks and limit their risks. Both these interventions will prevent an expansion of domestic credit and related effects mentioned earlier.

A commonly observed effect of a rise in net capital inflows is a rapid expansion of the commercial bank sector. This has been true of Thailand and Indonesia, where bank assets expanded rapidly from 73 per cent and 45 per cent of GDP, respectively, in 1988, to 102 per cent and 74 per cent of GDP, respectively, in 1993 (Folkerts-Landau *et al.* 1995). Table 7.3 gives some indicators of banking activity before and after capital account liberalization in India. Column 2 reveals that total assets of banks in India did not display an extraordinary expansion, but just a modest 3 per cent increase between

Table 7.3 Banking activity indicators, 1990–2000 (per cent GDP)

Year	Total assets	Bank credit to commercial sector	Investment in government securities	Net capital account	Net foreign currency assets of the banking sector	Foreign currency assets	Non-resident fixed deposits	Overseas foreign currency borrowing
1990–1	56.3	30.2	8.8	2.3				
1991–2	51.6	28.8	9.6	1.5				
1992–3	50.3	29.4	10.1	1.6				
1993–4	50.7	27.7	11.8	3.5				
1994–5	50.4	28.9	11.6	2.8				
1995–6	50.4	29.0	11.1	1.3				
1996–7	49.1	27.5	11.6	3.0				
1997–8	52.3	28.5	12.3	2.5				
1998–9	54.1	28.2	12.7	2.0	−0.75	2.25	2.91	0.08
1999–2000	56.7	30.0	14.2	2.3	−1.20	1.63	2.74	0.09
2000–1	59.4	30.9	15.6	1.9	−1.65	2.37	3.95	0.07

Sources: Reserve Bank of India (2001) and Reserve Bank of India (various issues) *RBI Bulletin*.

1990 and 2000. Private domestic credit in relation to GDP (column 3) did not show a rapid expansion either, though some co-movement with a surge in net capital inflow can be detected during the boom periods, 1993–5 and 1999–2000. In contrast, investments of banks in government securities can be observed to have increased steadily, almost doubling between 1990 and 2001. Standing at 15.6 per cent of GDP in 2001, they represent an increasing transfer of risk to the public sector; that is, the central bank.

The share of NRI deposits in relation to GDP remained constant at 0.5 per cent, the same level as in 1990, mainly because foreign currency deposits were still restricted to only non-resident Indians. Statistics regarding foreign-currency assets and liabilities of the banking system, available only from 1998–9 onwards, show that foreign currency liabilities of the banks have more than doubled between 1998–9 and 2000–1. At 1.65 per cent of GDP in March 2001, these are fairly modest in comparison to the levels in some East Asian countries during the capital inflow boom of the early 1990s. For example, foreign liabilities rose from 7 per cent to 19 per cent in Malaysia between 1990 and 1993, and from 3 per cent to 11.2 per cent in Thailand between 1987 and 1993. Both the cautious pace of reform and its sequencing have ensured that the increase in foreign liabilities is kept within limits.

Several factors account for this muted impact on the commercial banks. First, the magnitude of net capital inflows in India is small in comparison to the Asia-Pacific region, as shown in the section on the changing profile of India's capital account. Second, the sequencing of capital account liberalization has been ordered such that liberalization of capital account items directly concerning the banking sector followed relatively late in the process, with many important items still partially or completely restricted; for example, foreign currency deposits.

Last, but not least, is the insulation offered by the policy response of the monetary authorities. As analysed in the section on capital flows below, much of the net capital inflow into the country has been absorbed as foreign currency reserves. This would potentially represent an increase in domestic credit, were it not to be sterilized. While it is difficult to collect evidence on the magnitude of sterilization of credit in India during the capital inflow surge, various sources suggest that it is quite high. Kletzer and Kohli (2001) note that, for the period August 1995–December 2000, correlation between monthly increases in commercial bank credit to government and reserve inflow for the previous month is 0.48, while correlation between contemporaneous changes is −0.29. This indicates sterilization of reserve inflows by the Reserve Bank through an increase in public debt held by the financial sector. As shown in Table 7.3, investments by banks in government securities have risen steadily. This evidence suggests that the central bank used domestic credit policy to attain internal policy objectives while engaging in sterilized intervention to influence/maintain the exchange rate. Sterilization has several controversial implications, which we shall consider later.

Impact of portfolio capital flows on the capital market

This section examines the impact of portfolio capital flows on the equity market. To recall, equity inflows were liberalized at an early stage of reform. When capital started to flow into India, portfolio flows played an important role, exceeding FDI inflows for several years (see Table 7.1). As a share of the net capital account, portfolio flows contributed as much as 58.9 per cent in 1995. As a share of GDP, net investments of foreign investors in the equity market hovered in the range of 0.5–0.7 per cent during the 1993–6 boom period, and slackening afterwards. What has the impact been of portfolio equity flows on the capital market in India following liberalization?

In theory, capital market integration will result in a lower cost of funds due to diversification and an increase in the supply of capital. Other benefits of liberalization of trade in financial assets include expansion in the size of the market as the number of potential investors increases, improved liquidity and market depth, and increased efficiency in allocation of investments. As the link between local and foreign markets strengthens, the progressive integration of financial markets has the potential to increase the risk of volatility spillovers. Even if spillover effects are excluded, market volatility can increase in the country as the frequency of inflows and outflows increases. A rise in volatility can have a potentially destabilizing effect, especially if financial markets are thin, which is very often the case in developing countries. This can also lead to large variations in market liquidity, which can lead to higher volatility. Subsequent real effects of capital market liberalization documented in the literature relate to lending and investment booms.

Are any of the above effects visible in the case of Indian financial markets? As documented earlier, the opening of financial markets to foreign investors attracted significant amounts of private portfolio capital, which exceeded FDI in the early years. Figures 7.10 and 7.11 track movements in equity prices and net equity inflows. The stock market index shows a sharp increase *vis-à-vis* 1990 levels, and the peaks in the price–earnings ratio display a co-movement with the high inflow periods of 1992–5 and 1999–2000. This suggests that the entry of foreign investors possibly led to sharp increases in equity prices through a rise in demand for domestic equities. This is similar to the liberalization experience of other emerging markets. For example, the price–earnings ratio for Mexico rose five times between 1988 and 1993, and doubled in Hong Kong and Thailand between 1990 and 1993 (Folkerts-Landau *et al.* 1995) following the liberalization of equity flows.

Table 7.4 shows indicators of stock market growth, liquidity, turnover and prices in the stock market from 1990. Market capitalization measures the size of the capital market in relation to GDP, whereas the volume of domestic equities traded on the domestic exchange divided by GDP is a measure of market liquidity (Levine and Zervos 1998).

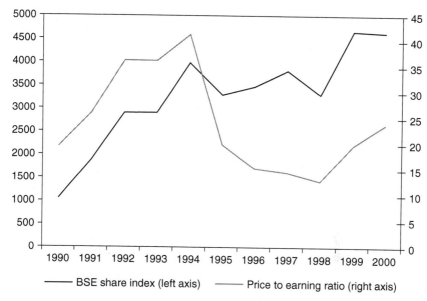

Figure 7.10 BSE share price index and P/E ratio
Source: Reserve Bank of India (2000).

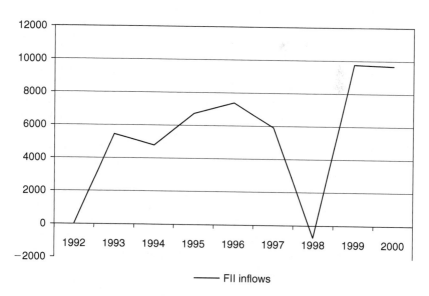

Figure 7.11 Foreign institutional investment (FII) inflows, 1992–2000
Source: Reserve Bank of India (2000).

Table 7.4   Liquidity and growth indicators

Year	Net FII investment in the Indian capital market[a]	Growth of the stock market[b]	Liquidity in the stock market[c]	Price/ earnings ratio	No. of listed companies
1990–1	–	16.0	6.3	19.7	2245
1991–2	–	49.5	11.0	44.3	2514
1992–3	–	25.1	6.1	29.3	2861
1993–4	0.6	42.8	9.8	46.8	3585
1994–5	0.5	43.0	6.7	30.4	4702
1995–6	0.6	44.3	4.2	17.3	5603
1996–7	0.5	33.9	9.1	14.6	5382
1997–8	0.4	36.8	13.7	15.2	5853
1998–9	−0.04	31.0	17.7	14.6	5848
1999–2000	0.5	46.7	35.0	22.7	5889
2000–1	0.4	26.2	45.9	19.7	5955

Notes: [a]Net equity investments (per cent GDP); [b]Market capitalization (per cent GDP); [c]Turnover (per cent GDP).
Sources: Reserve Bank of India (2001; *RBI Bulletin*) and The Stock Exchange, Mumbai.

Some apparent associations revealed by the time-series are noteworthy. One, the growth of the stock market as measured by the market capitalization to GDP ratio reveals a positive correspondence with net equity flows, indicating an expansion in the size of the equity market during periods of high inflows, as in 1993–5 and 1999–2000. The price–earnings ratio also displays a similar co-movement in these two periods, indicating that a surge in foreign capital inflow led to a rise in equity prices. For example, the price–earnings ratio jumped to 22.7 in 1999–2000 from a low of 14.7 in 1998–9, which was also a period when there was a net capital outflow from the country. Sharp swings in price movements can also cause large variations in market liquidity, though the volume of equities traded on the exchange in relation to GDP does not move with these price swings. Market liquidity, in fact, increased steadily over the 1992–2001 time-span, indicating no adverse effects from booms and reversals in capital inflows.

How has liberalization affected market prices, volatility and spillovers? Table 7.5 shows the unconditional correlations between monthly stock prices and returns over the 1992–2001 time-horizon to provide some indication of how the correlation structure has changed over time. These movements indicate that the opening up of the capital account made the stock markets more vulnerable to the vagaries of cross-border movements of capital. The table also shows that correlation between markets (Indian and US) has risen over time, and tends to be higher during periods of higher volatility. Increased correlation across markets is consistent with (though not definitive) evidence of the greater integration of financial markets.

Table 7.5   Volatility, spillover and effects on prices

Year	Equity flows and price/earnings ratio	BSE Sensex and lag of Dow Jones industrial average	Absolute volatility of the returns on the BSE Sensex	Relative volatility
1992–3	–	−0.43	10.6	1.8
1993–4	0.77	0.95	9.6	3.1
1994–5	0.72	−0.36	5.4	1.8
1995–6	−0.44	−0.19	7.2	2.9
1996–7	0.82	−0.19	7.7	2.1
1997–8	0.69	0.15	8.9	1.9
1998–9	0.05	0.33	7.8	1.2
1999–2000	0.08	0.49	8.6	1.6
2000–1	−0.38	0.17	8.0	1.8
2001–2[a]	0.67	0.53	6.8	1.2

Note: [a] Period is April 2001 to December 2001.
Sources: Reserve Bank of India (2001; *RBI Bulletins*), Dow Jones website: www.dowjones.com and author's calculations.

Absolute volatility, as measured by the standard deviation of total returns on the monthly Bombay Stock Exchange (BSE) index, rose during periods of high inflows, namely 1993–4 and 1999–2000, indicating an association with excessive price fluctuations. Volatility of stock prices also increases relative to that of the US when portfolio flows are excessively volatile, which is consistent with the view that volatility of portfolio flows into a country magnifies the sensitivity of stock prices to fluctuations in stock prices of larger equity markets. This reflects that the vulnerability of the local stock market to surges and reversals has increased after liberalization.

Policy implications and conclusion

The experience with transition to private capital flows in India shows that the key economic variables are affected greatly by these flows. Its experience also conforms to the stylized representational impact faced by economies of the Asian and Latin-American region. As the Indian economy becomes increasingly integrated with the rest of the world, a reasonable expectation would be that official external assistance will halt completely, and private inflows increase, perhaps even to match levels reached by other emerging markets. In such a scenario, what are the implications for economic policy?

As this chapter shows, the response of the exchange rate, the domestic monetary base and the domestic financial sector reveal the Indian economy's heightened vulnerability to exogenous factors, which may well be outside the country's control. For example, a negative capital account shock through changes in interest rates outside the country or a sudden shift of investors to locations offering higher returns could have a damaging impact on the economy. These features, combined with the new dependency on private capital flows, imply that economic policies have to be more responsible and geared not only towards attracting these inflows, but also the right type of private foreign capital. Further, policies have to be orientated towards sustaining and managing these transfers, to utilize them for productive absorption.

A disturbing feature in the Indian context is the distinct tilt towards portfolio rather than direct investment flows. It is well known that the composition of flows makes a significant difference, both in terms of impact[11] and smooth management. Portfolio flows are more volatile than direct investment flows, and because of their short-term, uneven nature, they are more difficult to intermediate.[12] Thus they have a greater impact on stock markets and domestic money supply, and can lead to consumption, stock market and real estate booms via sudden expansions in liquidity in financial markets. FDI, on the other hand, is long-term in nature; being embedded in plant and equipment investment, it is less susceptible to sudden withdrawals and leads to productive uses of capital and economic growth. Short-term flows therefore need to be matched by foreign capital inflows of a longer duration. But FDI does not reveal a stable, dominating trend in India so far. Therefore, this is a critical area for economic policy to concentrate on. The focus should be to revamp economic policies so as to attract private capital flows of the stable, productive variety that raise the productive capacity of the economy.

Preliminary evidence for India on the relationship between portfolio flows and some stock market indicators suggests that market prices are not unaffected by capital inflows. Correlation between domestic and foreign financial markets highlights India's vulnerability to external financial shocks, exposing the economy to sudden withdrawals of foreign investors from the financial market, which will affect liquidity and market volatility. India's financial markets, which are still relatively thin and underdeveloped, could pose a severe constraint on intermediating heavy volumes of volatile, short-term capital, necessitating excessive intermediation through the domestic banking sector.

Banks account for 64 per cent of the total financial assets of the Indian economy. Heavy inflows in many countries have been associated with sudden expansion in banks' liabilities, domestic monetary expansion, unscrupulous loans, and real estate and/or consumption booms. Moral hazard risks thus increase the likelihood of financial instability, which occurred during the Asian crisis. In such a scenario, a sound banking system is an essential prerequisite. The state of the Indian banking system, particularly the public-sector banks, is fragile. Many of them are undercapitalized, with large levels of non-performing loans on their balance sheets. Though India's financial reforms have consistently emphasized the strengthening of prudential regulation and supervisory standards, sector as well as borrower-specific exposure limits exist, and liquidity requirements are in place. The capacity of these institutions to assess, price and manage risks is doubtful. Moreover, regulatory reforms need to be supplemented with an appropriate incentive environment, which does not at present exist. These capacities can be created through structural changes and the institutional reform of these institutions, progress on which is as yet to gain momentum. For example, privatization and operational autonomy to public banks are two spheres of financial-sector reform that would address these features, but where progress has been very limited.

Policy issues also relate to real exchange rate appreciation and policy responses to manage private capital inflow. This chapter shows that capital inflows are associated with real appreciation, an area where conflicting policy choices are bound to arise. The option of a more flexible exchange rate policy, which has the advantages of insulating domestic money supply and discouraging speculation through increased exchange risk, carries with it the risk of appreciation. An implication of real appreciation is the loss of external competitiveness, which hurts exports. This could lower the profitability of the trading sectors of the economy and disrupt the process of trade liberalization that India is currently implementing. Moreover, there are real adjustment costs associated with exchange rate changes, which, if the inflows are temporary, can severely disrupt economic processes within the economy.[13] The policy option of protecting exports through subsidies, as a safeguard against adverse exchange rate movements, is also now constrained by the current environment of globalization and trade agreements.

The major policy issue here is how much the exchange rate should be allowed to fluctuate or adjust *vis-à-vis* the trade-off between the real economic costs of exchange rate fluctuations and inflation. However, a stable exchange rate is difficult to reconcile with simultaneous control of domestic money supply along with capital mobility. This is the familiar *macroeconomic policy trilemma* (Obstfeld and Taylor 2001), where the conflict facing policy-makers is the choice between a fixed exchange rate, capital mobility and an activist monetary policy, when only two of the three objectives can be chosen. While the popular policy response prescribed in this context is to float the exchange rate, it is an option that is at present not feasible, for reasons considered above.

A more realistic response could be the continued use of capital controls, particularly on short-term inflows. There is no doubt, particularly in the aftermath of the currency crises, that capital controls have re-emerged as a self-protection device to safeguard against heavy capital surge pressures. These can be effective in managing the external position, particularly in the short run, with some degree of success. In this regard, both Chile (1991) and Malaysia (1998) serve as useful case studies. Chile's unremunerated reserve requirements on short-term flows of less than one-year's maturity have been found to have tilted the composition of its inflows towards longer maturity. Similarly, Malaysia's capital controls in 1998 gave it a useful amount of time to restore and revive its domestic economy by enabling it to gear its monetary policy towards domestic objectives.[14]

Finally, in managing capital inflows to date, sterilization has been used regularly to limit the impact on domestic money supply. Preliminary evidence in this chapter shows a high degree of sterilization of capital inflows by the central bank. To sterilize or not is a controversial issue, and many academics have noted the pitfalls associated with sterilization policies (Calvo 1991; Spiegel 1995). Since it involves an exchange of foreign currency assets for domestic currency assets, the interest rate on the latter has to be kept high to limit central bank losses arising from interest differentials. This, however, would serve to attract further capital inflows, which could potentially be destabilizing in some situations. A more pertinent argument against sterilization is that it leads to an increase in public debt. These costs, termed 'quasi-fiscal costs' in the literature, because of a favourable interest differential for domestic bonds, can be substantial.[15] The substantial rise in commercial banks' holdings of government securities by the banking system in the 1990s, mentioned earlier in the chapter, suggests that the burden of quasi-fiscal costs in India could be quite high. In conjunction with existing levels of public debt, as well as the mounting burden of interest payments, the costs of using the sterilization option are likely to be severe.

The analysis in this chapter shows that, while the shift in external financing from aid transfers to private capital flows has raised the availability of external resources to the Indian economy, it has also imposed greater discipline through the increased vulnerability of the economy to negative capital account shocks, volatility and other risks. The presence of integrated financial markets also exposes the economy to correlated risks, which makes it necessary to distinguish between different types of private inflows, and develop sound and efficient domestic financial institutions with the capacity to intermediate such inflows. This transition points out the importance of self-protection policies that countries must evolve in order to mitigate the risks to themselves, while seeking to extract both static and dynamic gains from private capital flows.

Notes

The author is employed by the Reserve Bank of India. The views expressed, however, are the author's own and not those of the institution to which she belongs. I am grateful to Pranab Sen, T. N. Srinivasan, Kenneth Kletzer, Manmohan Kumar, Peter Clark, Paul Cashin, Christopher Towe and other participants in a seminar at the Fund's Research Department for useful comments. Part of this chapter was published as IMF Working Paper WP/01/192, 1 December 2001.

1 See Calvo *et al.* (1992); Corbo and Hernandez (1994); Khan and Reinhart (1995) and Koenig (1996), among others.

2 Empirical studies that have begun to appear on the subject assess the impact of capital inflows on output growth (Gruben and McLeod 1996); differential macro-economic effects of portfolio and foreign direct investment (Gunther *et al.* 1996); effects on monetary conditions, savings and investment (Kamin and Wood 1998); and the domestic financial sector (Henry 1999; Tesar 1999; Folkerts-Landau *et al.* 1995 and many others).

3 These figures exclude the years 1990–1 because of the balance of payments crisis, as a result of which there was extensive capital flight of non-resident Indian capital from India (see Government of India, various years).

4 Khan and Reinhart (1995) have pointed out that differences in composition of aggregate demand might account for this varied exchange rate response across the two regions as investment rose in the APEC region but consumption rose in Latin America. A similar investigation for India shows that the investment to GDP ratio increased by 3.5 per cent during the capital inflow boom in 1993–5. Private savings rose by an approximately similar amount, and consumption, private and public, declined. In the second episode (1996–7) when the inflows resumed, investment remained sluggish, showing only a marginal increase in 1997–8. Public consumption retained its upward trend; private consumption also rose, declining slowly thereafter. No clear-cut pattern is thus visible in the macro-economic statistics, apart from a steady increase in public consumption and an investment boom between 1993 and 1995. The role of composition of aggregate demand in curtailing a real appreciation is thus indeterminate during this period.

5 For example, after the flows had abated, by mid-1995, the central bank effected an adjustment in the nominal exchange rate in late 1995, bringing the real exchange rate closer to the March 1993 level. A similar policy response prevailed when the real exchange rate appreciated in response to capital inflows in 1996–7; the appreciation was reduced by 9 per cent in December 1997. These adjustments can be seen in Figure 7.3.

6 The Augmented Dickey–Fuller (ADF) test and Phillips–Perron statistics for net capital account and the real effective exchange rate are −4.00, −5.80 and −2.87 and −6.24, respectively. Critical ADF values are −3.68 (1 per cent), −2.97 (5 per cent), −2.62 (10 per cent) while Phillips–Perron values are −3.67 (1 per cent), −2.96 (5 per cent) and −2.62 (10 per cent), respectively. The REER is non-stationary according to the ADF test.

7 The stationarity of the real exchange rate is interesting; it follows the change in the exchange rate regime in 1993 and validates purchasing power parity for the period. The mean-reverting nature of the real exchange rate in the 'managed float' period might however, be associated with the purchasing power parity (PPP) rule by which the float is managed rather than a market determined movement of the REER. See Kohli (2002).

8 The λ_{trace} statistic is 23.1, which exceeds the critical value of 20 at 1 per cent, suggesting that the null hypothesis of no cointegrating vector be rejected.

9 The detailed VECM results are not reported here, but are obtainable from the author on request.

10 Conscious efforts made by the authorities to boost foreign exchange reserves through the mobilization of funds from non-resident Indians (NRIs), namely the Resurgent India Bonds (1998) and the Indian Millennium Deposit Bonds (2000)

are also to be noted at this point. These were targeted exclusively at NRIs and overseas corporate bodies predominantly owned by NRIs.

11 Some studies have shown both categories to hold equivalent time-series properties though. See Claessens *et al.* (1995).

12 Tentative evidence for India supports this hypothesis. Portfolio flows are more volatile than FDI, as measured by the standard deviation of the two series.

13 See Calvo and Reinhart (2000), who provide evidence as to why developing countries fear floating exchange rates.

14 Some authors (for example, Khan and Reinhart 1995) have argued that taxation of short-term flows is subvertible through over-invoicing and under-invoicing of imports and exports in the long run. On the other hand, there is some empirical evidence to suggest that capital controls had a persistent and sizeable effect on the composition of capital inflows in Chile, tilting them towards longer maturity (Gregorio *et al.* 2000).

15 Calvo *et al.* (1992) have estimated quasi-fiscal costs for Colombia at 0.5 per cent of GDP, while Khan and Reinhart estimate them to be between 0.25–0.5 per cent of GDP for Latin-American countries. Kletzer and Spiegel (1998) have extended the analysis further to incorporate the role that quasi-fiscal costs might play in monetary policy for a group of APEC countries. Though they find these to be small in their influence on central bank behaviour, they do find they might play a role in the abandonment of a sterilization programme amid a capital surge.

References

Acharya, S. (1999) 'Managing External Economic Challenges in the Nineties: Lessons for the Future', Paper presented at a seminar at ICRIER, 20 January.

Calvo, G. A. (1991) 'The Perils of Sterilization', IMF Staff Papers 38(4): 921–6.

Calvo, G. A., L. Leiderman and C. M. Reinhart (1992) 'Capital Inflows and Real Exchange Rate Appreciation in Latin America: The Role of External Factors', IMF Staff Papers, 40(1): 108–151.

Calvo, G. A. and C. M. Reinhart (2000) 'Fear of Floating'. Available at: www.puaf.umd.edu/papers/reinhart/papers.htm.

Claessens, S., M. P. Dooley and A. Warner (1995) 'Portfolio Capital Flows: Hot or Cold?', *The World Bank Economic Review*, 9(1): 153–74.

Corbo, V. and L. Hernandez (1994) 'Macroeconomic Adjustment to Capital Inflows: Latin American Style versus East Asian Style', World Bank Policy Research Working Paper 1377, Washington, DC: World Bank.

Dow Jones website. Available at: www.dowjones.com.

Edwards, S. (1999) 'Capital Flows to Latin America', in M. Feldstein (ed.), *International Capital Flows*, Cambridge, Mass.: National Bureau of Economic Research.

Gregorio, J. D., Edwards, S. and R. O. Valdes (2000) 'Controls on Capital Inflows: Do They Work?', *Journal of Development Economics*, 63: 59–83.

Folkerts-Landau, D., G. J. Schinasi, M. Cassad, V. K. Ng, C. M. Reinhart and M. G. Spencer (1995) 'Effect of Capital Flows on the Domestic Financial Sectors in APEC Developing Countries', in M. S. Khan and C. M. Reinhart (eds), 'Capital Flows in the APEC Region', IMF Occasional Paper No. 122, Washington, DC: IMF.

Glick, R. (ed.) (1998) *Managing Capital Flows and Exchange Rates: Perspectives from the Pacific Basin*, Cambridge: Cambridge University Press for the Federal Reserve Bank of San Francisco.

Government of India (various years) *Economic Survey 1990–91; Economic Survey 1991–92*, Delhi: Ministry of Finance of the Government of India.

Government of India (various years) *Indian Public Finance Statistics*, various issues, Delhi: Department of Economic Affairs, Ministry of Finance.

Gruben, W. C. and D. McLeod (1996) 'Capital Flows, Savings and Growth in the 1990s', Unpublished manuscript, Federal Reserve Bank of Dallas (cited in Kamin and Wood (1998)).

Gunther, J. W., R. R. Moore and G. D. Short (1996) 'Mexican Banks and the 1994 Peso Crises: The Importance of Initial Conditions', *North American Journal of Economics and Finance* 7(2): 125–33 (cited in Kamin and Wood (1998)).

Henry, P. B. (1999) 'Do Stock Market Liberalizations Cause Investment Booms?', Research Paper Series, Paper 1504R, Stanford, Calif.: Graduate School of Business, Stanford University.

International Monetary Fund (IMF) (various years) *International Financial Statistics*, various issues, Washington, DC: IMF.

Joshi, V. and I. M. D. Little (1994) *India: Macroeconomics and Political Economy*, Oxford: Oxford University Press.

Kamin, S. B. and P. R. Wood (1998) 'Capital Inflows, Financial Intermediation, and Aggregate Demand: Empirical Evidence from Mexico and Other Pacific Basin Countries', in R. Glick (ed.), *Managing Capital Flows and Exchange Rates: Perspectives from the Pacific Basin*, Cambridge: Cambridge University Press for the Federal Reserve Bank of San Francisco.

Khan, M. S. and C. M. Reinhart (eds) (1995) 'Capital Flows in the APEC Region', IMF Occasional Paper, Washington, DC: IMF.

Kletzer, K. and R. Kohli (2001) 'Financial Repression and Exchange Rate Management in Developing Countries: Theory and Empirical Support from India', ICRIER Working Paper 71, June, New Delhi: ICRIER.

Kletzer, K. and M. M. Spiegel (1998) 'Speculative Capital Inflows and Exchange Rate Targeting in the Pacific Basin: Theory and Evidence', in R. Glick (ed.), *Managing Capital Flows and Exchange Rates: Perspectives from the Pacific Basin*, Cambridge: Cambridge University Press for the Federal Reserve Bank of San Francisco.

Koenig, L. M. (1996) 'Capital Inflows and Policy Responses in the ASEAN Region', IMF Working Paper, Washington, DC: IMF.

Kohli, R. (2000a) 'Aspects of Exchange Rate Behaviour and Management in India: 1993–98', *Economic and Political Weekly*, 35(5), 29 January–4 February.

Kohli, R. (2000b) 'Real Exchange Rate Stabilization and Managed Floating: Exchange Rate Policy in India, 1993–99', ICRIER Working Paper 59, October, New Delhi: ICRIER.

Kohli, R. (2001) 'Capital Flows and their Macroeconomic Effects in India', IMF Working Paper WP/01/192, Washington, DC: IMF. (An earlier version published as ICRIER Working Paper 71, March 2001.)

Kohli, R. (2002) 'Real Exchange Rate Stationarity and Managed Floats: Evidence from India', *Economic and Political Weekly*, 37(5), 2–8 February.

Levine, R. and S. Zervos (1998) 'Stock Markets, Banks, and Economic Growth', *American Economic Review*, 88(3): 537–58.

Obstfeld, M. and A. M. Taylor (2001) 'Global Capital Markets: Growth and Integration: Japan', US Center Sanwa Monographs on International Financial Markets (Manuscript in progress). (Cited in A. M. Taylor, 'A Century of Purchasing Power Parity', NBER Working Paper 8012, November 2000).

Reserve Bank of India (2000) *Annual Report*, 1999–2000, Mumbai.

Reserve Bank of India (various years) *Report on Currency and Finance*, various issues, Mumbai.

Reserve Bank of India (various years) *Handbook of Statistics*, various issues, Mumbai.

Reserve Bank of India (various years) *RBI Bulletin*, various issues, Mumbai.

Spiegel, M. M. (1995) 'Sterilization of Capital Inflows through the Banking Sector: Evidence from Asia', *FBRSF Economic Review*, 3.

Tesar, L. L. (1999) 'The Role of Equity in International Capital Flows', in M. Feldstein (ed.), *International Capital Flows*, Cambridge, Mass.: National Bureau of Economic Research.

World Bank (1999) *World Development Indicators* 1999 (CD-ROM), Washington, DC: World Bank.

World Bank (various years) *Global Development Finance, Country Tables*, various issues, Washington, DC: World Bank.

8
The Millennium Challenge Account: Transforming US Foreign Assistance Policy?

Steven Radelet

Introduction

In January 2004, the United States established a new foreign assistance programme called the Millennium Challenge Account (MCA) designed to provide substantial new funding to a select group of low-income countries that, in the administration's view are 'ruling justly, investing in their people, and encouraging economic freedom'.[1] In principle, the MCA could bring about the most fundamental changes to US foreign assistance policy since the Kennedy administration, although that outcome is far from certain. The significance of the proposed programme lies partly in its scale: the administration's proposed annual funding of US$5 billion, if realized, would represent almost a 40 per cent increase over the 2002 US foreign aid budget of US$13 billion, and a near doubling in the amount of aid that focuses strictly on development objectives. Perhaps even more important than its size, however, is that the new programme (on paper, at least) brings with it the opportunity to improve significantly the allocation and delivery of US foreign assistance.

Traditional foreign aid programmes around the world have been criticized in recent years for a variety of reasons. Berg (2002) provides an overview of the perceived key weaknesses of aid, along with a critique of the main proposals aimed at redressing them. Among the most common criticisms of aid are the following:

- Donor agencies are faced with multiple and often conflicting goals, encompassing everything from supporting political allies, encouraging growth, improving health and education, strengthening the environment, responding to humanitarian emergencies, and distributing surplus agricultural production as food aid.
- Too much aid is directed at the wrong countries. Critics charge that significant amounts of aid are directed at countries that either are not the

poorest countries, or that do not have policies and institutions conducive to using aid effectively or enhancing development more broadly (Collier and Dollar 2002).

- Aid programmes do not reflect local priorities because they do not involve recipients (government and non-government entities) sufficiently in their design, and because they 'earmark' significant funds for their own priorities, leading to a lack of local 'ownership' of and commitment to donor-financed programmes.

- Aid programmes are heavily bureaucratic, ensuring that most aid never reaches its intended recipients (Easterly 2002). Significant amounts of aid are 'tied' to purchases of goods and services in the donor country, reducing the ultimate value of the aid to the recipient. Moreover, the large bureaucracy imposes high costs on recipients, since a relatively small number of capable staff must review countless donor documents and host hundreds of donor missions per year. For example, a United Nations study found 1,500 projects in Burkina Faso and 850 in Bolivia (as cited in Brainard *et al.* 2003: 10).

- Donor activities are not well harmonized, with multiple donors financing similar projects, each with their own independent design, implementation, monitoring and evaluation systems. The lack of harmonization leads to duplication, higher administrative costs for the recipients, and less effective aid flows. For example, in Tanzania in the early 1990s, donors were implementing 15 separate health projects at the same time (van de Walle 2001).

- Monitoring and evaluation systems are badly flawed. Donors rarely measure results accurately, so that there is little historical systematic information about what works and what does not. This lack of information makes it harder to allocate new funds efficiently, and increases the perception that aid is ineffective.

The Bush administration sees the MCA as addressing some (although not all) of these criticisms because it is supposed to differ from current programmes in four critical ways. First, it has narrower and more clearly defined objectives, aimed primarily at supporting economic growth and development and not other foreign policy goals. Second, it is providing assistance to a select group of low-income countries that in the administration's judgement are implementing sound development policies, in an attempt to make the aid funds sent to those countries more effective. Third, the programme is designed to have lower bureaucratic and administrative costs than current aid programmes. Towards that end, in January 2004 it established a new government corporation called the Millennium Challenge Corporation (MCC) to administer the programme. Fourth, the administration plans to give recipient countries a greater say in programme design, implementation and evaluation in order to improve programme efficiency and effectiveness.

In many ways, the MCA is a promising new programme. However, much work needs to be done to turn that promise into reality, and it is quite possible that the programme will never reach its potential. Many of the details on how the new programme will operate remain uncertain. Congress passed enabling legislation for the new programme in January 2004, and with it provided US$1 billion in funding for the first year of its operation. In early May 2004 the administration announced the first group of sixteen qualifying countries. At the time of writing (late May 2004), it has not yet made fully clear its plans for operations on the ground in recipient countries, how programmes will be evaluated, or how the MCA will co-ordinate its programmes with other existing US aid agencies, particularly USAID. Some of these details will be worked out during the first year of the programme as it goes through its start-up phase. At the moment, however, the MCA remains more of a promise than a reality.

Nevertheless, even if the programme is implemented basically as designed, it will not address all the criticism of foreign aid. Most obviously, by introducing a new bilateral programme, the MCA does little institutionally to improve the co-ordination or harmonization of aid programmes.[2] Indeed, there is significant danger that the MCA could add to co-ordination problems, both within the US government and across donor programmes by simply adding one more programme to the mix. Moreover, the MCA by itself will constitute only one part of an overall foreign assistance programme, since it is designed to operate in a relatively small number of developing countries. To date, the administration has not developed clear foreign assistance strategies for countries that do not qualify for the MCA, or for failed states that might be breeding grounds for terrorism and international crime. As such, it is incomplete as a new foreign assistance strategy.

Narrower objectives

US foreign assistance, along with that from other governments, suffers from trying to do too many things at once. There are multiple objectives and purposes, often leading to a lack of coherence in everything from broad strategic planning to specific programmes on the ground. For example, the US Foreign Assistance Act of 1961, as amended, specifies a remarkable thirty-three different goals and seventy-five priority areas for US foreign aid: Carol Lancaster (2000) has classified six different broad purposes of US foreign assistance:

- *Promoting security*, including containing communism, peacekeeping in the Middle East, and, more recently, supporting the war on terrorism.
- *Promoting development*, such as financing investments in health, education, infrastructure aimed at raising incomes, reducing poverty, and improving standards of living. The MCA is most closely aligned with this objective.
- *Providing humanitarian relief* in both natural disasters and civil conflicts.

- *Supporting political and economic transitions* towards free markets and democracies in former socialist economies.
- *Building democracies*, both as an end in itself and as a means towards other ends, such as the protection of human rights or the cessation of civil conflict.
- *Addressing transnational problems*, such as high population growth, food insecurity, and health problems such as HIV/AIDS and malaria.

These objectives are all important and legitimate goals for US foreign aid and foreign policy more broadly. Problems arise, however, when one programme attempts to meet multiple, sometimes conflicting objectives simultaneously, leading to a lack of coherence in everything from broad strategic planning to specific programmes on the ground. The most obvious conflict arises between diplomatic and security goals, on the one hand, and long-term development goals on the other.

The tension between these goals is a prime reason that aid has had a mixed impact on growth and poverty reduction. When legitimate security goals drive the allocation of resources (such as Cold War politics, or current funding for Pakistan as part of the war on terrorism), much less should be expected in terms of achieving development. It should hardly be surprising that aid delivered during the Cold War or to support Middle East peace has achieved weak development results, because that was not its chief goal. No one seriously believed that Zaire's Mobuto Sese Seko was using American largesse to vaccinate children and train teachers. And while Egypt has used some of its aid for development purposes, much has been wasted or diverted to other purposes. Aid to Egypt, however, has helped to maintain the ceasefire with Israel agreed to at the 1978 Camp David Accords, clearly an important achievement.

The MCA's sharper focus on economic growth and poverty reduction is intended to reduce these tensions, though they can never be fully eliminated. As a result, the MCA should be more able to define specific goals, ensure that resources are better allocated to meet those goals, and allow for a stronger and clearer evaluation of results. This should help to ensure that both recipient countries and the American public get better outcomes from its foreign assistance programme. Of course, much depends on the extent to which the programme is able to maintain its focus on growth and is not used simply to support political allies.[3] This, in turn, will depend on the process used to select countries for the programme, the subject to which I now turn.

Selecting for success?

A central tenet of the MCA is that aid can be more effective if it is focused on nations with governments that are committed to economic development and poverty reduction. This idea seems to make sense: foreign assistance should go much further where governments are dedicated to building better schools and clinics, creating good jobs, and rooting out corruption than in countries with dishonest or incompetent governments. In reality, of course, whether or not the idea works in practice will depend on the details of implementation. 'Country selectivity' has gained much currency in recent years, based to a large extent on the research of World Bank economists Craig Burnside, David Dollar and Paul Collier, which concludes that aid has a positive relationship with growth in countries with good policies and institutions, and little effect in other countries (World Bank 1998; Burnside and Dollar 2000; Collier and Dollar 2002).

However, these studies have come under attack from two directions. Several studies challenge the finding that the positive aid/growth relationship depends on good policies, finding instead that aid is positively correlated with growth (with diminishing returns) regardless of the policy environment (see, for example, Hansen and Tarp 2000). Clemens *et al.* (2004) find a strong and robust relationship between some components of aid and economic growth in the short and medium term that does not depend strictly on the policy environment. From another direction, other studies have found that the Burnside and Dollar results are not robust to new data points and different time frames, and do not find a clear relationship between aid and growth (Easterly *et al.* 2003).

While the statistical debate continues, the 'country selectivity' idea seems intuitively correct to development specialists from a variety of backgrounds who believe that aid is more likely to work in countries with governments that are committed to development – including some aid critics. For example, few believe that aid did any good in Zaire under the disastrous leadership of Mobuto Sese Seko, but it played an important supporting role in well-governed Botswana's very rapid development. Helen Hughes (2003), while strongly criticizing the Australian aid programme, argues that its 'best projects and programmes have been in countries like Thailand and Indonesia that were sharply focused on growth in the 1970s and 1980s'.

Partly because of these beliefs, the Burnside, Dollar and Collier research has influenced several donors strongly, including the World Bank, the Asian Development Bank, and the African Development Bank. All three banks have adopted a performance-based allocation (PBA) system for distributing their concessional loans among eligible borrowers. In the World Bank, a country's allocation depends primarily on its country policy and institutional assessment (CPIA) score, through which Bank staff rank countries on twenty different policy and institutional criteria. Other factors determining allocation are the performance of the country's loan portfolio with the Bank, its average income, and its population (World Bank 2003a, 2003b). The Asian and African Development Banks use similar, albeit not identical, systems (ADB 2001; AfDB 2001).

There is no question that the idea of 'country selectivity' and the Burnside, Dollar and Collier research are at the core of the MCA country selection process. However, the general idea that good policy matters in making aid more effective takes us only so far. Putting this idea into practice raises an immediate challenge: how should donors determine whether potential recipient countries meet the standard of 'good policy?' This question has been the focus of much debate on PBA systems at the multilateral development banks (MDBs), particularly on the choice of indicators, their measurement, weighting, and exceptions to the rules. With respect to the MCA, specifically, are the administration's criteria of 'ruling justly, investing in their people, and establishing economic freedom' the right ones? And if so, how, precisely, should the US government determine which countries meet these criteria?

At the most general conceptual level, it is hard to argue against the three broad criteria. Surely donors should be inclined to provide more support, all else being equal, to countries with better governance – in the sense of a less corruption, more effective government, and stronger support for democracy. Moreover, recent empirical evidence suggests that countries with better governance have better development outcomes, in the sense of faster economic growth, increased adult literacy, and lower infant mortality (Kaufmann *et al.* 1999).[4] Similarly, few development experts would argue about the merits of low-income countries 'investing in their people' to the extent that means investments in basic health and education. 'Investing in economic freedom' is more contentious: although there clearly has been a consensus to move towards more open and flexible markets in low-income countries since the 1980s, debate continues on how far this trend should go, and which markets should be liberalized. In all three areas, then, the devil is in the details, as has been discovered in other PBA systems. While most development experts would not argue forcefully against the broad thrust of the three criteria, all would ask: precisely what do they mean, and how should they be measured?

To address this issue, the administration uses sixteen specific indicators (see Table 8.1), grouped into the three broad categories. According to the administration's methodology, countries must score above the median (calculated for all broadly eligible countries) on half or more of the indicators in each of the three groups to qualify for the MCA (MCC 2004a). That is, countries must surpass the median in three of the six 'ruling justly' indicators, two of the four 'investing in people' indicators, and three of the six 'establishing economic freedom' indicators. In addition, a country must score above the median on corruption, regardless of how well it does on all the other indicators.

The administration has stressed that the list produced by the sixteen indicators will not be final – the board of directors of the new MCC can modify the final list under certain circumstances. Specifically, in making its final decisions, the board will be 'empowered to take account of data gaps, lags, trends, or other material information, including leadership, related to economic growth and poverty reduction' (MCC 2004a). This last step introduces some

Table 8.1   Eligibility criteria for the MCA

Indicator	Source
I Ruling justly	
1 Control of corruption	World Bank Institute
2 Rule of law	World Bank Institute
3 Voice and accountability	World Bank Institute
4 Government effectiveness	World Bank Institute
5 Civil liberties	Freedom House
6 Political rights	Freedom House
II Investing in people	
7 Immunization rate: DPT and measles	WHO/World Bank
8 Primary education completion rate	World Bank
9 Public primary education spending/GDP	World Bank
10 Public expenditure on health/GDP	World Bank
III Economic freedom	
11 Country credit rating	Institutional Investor
12 Inflation	IMF
13 Regulatory quality	World Bank Institute
14 Budget deficit/GDP	IMF/World Bank
15 Trade policy	Heritage Foundation
16 Days to start a business	World Bank

Note: To qualify, countries must be above the median on half of the indicators in each of the three sub-groups, and above the median on corruption.
Source: MCC (2004a).

subjectivity into the selection process, which is probably necessary, given the weaknesses in the data. However, this discretion opens up the possibility that the ultimate list of qualifying countries will become politicized. There is little question that, to some degree, some pressure to put political allies on the eligibility list is inevitable. But the system has checks and balances that will modify this impulse in key ways. Most importantly, the selection system that the administration is using is very public and transparent, and uses public data (not secret US data). To the extent that it deviates from this list, it will have to answer to public scrutiny from Congress and other interested parties. (This public selection system is one way in which the MCA goes beyond the multilateral development banks' PBA system, since the MDBs' country policy performance scores are not publicly available.) This public check will not completely prevent the administration from making some changes, but it will make it much more difficult, and to some extent should modify potential abuse of the selection process.

The pool of countries eligible to compete for MCA funding will increase gradually during the first three years (MCC 2004b). In the first year (fiscal year 2004), it includes countries that have both an average annual per capita income below US$1,435 and are eligible for concessional borrowing from the World Bank. There are seventy-five countries in this group. In the second year (FY 2005) the pool of eligible countries will expand slightly to include all eighty-seven countries with average per capita incomes below US$1,435, regardless of their borrowing status with the World Bank. The administration plans to expand the pool of eligible countries sharply in FY 2006 (in line with the increase in annual funding to the targeted US$5 billion) to include the twenty-eight nations with average per capita incomes between US$1,435 and US$2,975. This group of countries would be judged separately from the eighty-seven countries with average incomes below US$1,435, with separate median scores to assess country qualification. Adding this last group of nations is controversial, with some analysts (including me) believing that the programme should remain focused on the poorest, least developed countries of the world and should not be expanded to include countries that have access to private capital markets.

In May 2004, the administration announced the sixteen qualifying countries for the first year as Armenia, Benin, Bolivia, Cape Verde, Georgia, Ghana, Honduras, Lesotho, Madagascar, Mali, Mongolia, Mozambique, Nicaragua, Senegal, Sri Lanka and Vanuatu.[5] In selecting this list of countries, the administration remained fairly true (but not 100 per cent) to its selection methodology. Table 8.2 shows the countries actually chosen (column 1) alongside those that would have qualified if a very strict interpretation of the quantitative selection process had been used. Of the sixteen countries selected, thirteen passed the selection criteria completely (meaning that they scored above the median on half of the indicators in each of the three groups, including scoring above the median on control of corruption). These countries include Armenia, Benin, Cape Verde, Ghana, Honduras, Lesotho, Madagascar, Mali, Mongolia, Nicaragua, Senegal, Sri Lanka and Vanuatu.

Three countries were added to the list that did not strictly meet the qualifying criteria: Bolivia, Georgia and Mozambique. Four others that cleared sufficient hurdles were dropped from the final list: Bhutan, Guyana, Mauritania and Vietnam. Three of these (Bhutan, Mauritania and Vietnam) were the only three non-democracies to qualify strictly on numbers. Although the administration has not stated publicly why these countries were dropped, apparently it was because they were not considered to be democracies. Thus, while being a democracy is not strictly a qualification criterion for the MCA, the administration has sent a strong signal that few, if any, non-democracies will qualify for the programme. Lucas and Radelet (2004) provide more discussion on the details of the countries that were added to on dropped from the final list of qualifiers.

In 2005, as the list of countries eligible to compete expands slightly, some additional countries may qualify, and the list will expand further in 2006. In particular, according to an earlier analysis (Radelet 2003b), the Philippines

Table 8.2 MCA qualifying countries and countries that pass the indicators test

MCA qualifying countries for 2004	Countries that strictly pass the MCA indicators test
Armenia	Armenia
Benin	Benin
Bolivia	**Bhutan**
Cape Verde	Cape Verde
Georgia	Ghana
Ghana	**Guyana**
Honduras	Honduras
Lesotho	Lesotho
Madagascar	Madagascar
Mali	Mali
Mongolia	**Mauritania**
Mozambique	Mongolia
Nicaragua	Nicaragua
Senegal	Senegal
Sri Lanka	Sri Lanka
Vanuatu	Vanuatu
	Vietnam

Countries that miss passing the indicators test by one indicator

Bangladesh	Indonesia
Bolivia*	Kenya
Bosnia and Herzegovina	Kiribati
Burkina Faso	Malawi
Djibouti	Moldova
East Timor	Nepal
Georgia*	São Tomé and Príncipe
India	Tonga

Note: The three countries in **bold** type passed the indicators test but were not selected by the MCC board of directors as qualifying countries. The two countries marked with an asterisk were selected to qualify even though they did not pass the indicators test. In addition, Mozambique was also chosen, even though it missed passing the indicators test by two indicators.

Source: Millennium Challenge Corporation press release, 6 May 2004. Available at: www.mcc.gov/Documents/PR_Eligible.pdf; and Radelet (2004b).

and Swaziland may be added in 2006, whereas in 2007 South Africa, Namibia, Bulgaria, Jordan and Belize are possible qualifiers. As Table 8.2 shows, many other countries miss qualifying by just one of the indicators. Several of these countries could easily qualify within the first few years by improving their scores in that one deficient area. Thus it is quite conceivable that 20–25 countries could qualify for the MCA by its fourth or fifth year of operation.

The relatively large MCA budget, combined with the small number of qualifying countries, should provide ample incentive for countries to try to qualify. For the first year, Congress has approved US$1 billion in funding. With sixteen countries qualifying for the programme, the average country could receive US$63 million. This is equivalent to about a sixth of the average total capital inflows (from aid and other sources) of US$384 million per country for IDA-eligible countries (Radelet 2003b). Ultimately, if the MCA receives a total budget of, say, US$3 billion (a figure more likely than the US$5 billion proposed by the president), and twenty-five countries qualify, the average per country would reach US$120 million per year, equivalent to about a third of current capital inflows.

This list of countries named as qualifiers in the first years is not perfect, and there are understandable debates about the merits and demerits of including particular countries. But it is a reasonable start towards an objectively-based, non-political and selective programme. Weaknesses and inconsistencies in the data result in some countries appearing on the list that probably should not qualify, and there are a few nations that just miss out, despite having a strong record of using aid effectively. Some changes to the selection criteria could undoubtedly improve it. For example, some of the weakest indicators (such as the trade index) could easily be improved over time. The aggregation methodology of counting the number of median scores surpassed could be replaced with a simple aggregation method of normalizing scores and then adding them into a composite score, which (while not perfect) leads to fewer anomalies. In addition, the criterion to drop all countries with corruption scores below the median should be modified, since the underlying data are not robust enough to make such clear judgements. Detailed discussion of these and other proposals to improve the selection procedure are beyond the scope of this chapter, and have been covered extensively elsewhere (Radelet 2003b). Nevertheless, despite these possible adjustments, the proposed system provides a reasonable way to begin distinguishing between nations that show a strong commitment to development and those that do not, and to, at least partially, de-politicize the process of allocating foreign assistance.

Beyond selection: improving the aid bureaucracy

The US foreign aid system is bogged down by a heavy bureaucracy, overly restrictive legislative burdens and conflicting objectives. As with most donors, the US delivers aid in basically the same way in countries with competent, committed governments as in countries with high levels of corruption and poor development policy. The Bush administration claims it will make the MCA different, and it started by creating a new 'government corporation' – the MCC – to run the MCA, designed to reduce administrative costs and increase effectiveness.

The MCC only became legally operational in late January 2004, and at the time of writing (May 2004) is still not fully staffed, so details on its structure and operations remain somewhat uncertain. The MCC will be governed by a nine-person board of directors chaired by the secretary of state and including three cabinet members, the head of USAID, the CEO of the MCC, and four non-government members. Some staff will be drawn from a variety of government agencies for a limited term, while others will be hired from outside the government. The MCC's biggest advantage is that it starts with a clean slate and therefore may be able to avoid the bureaucratic procedures and multiple congressional mandates that weaken current aid programmes. Its status as separate from any existing department could make it more flexible and responsive, and could help it to attract some top-notch talent.

Establishing a new corporation, however, entails certain risks. Dividing the US foreign-assistance programme into two major agencies (USAID and the MCC), in addition to several smaller agencies such as the Peace Corps, could impede co-ordination and increase redundancy. Furthermore, the administration hopes to keep the MCC small, but its projected staffing level of somewhere between 100 and 200 people seems inordinately insufficient for a programme with an annual budget of US$5 billion. It is also not clear who will represent the MCC on the ground in the qualifying countries. Presumably, it will contract-out many services, such as monitoring and evaluation, or it might try to work through USAID staff in each country. Nevertheless, there is a risk that the new agency will be understaffed and thus unable to deliver the high-quality operations that will be expected. In addition, having the secretary of state serve as chairman of the board of the MCC could give the department too much control over qualification and allocation decisions, which could compromise the objectivity of the MCA in favour of other foreign policy goals. In short, over time the MCC could, by facing all of the obstacles that are currently facing USAID, especially if in the meantime the administration does not try to rectify the weaknesses within USAID itself.

Thus one of the biggest concerns is the impact of the MCC on USAID and the relationship between the two organizations. The MCC is likely to draw staff and resources from USAID, further weakening the agency, possibly risking some resentment, and making co-operation more difficult. Many issues remain uncertain. For example, will USAID continue to operate in the MCA countries, or will it pull out once a country qualifies? On the one hand, having both institutions operating in the same country could be confusing for recipient countries and duplicate services unnecessarily. But on the other hand, there may be some projects and programmes that USAID is better positioned to administer with its prior experience and established operations on the ground in these countries. This issue could prove particularly tricky for borderline countries that qualify for the MCA for several years, then fail to qualify, and then qualify again. Switching back and forth between MCA and USAID programmes could be very cumbersome. Similarly, will the MCC operate under new or existing foreign assistance guidelines for procurement of goods and services and other operations? Although more flexible guidelines might seem useful for the MCC, if the two agencies are operating under vastly different rules in the same country, it could lead to serious confusion.

The administration has not yet addressed these questions. If not resolved carefully through strong planning and co-ordination, the difficulties in operating two foreign assistance programmes from two very different parts of the US government are sure to become apparent, and could significantly undermine both MCA and USAID programmes.

Designing better programmes

Similarly, programme design, implementation and evaluation – all of which will be critical – have yet to be developed. Currently, most US foreign assistance is delivered through a country-programming approach in which USAID staff members develop a country strategy, design specific interventions, and evaluate the outcomes. This top-down approach has many shortcomings, including the absence of recipient-nation ownership of specific projects, only partial co-ordination (at best) with the recipient country's overall development strategy, a heavy requirement of USAID staff, and little competition between proposed projects. This approach (or parts of it) might make sense in countries with weak governments that show little commitment to development, but it makes little sense for the MCA. Because MCA-recipient nations have an established record of good development policies, the administration should give to them much more of the responsibility for programme design so that MCA-funded programmes are more consistent with their development strategies (Radelet 2003b).

Apparently, they are prepared to do just that, in ways that will differ significantly from current programmes. The new corporation will draw on the approach used by many foundations, in which recipients write proposals for various activities and only the best ideas in fact receive funding. Countries selected for the programme must develop a proposal describing the ways in which they would like to use MCA funds. Each proposal must describe the basic objectives, the justification for placing a high priority on the proposed activities, the consultative process between the government and non-government groups (civil society, NGOs, private sector and so on) in preparing the proposal, the strategy for implementing the programme, the costs, the contributions by other donors, and specific quantitative indicators of progress (MCC 2004c). The MCC expects that at least some of the activities in the proposal would be carried out by civil society or the private sector. Proposals could focus on one specific activity, but could also include several different separable activities (for example, building rural roads, water supplies, primary schools). Not all proposals would be accepted: the MCC believes that some will be accepted, some will be sent back for revision, and some will be rejected. The proposals that are accepted would provide the foundation for a three-year 'compact' agreement between the MCC and the recipient government that would lay out the commitments on both sides to carry out the specific activities and provide funding.

This approach is similar to that being used by some other new aid organizations, including the Global Alliance for Vaccines and Immunizations (GAVI) and the Global Fund to Fight AIDS, Tuberculosis, and Malaria (GFATM). It could also provide a process through which the US government could provide direct budget support and finance aid programmes (including recurrent costs) in addition to specific projects. This approach would be consistent with the recent efforts of other donors towards the 'pooling' of funds and towards sector-wide approaches (SWAps) to financing health and education programmes.[6]

This approach places the responsibility for development programmes where it belongs – with recipient nations, and not with aid agencies. If such an approach were implemented in a serious, non-superficial way, it would ensure that recipient governments and other agencies within MCA-recipient countries set their own priorities and develop their own strategies. It would also increase recipient-nation ownership of and commitment to development programmes, which could lead to better results. One key concern is that many MCA countries will initially lack the capacity to develop strong proposals and programmes, but the only way they will develop these capacities is if they are given the responsibility to do so, along with some funding for technical assistance in the early years.[7] Obviously, this approach can only work in those countries that have shown, and continue to show, a real commitment to development.

The final, and perhaps most crucial, element for the MCA to succeed is a serious monitoring and evaluation (M&E) process. Most aid agencies have weak and rather superficial M&E processes, and if the MCA follows this pattern, it is doomed to fail. Effective M&E is critical for keeping funded programmes on track to meet their goals; guiding the allocation of resources towards successful activities and away from failures; and ensuring that the lessons learned from ongoing activities – both successes and failures – inform the design of new projects and programmes.

Two distinct kinds of M&E are required: tracking finances; and monitoring substantive targets. Financial accountability should ensure that funds are spent where they are supposed to be spent, the project remains within budget, regulations on procurement and payment are followed, and funds are not stolen. Substantive accountability focuses on attaining specified benchmarks, such as purchasing a certain number of textbooks, training so many teachers, building a designated number of schools, increasing test scores by a certain amount, or increasing a school's graduation rate. Monitoring and evaluation must be incorporated into projects and programmes from the outset, not added as an afterthought halfway through the process. Both internal (carried out by the grantees) and external audit (carried out directly by the MCC or a contractor for the MCC) will be needed to ensure monitor compliance and high standards. A small number of programmes should be evaluated through randomized trials, as suggested by Kremer (2003) and others.

Of course, providing recipients with a greater say in programme design, implementation and evaluation entails some risks. Giving recipients greater flexibility can only work in countries that demonstrate the strongest commitment to development – exactly the MCA's target countries. With that greater flexibility, however, should come greater responsibility. The US should expect strong results from the MCA and hold grantees accountable for achieving the goals specified in their programmes. It should fund generously programmes that achieve results, and reduce funding for programmes that do not.

These issues and concerns go well beyond the MCA, since introducing a new MCA (even if it runs well) will not constitute a complete foreign assistance strategy for the US. Since only a small number of countries will receive MCA funding, the new programme is at best only a partial strategy for US foreign assistance. Indeed, because the MCA focuses on those countries with governments that have shown the strongest commitment to development, it essentially deals with the easiest cases among poor countries.

To really make US foreign aid work effectively, the Bush administration should develop comparable strategies for different groups of nations that fail to qualify for MCA funding, whether they just miss qualifying or are failed states mired in perpetual conflict. More broadly, the United States and other donors need to develop different approaches for different country circumstances, with varying design procedures, delivery mechanisms, objectives and M&E processes (Radelet 2004a). For example, in countries that just miss qualifying for the MCA, allowing recipients to write limited proposals focused on the specific areas where they fall short of qualification could strengthen traditional aid programmes. In countries with weaker governments, donor funding should continue to concentrate on specific projects, but with streamlined contracting and procurement procedures to make projects more cost effective. Where governments are weak (or part of the problem), aid should be channelled through NGOs and other service providers on the ground. In some circumstances, no aid should be provided at all. Of course, the risks will be greater and the results weaker in these countries. In effect, the MCA should be seen as just one of several tools available to address US goals in low-income countries.

Conclusion: a unilateral approach

The Bush administration's approach to foreign assistance has been decidedly unilateral. There are two major foreign aid initiatives: the MCA and the 'Emergency Plan for AIDS Relief', which will provide US$10 billion in new funds (in addition to US$5 billion already in the pipeline) up to 2009 fight HIV/AIDS around the world, with a special focus on Africa and the Caribbean.[8] Of the US$15 billion total in HIV/AIDS funding, the administration plans to provide just US$1 billion up to 2009 to the new multilateral GFATM. The rest of the funding will go through US bilateral programmes. The MCA is completely unilateral, and there has been very little consultation between the administration and other major donors to the programme. The proposed structure of these initiatives reveals the administration's distrust of both its own institutions and multilateral aid agencies.

With the MCA, the administration could have spearheaded a multilateral initiative with the same basic design: choosing countries selectively, delivering aid more efficiently with more recipient-country input, a smaller bureaucracy, and results-based management. There are three possible reasons why the administration chose the unilateral route:

- *Political.* In the face of mounting criticism that the US does too little to fight global poverty, the administration wanted to announce a significant, clearly American initiative at the International Conference on Financing for Development in Monterrey in March 2002. A multilateral effort, even if spearheaded by the US, would quickly have lost much of its brand identification as a US initiative.
- *Substance.* In two key areas of the MCA – country selection and the expectation of results – the administration does not have faith that the multilateral institutions will maintain high standards. It does not find convincing the claims by the World Bank that it has become more selective in its allocation decisions in recent years. Many in the administration believe that to turn the MCA over to a multilateral organization would doom it to large bureaucratic costs and weak results. In the administration's view, the US would be expected to be the largest donor but would cede much of its control to the other donors. For better or for worse, given a unilateral approach, the US can maintain complete control over all aspects of the programme. Hughes (2003) argues similarly about Australian aid, concluding that the bulk of it should be provided unilaterally, as she believes the multilateral institutions have failed to maintain high standards.
- *Ideological.* The unilateral approach to foreign aid is part of a much larger pattern of the administration's scepticism about multilateral approaches to foreign policy. There are many other examples, including terminating negotiations on the Kyoto Protocol on Climate Change, rejection of the Rome Statute of the International Criminal Court, and withdrawal from the antiballistic missile (ABM) treaty.

Several arguments in favour of a multilateral approach are laid out most clearly by van de Walle (2003) and Sperling and Hart (2003). First, a multilateral approach would be less cumbersome and confusing to recipient countries that are overwhelmed by the myriad proposal processes, financial mechanisms and reporting systems used by different donors. In September 2002, when former US Secretary of the Treasury Paul O'Neill asked Gerald Ssendaula, the Ugandan finance minister, what the biggest problem was with aid delivery, he replied 'It's too expensive', referring to the high bureaucratic costs of aid. A unilateral MCA would add one more to the mix rather than ease the burden for recipients. Second, a multilateral approach would provide the opportunity to better leverage US funds, since other donors would contribute more for each dollar that the US spends. While some donors may respond to the MCA by increasing their own aid allocations, they are likely to do so less than they would through a multilateral effort. Third, a multilateral approach reduces the pressure to allocate funds to diplomatic and strategic partners. However, the MCA's public selection process goes some distance towards easing these concerns. Moreover, multilateral organizations are far from immune to political pressures. They tend to take a different form, in which each member receives funding regardless of their commitment to good development policies, but the pressures exist none the less. Fourth, a multilateral approach would be less immune to earmarking, tied aid and other burdens imposed by Congress, although it would be subject to its own bureaucracy.

Under a best-case scenario, it is possible that a unilateral MCA could have a positive impact on other donors and on donor harmonization. By itself, the MCA, at US$5 billion, will be the equivalent of 9 per cent of current worldwide ODA flows of US$58 billion, not an overwhelming share but far from insignificant. Its proposed recipient-driven, programme-based approach could influence other donors to try similar strategies. Moreover, recipient proposals used for the MCA could be the basis for other donors co-financing similar activities. For example, consider the Education for All (EFA) initiative, in which donors agreed in the year 2000 to provide funding for countries that produced strong education strategies. The EFA strategies could be the basis for MCA funding in qualifying countries, with the US and other donors financing co-operatively parts of the same basic education plan.

Much will depend on the extent to which the new corporation is willing to work co-operatively with recipient governments and other donors to reduce the administrative burden on aid recipients. If the US stridently insists on using its own unique proposal format and reporting systems, the MCA will set back recent efforts to improve co-ordination. If, however, there is a serious effort to establish rigorous procedural norms that a majority of donors can accept, including expecting high performance standards, the MCA could be a small step in the right direction of improving donor harmonization and the performance of foreign aid.

At the time of writing, the MCA is only in its very early stages, having finally received approval and budgetary authority for its first year of operation. Many aspects of the programme are promising: its de-politicized country selection process (which should moderate, albeit not fully eliminate, political pressures in the selection process); its relatively large funding (US$1 billion in the first year); its country-owned proposal process; and its emphasis on achieving results. Of course, there is a very real possibility that the programme will not live up to its promise, and will ultimately operate like many other aid programmes, so some scepticism is warranted. But the MCA clearly signals a fundamental shift in the thinking behind US foreign aid programmes, holding out the possibility of larger and more effective foreign aid in the years to come. Working to achieve that goal is surely in America's best interests, as well as in the interests of low-income countries around the world.

Notes

An earlier version of this chapter with the same title was published in March 2004 by the Australian National University in its journal of policy analysis and reform, *Agenda*, 11(1): 53–70. Some parts of this chapter are drawn from an earlier paper 'Will the Millennium Challenge Account Be Different?', *The Washington Quarterly* (Spring 2003: 171–88), and from *Challenging Foreign Aid: A Policymaker's Guide to the Millennium Challenge Account.*

1 For more details, see the MCC website at www.mcc.gov. President Bush's speech that originally proposed the programme can be downloaded from www.whitehouse.gov/news/releases/2002/03/20020314-7.html.
2 Note that not all critics see too little harmonization as the problem. In particular, Easterly (2002) calls for more competition between donor agencies, rather than greater co-operation.
3 For a discussion of how the MCA fits into broader US foreign policy objectives, such as the war on terrorism, see Radelet (2003c).
4 As with any relationship, there are some exceptions to the rule. Some analysts point to China as a country with poor governance and strong development outcomes. China does score poorly on democracy-related indicators, but on other governance indicators (for example, political stability, government effectiveness, corruption, regulatory quality, and even rule of law), it scores well above the average for countries at similar levels of income (see World Bank Institute governance database at www.worldbank.org/wbi/governance/govdata2002/index.html).
5 See the press release announcing the countries at www.mcc.gov/Documents/ PR_Eligible.pdf
6 Berg (2002) argues against the movement towards aid-funded programmes (rather than projects) that underlies SWAps.
7 Berg (2002) argues that donors continually underestimate the depth of the capacity-building problem in developing countries. An earlier paper (Berg 1993) deals with this issue in depth and analyses the pitfalls and limitations of technical assistance.
8 The administration's major multilateral aid initiative is to push the World Bank and the regional banks towards providing more of their funds as grants. The US pledged an 18 per cent increase in its funding for the World Bank's concessional window over three years as part of the negotiations, conditional on the Bank meeting certain performance requirements.

References

African Development Bank (AfDB) (2001) 'Performance-based Allocation of ADF Resources'. Available at: www.adb.org/Documents/Policies/ADF/Performance_Based_ Allocation.

Asian Development Bank (ADB) (2001) 'Policy on Performance-based Allocation for Asian Development Fund Resources'. Available at: www.adb.org/documents/policies/ ADF/performance_based_allocation/default.asp.

Berg, E. (1993) *Rethinking Technical Cooperation: Reforms for Capacity Building in Africa*, New York: UNDP.

Berg, E. (2002) 'Increasing the Effectiveness of Aid: A Critique of Some Current Views', Paper prepared for the Expert Group Meeting, Department of Economic and Social Affairs, United Nations, 24–25 January.

Brainard, L., C. Graham, N. Purvis, S. Radelet and G. Smith (2003) *The Other War: Global Poverty and the Millennium Challenge Account*, Washington, DC: Brookings Institution and Center for Global Development.

Burnside, C. and D. Dollar (2000) 'Aid, Policies, and Growth', *American Economic Review*, 90(4): 847–68.

Clemens, M., S. Radelet and R. Bhavnani (2004) 'Counting Chickens When They Hatch: The Short-Term Effect of Aid on Growth', CGD Working Paper 44, Washington, DC: Center for Global Development.

Collier, P. and D. Dollar (2002) 'Aid Allocation and Poverty Reduction', *European Economic Review*, 45(1): 1–26.

Easterly, W. (2002) 'The Cartel of Good Intentions: Bureaucracy versus Markets in Foreign Aid', CGD Working Paper 4, Washington, DC: Center for Global Development.

Easterly, W., R. Levine and D. Roodman (2003) 'New Data, New Doubts: Revisiting "Aid, Policies and Growth"', CGD Working Paper 26, Washington, DC: Center for Global Development.

Hansen, H. and F. Tarp (2000) 'Aid Effectiveness Disputed', *Journal of International Development*, 12(3): 375–98.

Hughes, H. (2003) 'Aid Has Failed the Pacific', *Issue Analysis*, 33, Sydney: The Centre for Independent Studies. Available at: www.cis.org.au/issueanalysis /ia33/ia33.htm.

Kaufmann, D., A. Kraay and P. Zoido-Lobatón (1999) 'Governance Matters', WB Policy Research Working Paper 2196 (October), Washington, DC: World Bank.

Kremer, M. (2003) 'Randomized Evaluations of Educational Programs in Developing Countries: Some Lessons', *American Economic Review*, 93(2): 102–6.

Lancaster, C. (2000) *Transforming Foreign Aid: United States Assistance in the 21st Century*, Washington, DC: Institute for International Economics.

Lucas, S. and S. Radelet (2004) 'An MCA Scorecard: Who Qualified, Who Did Not, and the MCC Board's Use of Discretion'. Available at: www.cgdev.org/Research/MCA.cfm.

Millennium Challenge Corporation (MCC) (2004a) 'Report on the Criteria and Methodology for Determining the Eligibility of Candidate Countries for Millennium Challenge Account Assistance in FY 2004'. Available at: www.mca.gov/Documents/ methodology_report.pdf (downloaded March 2004).

Millennium Challenge Corporation (MCC) (2004b) 'Report on Countries That Are Candidates for Millennium Challenge Account Eligibility in FY 2004 and Countries That Are Not Candidates Because of Legal Prohibitions'. Available at: www.mca.gov/ Documents/candidate_report.pdf (downloaded March 2004).

Millennium Challenge Corporation (MCC) (2004c) 'Guidance for Developing Proposals for MCA Assistance in FY 2004'. Available at www.mcc.gov/Documents/Compact_Proposal_Guidelines.pdf (downloaded May 2004).

Radelet, S. (2003a) 'Will the Millennium Challenge Account Be Different?', *The Washington Quarterly*, Spring: 171–88.

Radelet, S. (2003b) *Challenging Foreign Aid: A Policymaker's Guide to the Millennium Challenge Account*, Washington, DC: Center for Global Development.

Radelet, S. (2003c) 'Bush and Foreign Aid', *Foreign Affairs*, 82(5): 104–17.

Radelet, S. (2004a) 'Aid Effectiveness and the Millennium Development Goals', CGD Working Paper 39, Washington, DC: Center for Global Development.

Radelet, S. (2004b) 'Which Countries Are Most Likely to Qualify for the MCA? An Update Using MCC Data', Washington, DC: Center for Global Development.

Sperling, G. and T. Hart (2003) 'A Better Way to Fight Global Poverty: Broadening the Millennium Challenge Account', *Foreign Affairs*, 82(2) (March/April): 9–14.

van de Walle, N. (2001) *African Economies and the Politics of Permanent Crisis, 1979–1999*, Cambridge: Cambridge University Press.

van de Walle, N. (2003) 'A Comment on the MCA Proposals', Washington: Center for Global Development. Available at: www.cgdev.org/briefs/vandewalle_20030109.pdf.

World Bank (1998) *Assessing Aid: What Works, What Doesn't, and Why*, Washington, DC: World Bank.

World Bank (2002) *A Case for Aid: Building a Consensus for Development Assistance*, Washington, DC: World Bank.

World Bank (2003a) *IDA's Performance-Based Allocation System: Current and Emerging Issues*, WB Report 27082 (October), Washington, DC: World Bank.

World Bank (2003b) *Allocating IDA Funds Based on Performance: Fourth Annual Report on IDA's Country Assessment and Allocation Process*, Washington, DC: World Bank.

9
Debt Relief: The Development and Poverty Impact

Tony Addison

Introduction

No development issue has quite captured the public imagination in the same way as debt relief. The juxtaposition of the billions of dollars owed and the grinding poverty of the countries concerned deliver an easy campaigning slogan and a seemingly straightforward policy recommendation: cancel the debt. But at the same time debt is also a complex issue, evident in measuring the stream of principal and interest payments over time (the net present value – NPV – of debt with, in turn, its assumptions about discount rates), the arcane language of 'decision points' and 'completion points', the vexed question of what we mean by 'debt sustainability (and the assorted ratios of debt-to-exports, debt-to-GDP, and debt-to-revenue), not to mention the interconnections with Poverty Reduction Strategy Papers (PRSPs) and the Millennium Development Goals (MDGs). Successive debt relief initiatives from the 1980s onwards with, since the mid-1990s, the heavily indebted poor countries (HIPC) initiative (later 'enhanced') and now the Multilateral Debt Relief Initiative (MDRI) have steadily become more generous – but just how generous remains a matter of dispute. And not all indebted poor countries are HIPCs, and not all poor countries have large debts. The issue of horizontal equity across countries as well as the problem of moral hazard therefore arise.

We are now in the middle of another large shift in the debt landscape as the debt-cancellation announced at the 2005 G8 summit in Gleneagles, Scotland comes to fruition in the form of the MDRI. This chapter discusses how the poor-country debt crisis arose as a result of low growth, uncoordinated donor-lending and the absence of a market that could mark down the debt's value and the implications of the HIPC initiative and MDRI for aid flows. I then turn to the development and poverty impact of debt relief, discussing the debt overhang and fiscal effects together with the respective roles of economics and politics in determining the amount of debt relief – and some of the dangers and opportunities that lie ahead. The chapter concludes by

216

emphasizing the importance of getting poor countries connected effectively to the international capital market, where they can share in the growth of global portfolio flows and foreign direct investment (FDI).

The present situation

Much ink has been spilled on the causes of high-indebtedness in poor countries and ways to resolve it (Box 9.1 presents a small selection of views). But the issue ultimately comes down to this; successful sovereign debt management depends on a country's ability to achieve high growth and foreign-exchange generation – thereby containing debt-to-GDP, debt-to-exports and debt-to-revenues at reasonable ('sustainable') levels. Otherwise the fiscal position becomes unsustainable.[1] This is the lesson of the 1980s: heavy debtors such as South Korea managed to outgrow their debts in ways that the more inward-orientated Latin American economies did not, and Africa is fundamentally the same.

Box 9.1   Viewpoints on debt and debt relief

'There is a compelling economic argument for borrowing when the rate of return on these investments exceeds the cost of capital. And there is a corresponding compelling political argument: the gains from borrowing will be felt now, while the problems of repayment will occur under someone else's watch' (Joseph Stiglitz 2005: 21).

'[T]he current system's dysfunctionality arises in part from the fact that donors are involved too intrusively in a country, in the name of aid effectiveness ... deep debt relief will be an important step on the road to achieving greater toughness and more of an arm's length relationship on aid flows' (Ravi Kanbur 2000: 422).

'[D]ebt problems can in large part be attributed to uncoordinated lending associated with a poorly functioning international institutional framework ... It is hard to explain the debt and financing problems of low-income countries in the context of a single (altruistic) lender or donor ... Such a lender would presumably have lent prudently and avoided excessive debt build-ups' (Stijn Claessens 2005: 140–1).

'The entire edifice of loans is built upon presumptions of high rates of growth that will not occur unless more fundamental reform takes place within financial institutions and LDC economies as a whole ... USAID abandoned sovereign loan programmes 25 years ago. A number of other donors continue to lend money to countries that cannot repay them' (Andrew Natsios 2006: 137).

'Debt forgiveness grants aid to those recipients that have best proven their ability to misuse that aid. Debt relief is futile for countries with unchanged government behavior. The same mismanagement of funds that caused the high debt will prevent the aid sent through debt relief from reaching the truly poor' (Bill Easterly 2001: 136).

'For all the [Africa] Commission's many sensible recommendations, it is a reminder of how previous plans died when exposed to rich country self-interest ... Yet great scepticism is justified for any proposals driven by London, which continues to leach African wealth such as the billions of dollars processed through British financial institutions by the late Nigerian dictator General Sani Abacha and his associates' (Michael Peel 2005: 2).

'Debt sustainability has, until now, been narrowly assessed according to a country's ability to pay in terms of its export earnings – regardless of other demands on public funds. This prevents governments in many developing countries meeting the basic needs of their citizens. A new approach to debt sustainability is urgently needed in order to reduce poverty and promote sustainable development' (New Economics Foundation 2006: 5).

'Given the extent of looting and repression by many dictators, it seems plausible that the efficiency gains from preventing odious debt are much larger than the efficiency gains from solving debt overhang. Loan sanctions against such dictators could potentially prevent some of this borrowing' (Seema Jayachandran and Michael Kremer 2006: 91).

Of the forty HIPCs, thirty-three are in Sub-Saharan Africa (SSA). Africa's growth is improving, but Africa is far from achieving any big breakthrough; total factor productivity (TFP) has been negative for the three decades 1970–80, 1980–90 and 1990–2000 (the only region for which this is the case) with the two big sources of productivity growth – capital deepening and labour productivity growth – being negative since 1980 (see TFP calculations by Crafts 2006: 26). Whatever the desirability of the Bretton Woods institutions' reforms in terms of economic efficiency and poverty reduction, they do not appear (as yet) to have pushed Africa on to any kind of growth fast-track. Environmental fragility, tropical diseases, limited human capital and inadequate physical infrastructure all constrain growth. And the production of tradables (both exportables and import-substitutes) does not recover quickly when high political uncertainty discourages private investment – particularly in the 'post-conflict' debtors.

When private creditors hold the debt of an individual, company or country in default, the loan is eventually written down on the creditor's books. The Brady Plan ultimately reduced Latin America's debts in this way, with the price of a country's debt reflecting the secondary market's assessment of repayment prospects (including the government's chances of reducing absorption below national income to make the requisite net transfer abroad, and the limit on how far consumption has to fall before the political pain becomes unbearable). In contrast, Africa's debt is mainly the legacy of concessional loans given during the 1980s to support 'structural adjustment', together with earlier aid-project lending (Nigeria has the largest commercial debt). This includes bilateral debt, but most importantly, money owed to the International Development Association (IDA), the IMF and the African Development Bank. Official creditors have maintained the debt at its full value on their books until written off (debt relief is valued at its NPV using a discount rate to take account of its grant element). Therefore official debt is always larger – and any debt relief always looks more generous – than would be the case in a secondary market. Some imputations of the market value of HIPC debt put it as low as 28 cents in the dollar (Cohen 2000: 22).

Successive debt initiatives

This is not the place for a detailed history of debt relief (instead, see Birdsall and Deese 2005). Suffice it to say that, by the mid-1990s, the debt build-up was alarming and the HIPC initiative was launched in 1996 and significantly enhanced in 1999 (Kanbur 2000; Addison *et al.* 2004). The main criterion for eligibility is a high debt-to-export ratio (originally set at 250 per cent and later reduced to 150 per cent, in 1999) and high ratios for debt-to-GDP and debt-to-revenue are also included in the IMF and World Bank's overall assessment of debt sustainability. Many observers have argued that these debt-sustainability criteria are essentially arbitrary (see, for example, Sachs 2002: 276). Given the uncertainties associated with predicting the trajectory of the main foreign-exchange earner – commodities – it is difficult to disagree with this assessment, and the concept of debt sustainability will always be a 'grey area' (this is not, however, to deny the importance of further technical work in refining debt sustainability, since benchmarks are needed around which to construct a debate about each country's prospects: see, for example, Kraay and Nehru 2006). The criteria have become more generous over time, notably with the enhanced HIPC initiative and most recently with the introduction of the MDGs, which must now be taken into account in debt assessment (Vallée and Vallée 2005). And debt relief has come to be seen as not just an economic instrument but also as a tool for encouraging political transition, including conflict resolution (Addison and Murshed 2003). With a PRSP in place (criticism of the first PRSPs has led to a more participatory process in recent years) and the IFIs satisfied with the pace of economic reform, a country reaches decision point: debt relief is provided first by reducing interest payments (at decision point) followed by cutting the debt stock itself (at completion point).

Who is in, and who is out, of the HIPC initiative raises questions of horizontal equity among debtors, as well as 'moral hazard'. There is a group of non-HIPC debtors who may be eligible for HIPC inclusion; these are the so-called 'sunset clause' countries and four of them (Eritrea, Haiti, the Kyrgyz Republic and Nepal) were recently reclassified as HIPCs. There are also 'grey zone' countries (Bangladesh, Bhutan, Sri Lanka and Tonga) whose debt ratios fall within a 10 per cent range around the HIPC thresholds (IMF and World Bank 2004; IMF and World Bank 2005: 2).

Nigeria's status has been an anomaly until the recently concluded debt relief agreement. Despite Africa's largest external debt, Nigeria's classification as an 'IDA-blend' country put it outside the HIPC initiative (it has now been reclassified as IDA-only as part of the debt-relief package).[2] Only 8 per cent of its US$34 billion debt is multilateral; and 80 per cent is owed to Paris Club creditors – and most of that to just three countries: France, Germany and the UK (Moss *et al.* 2005). Payments to Paris Club creditors alone exceeded public spending on health, and many Nigerians asked why Iraq and not Nigeria was receiving debt relief. By 2005, the need for economic reform – improving the fiscal management of oil revenues, for example – was being submerged by increasingly strident calls for debt repudiation along the lines of Argentina. For donors, it became urgent to help President Olusegun Obasanjo's team of modernizing technocrats to gain acceptance for reform, and the 2005 Africa Commission report backed extension of debt relief to Nigeria under a wider 'debt compact', arguing, essentially, that the deep poverty of Nigeria's 130 million people could not be ignored. In summary, Nigeria illustrates the fact that the political dimension of debt relief is as important as its economic dimension. A strong global oil price enabled Nigeria to build its foreign exchange reserves (to about 60 per cent of its external debt) thereby facilitating the buy-back in 2006 of a substantial portion of the commercial debt at a discount (see further discussion below).

The Multilateral Debt Relief Initiative

The 2005 summit of G8 leaders proposed full cancellation of the debt owed to the three multilateral lenders by countries that have reached, or will eventually reach, their completion points under the enhanced HIPC initiative. The IFIs subsequently fleshed out the G8 proposal, resulting in MDRI, which began on 1 July 2006. In essence, countries at completion point get their debts reduced to the level defined as sustainable under the Enhanced HIPC Initiative, and then the remainder owed to the IMF, the World Bank and the AfDF cancelled under MDRI.[3] Low-income non-HIPCs are also eligible for MDRI, at least in the case of IMF debts (eligibility for full cancellation of IMF debts has been extended to all countries with a per capita income of less than US$380, on the basis of the Fund's principle of 'uniformity in resource use').[4]

Table 9.1 Enhanced HIPC initiative: list of participating and potentially eligible countries

Completion point countries (20) currently eligible for MDRI	Decision-point countries (9)	Pre-decision-point countries (11)
Benin	Burundi	Central African Republic
Bolivia	Chad	Comoros
Burkina Faso	Democratic Republic of	Côte d'Ivoire
Cameroon	the Congo (DRC)	Eritrea
Ethiopia	Republic of Congo	Haiti
Ghana	(Congo-Brazzaville)	Kyrgyz Republic
Guyana	The Gambia	Liberia
Honduras	Guinea	Nepal
Madagascar	Guinea-Bissau	Somalia
Malawi	São Tomé and Príncipe	Sudan
Mali	Sierra Leone	Togo
Mauritania		
Mozambique		
Nicaragua		
Niger		
Rwanda		
Senegal		
Tanzania		
Uganda		
Zambia		

Notes: *To reach decision point*, countries must have: a track record of macroeconomic stability; have prepared an Interim Poverty Reduction Strategy (through a participatory process); and cleared any outstanding arrears. The amount of debt relief required to bring debt indicators to HIPC thresholds is calculated. Then countries start to receive debt relief on a provisional basis.
   To reach completion point, countries must: maintain macroeconomic stability (under a PRGF-supported programme); undertake structural and social reforms; implement a Poverty Reduction Strategy satisfactorily (for one year). The country's creditors then provide debt relief irrevocably.
Source: www.worldbank.org.

Among the forty HIPCs, twenty are initially eligible for 100 per cent debt cancellation (see Table 9.1); that is, they are at their completion point (Benin, Bolivia, Burkina Faso, Cameroon, Ethiopia, Ghana, Guyana, Honduras, Madagascar, Malawi, Mali, Mauritania, Mozambique, Nicaragua, Niger, Rwanda, Senegal, Tanzania, Uganda and Zambia).[5] Cameroon and Malawi were granted completion point status in 2006 after further economic reform, particularly in the area of public expenditure management (Mauritania was included earlier, with full debt cancellation also being a condition of full debt relief). Two low-income non-HIPCs (Cambodia and Tajikistan) also receive MDRI relief of their IMF debts.

Of the remaining twenty HIPCs, nine have reached their decision point and will be eligible for debt cancellation once they complete their reforms (see Table 9.1). Of the countries at decision point, the Bank and IMF consider that two (São Tomé and Príncipe, and Sierra Leone) could reach completion point soon (IMF and World Bank 2006: 1). The remaining decision-point countries have stalled on economic reform in one way or another (usually in fiscal management), and at the time of writing, Chad is suffering a very serious political crisis. The eleven pre-decision-point countries are in a range of complex political situations: Eritrea (tense relations with Ethiopia following the 1998–2000 border war); Haiti (hesitant post-conflict reconstruction and democratization); Nepal (civil war); Somalia (no internationally recognized government); Sudan (peace agreement with the southern secessionists but genocide in Darfur); and Côte d'Ivoire (tentative peace).

For the completion-point countries, MDRI amounts to US$37 billion in debt relief over forty years (World Bank 2006), somewhat lower than the estimate in late 2005 of US$42.5 billion (IMF and World Bank 2005). The average NPV debt-to-export ratio of these eighteen countries will fall from 180 per cent (after HIPC relief) to about 52 per cent after implementation of MDRI (IMF and World Bank 2005: 2). Following completion, annual gross assistance flows from the IDA and AfDF to a country will be reduced by the amount of debt relief during the year that debt relief takes place, and subsequent aid flows then depend on a country's performance. Since debt-savings are netted out of future IDA flows, there is no net impact on cash flow. We now turn to debt relief's relationship to the bigger picture for official development assistance (ODA).

The implications for aid flows

Debt relief (both HIPC and non-HIPC) is having a significant impact on the volume of ODA. Debt relief accounted for most of the increase in aid over 2004–5: ODA from OECD-DAC members rose by 31.4 per cent, to US$106.5 billion, in 2005, with aid in the form of debt relief grants increasing by more than 400 per cent (see Table 9.2 using data from OECD-DAC). A large portion of the increased debt relief is accounted for by debt forgiveness grants for Iraq and Nigeria (US$14 billion and US$5 billion, respectively), debt relief that is outside the HIPC initiative.[6] OECD-DAC predicts that total ODA will fall over 2006–7 as debt relief declines.

OECD-DAC includes debt relief for Nigeria and Iraq in the 2005 ODA total. Most of the debt relief for these two countries counts as debt relief because the original loans went out as 'other official flows' (OOF) and not as ODA. Consequently, the write-down can count as ODA, whereas if a concessional loan goes out as ODA, its write-down does not count as ODA again. However, a coalition of NGOs (including Oxfam, ActionAid and Save the Children) argues that this inflates the EU aid effort in particular, since much of this

Table 9.2   Share of debt relief grants in net official development assistance (preliminary data for 2005)

	ODA US$ millions, current	Of which: debt relief grants	Percentage change 2004 to 2005[a] without debt relief grants
Australia	1,666	9	6.1
Austria	1,552	901	9.0
Belgium	1,975	471	17.2
Canada	3,731	455	17.8
Denmark	2,107	20	0.8
Finland	897	150	11.6
France	10,059	3,199	0.0
Germany	9,915	3,573	−9.8
Greece	535	–	11.4
Rep. of Ireland	692	0	11.4
Italy	5,053	1,680	40.0
Japan	13,101	3,553	12.1
Luxembourg	264	–	8.4
Netherlands	5,131	410	16.6
New Zealand	274	–	18.7
Norway	2,775	25	12.6
Portugal	367	3	−65.1
Spain	3,123	498	13.7
Sweden	3,280	53	20.3
Switzerland	1,771	224	0.1
United Kingdom	10,754	3,699	−1.7
United States	27,457	4,073	16.2
Total DAC	106,477	22,995	8.7
Memo: items included in the above			
EC	9,629	–	8.7
DAC EU countries combined	55,704	14,657	3.8
G7 countries	80,068	20,232	8.9
Non-G7 countries	26,409	2,763	8.3
Non-DAC countries			
Czech Republic	131	10	15.8
Korea	744	–	57.1
Poland	283	0	101.0
Slovak Republic	56	–	87.7

Note: [a]Taking into account both inflation and exchange rate movements.
Source: OECD–DAC website, www.oecd.org/dac, 30 March 2006.

relief is for export credit debts – the purpose of which was to subsidize the commercial operations of European companies during Iraq and Nigeria's dictatorships (Eurodad 2006). Thus, while this debt relief for Iraq and Nigeria meets some of the ODA classification criteria (both are on the list of DAC recipients, the relief contains a grant element, and it is given to governments) its purpose was not developmental (a key ODA criterion) in the view of the NGO coalition.[7] Accordingly, ActionAid (2005) labels such debt relief 'phantom aid'.

Whether debt relief should be counted as aid is a thorny issue, and OECD-DAC plans to reopen the debate about what constitutes aid in 2007. One line of argument focuses on the budgetary space that increases by the relief of export credit debts (or indeed, loans given for military and political purposes) which is then available for development spending: it is not the *purpose* of the original loan that matters so much in deciding whether debt relief constitutes aid, but whether the release of *resources* is for development (a key DAC criterion for ODA). The counter-argument is that, by defaulting, the country unilaterally releases those resources for development, irrespective of whether the creditor keeps the debt on its own books. Essentially, creditors are maintaining the full value of the loan on their books (and for much longer than any private creditor would do) irrespective of whether the debtor can realistically pay, and then counting the write-downs in the value of those assets as aid. Accounting regulations force commercial lenders eventually to write-down the value of non-performing loans, and if official lenders had followed this practice – perhaps imputing a value to the debt using the commercial debt market as a guide – then donors would not today be able to make such large claims of generosity. The fundamental point is: did the debt stand any chance of being paid? It is this larger, systemic issue that underlies the principle adopted in the 2002 Monterrey Consensus that debt relief should not detract from, but should be additional to, ODA.

The scale of debt relief has given rise to much discussion (and some alarm) over the impact on the capital base of IDA. The cost to IDA of MDRI is US$42.5 billion over forty years (rising to US$56.5 billion if the 'sunset countries qualify as HIPCs).[8] Debt relief yet to be provided under the HIPC initiative is US$11.7 billion. IDA's assets stand at US$144.5 billion. MDRI and the remaining HIPC initiative debt relief will together reduce IDA's capital base by about 37 per cent over forty years if not replenished (46 per cent if the sunset countries are included). The financial impact in the first decade (2007–16) of MDRI is also sizeable: US$8.9 billion which, together with HIPC initiative relief, amounts to some 14 per cent of IDA's capital base. Note that MDRI's first decade ends just after the MDG target-date (2015), so any reduction in IDA would reduce the chances of the MDG's success.[9] However, while MDRI's impact on IDA's capital base appears dramatic it must be set in the context of IDA's replenishment.

With regard to replenishment, the G8's commitment to preserving multi-lateral financing while cancelling debt is somewhat ambiguous, and three levels of 'commitment' can be observed. First, there are 'unconditional' commitments to replenish IDA in its next round. This is money that is budgeted and available. Then there are conditional 'commitments': money that is, in principle, available but has to be allocated by finance ministries. Finally, and weakest of all, are 'political commitments' to maintain IDA funding at its present level over the next forty years (these must be ratified by parliaments so that the finance minister can write to the multilateral lenders making the commitment). Smaller donors are worried that the political comments of the G8 donors (who account for about 75 per cent of IDA) are too vague, and that, *ex post*, there will be a sizeable IDA shortfall. In summary, whether debt relief has a negative long-term impact on IDA's financial standing depends on the future course of replenishments, and there could well be some tension within the donor community over this. We must therefore hope that the ethical imperative of ensuring sufficient finance to meet the MDGs prevails in future decisions on IDA's replenishment.

The impact of debt relief

The development impact of debt relief works through two major channels. One is the impact on incentives for private investment, since a large debt-overhang is almost always associated with macroeconomic disequilibrium (which in its turn distorts and undermines private investment incentives) and therefore debt relief should stimulate investment when associated with economic reform. But the scale of this effect is difficult to pin down, not least because *expectations* play a critical role in private investment decisions – and the high uncertainty that continues when reform is hesitant can dampen any positive investment response from debt relief per se. Sudden shifts in property rights are also problematic. The government of Bolivia recently nationalized the natural gas industry (the largest sector for FDI), arguing that their earlier privatization was unconstitutional. This could discourage foreign capital inflow, thereby offsetting the positive investment impact of reaching completion point status under the HIPC initiative.[10]

The relief of commercial sovereign debt – the focus of the 1980s debt overhang literature – will usually generate fresh inflows of private capital (both portfolio and FDI) to finance physical investment, since country-risk premiums fall upon relief. Relief of official debt can do this if the country has a sovereign credit rating (or makes it easier to obtain one). This has been a big consideration in the Nigerian debt deal; Nigeria was able to obtain a sovereign rating of BB– from Fitch and Standard & Poor's (the same rating as Ukraine and Venezuela). However, for the smaller and poorer debtors, there can be no certainty that they will become any more attractive for private capital (which may in any case have earlier discounted the value of debt relief when the prospects of eventual repayment were judged to be low). Their prospects for new inflows to finance new investment then depend on new ODA flows, which will mainly fund public infrastructure investment (thereby having an indirect stimulative effect on private investment). The empirical literature generally finds that ODA 'additionality' is important in determining whether debt relief has a significant and positive effect on investment and growth (Hansen 2004).

Fiscal management and governance

The fiscal effect of debt relief is the second major channel connecting debt to development. By releasing resources that would otherwise be spent on debt servicing, spending on poverty alleviation and on development is expected to rise (although the standard comparison of such spending with debt servicing almost always overestimates the benefit, since the debt is unlikely ever to be fully serviced: this follows from the 'market-value' point made earlier). But the weak part in this channel is the fiscal system itself. Poor countries need good systems of public expenditure management and domestic revenue mobilization if they are to invest effectively in the services and infrastructure of most benefit to the poor (and national development, more broadly), meet the recurrent costs of those investments, and build effective and democratically-accountable states. On the fiscal deficit side, they need to be able to run expansionary fiscal policies without financing these through inflationary monetary expansion. Over time, the domestic debt market can grow (and the attractiveness of their debt to foreign investors can increase), thereby providing more scope for bond-financed public-spending growth – and reducing their very high dependence on ODA to meet the expenditure–revenue gap. None of this is easy to achieve, requiring as it does major institutional overhaul in the context of often chronically weak states (Kayizzi-Mugerwa 2003). Nevertheless, it remains imperative. Difficulties in fiscal reform are preventing Burundi, Chad, DR Congo, the Gambia, Guinea and Guinea-Bissau (all decision-point countries) from reaching HIPC completion (IMF and World Bank 2006: 2).

For the HIPCs that have reached the decision point, the data suggest a rise in poverty-reducing expenditure, as classified by the IMF and the World Bank (2006: 29), and reproduced here in Table 9.3. This is welcome news, but all such numbers must be treated with caution; budgeted resources frequently do not reach intended beneficiaries (Reinikka and Svensson 2002) and, in contrast to the conclusions of the Bank–Fund study just cited, Chauvin and Kraay (2005) find little evidence that debt relief has had a positive effect on the level and composition of public spending in HIPCs. And even well-spent money may not achieve the desired outcomes. Take health, for example. More funding for training health personnel will show up as a desirable rise in health expenditure, but whether health indicators improve proportionately to spending depends on the effectiveness of those personnel (that is, on the health-care system in which they operate) and, indeed, on whether they remain in their own country once trained. There are more Malawian doctors in my home city – Manchester – than in all of Malawi.[11] Much of the discussion of MDG-financing assumes that the key factor in MDG service

Table 9.3 Summary of poverty-reducing expenditure by the 29 countries that have reached the decision point

	1999	2000–1	2002	2003	2004	2005	2006	2007	2008
	Average		Actual			Preliminary		Projected	
Poverty-reducing expenditure[a]	(US\$, millions)								
African countries	4,140	4,466	5,491	7,077	8,333	10,776	12,114	13,273	13,978
Latin-American countries	1,800	1,963	2,055	2,074	2,378	2,717	3,000	3,174	3,369
Total	5,940	6,428	7,546	9,151	10,712	13,493	15,114	16,446	17,347
Ratio of poverty-reducing expenditure to government revenue[b]	(Percentages)								
African countries	38.6	40.4	41.9	43.1	43.0	45.7	46.7	47.5	46.0
Latin-American countries	47.6	49.6	52.3	50.7	49.8	47.9	49.4	49.7	50.0
Total	40.0	42.7	44.3	44.6	44.3	46.1	47.2	48.0	46.7
Ratio of poverty-reducing expenditure to GDP[b]									
African countries	5.5	5.6	6.1	6.8	7.0	8.0	8.3	8.4	8.3
Latin-American countries	10.8	10.2	10.7	10.4	11.0	11.5	11.7	11.8	11.8
Total	6.4	6.5	6.9	7.4	7.6	8.5	8.8	8.9	8.8

Notes: [a] Data are not available for all countries, for all years. The following data are missing: Burundi 1999; DR Congo 1999–2001; Republic of Congo 1999–2002 and 2005–10; Guinea-Bissau 1999–2001; Sierra Leone 1999; and São Tomé and Príncipe for 2000. No data replacement methodology was applied. The coverage of poverty-reducing expenditure varies across countries, but is generally consistent with the definition in the PRSP and the budget. In some countries, the definition of poverty-reducing expenditure has evolved over time to include more sectors; therefore, some of the increase in such spending over the 1999–2003 period may reflect changes in the definition.
[b] Weighted averages.

Sources: World Bank and IMF (2006) using HIPC country documents; and World Bank and IMF staff estimates.

supply – skilled labour – is a fixed, rather than a mobile factor. This is not an argument for giving up: instead, we must redouble efforts to ensure that pro-poor services really do improve.

A great deal comes down to 'governance'. Donors continue to struggle with recipient corruption, strategies wavering between using aid to induce reform (for example, establishing anti-corruption commissions) to withholding aid to punish corrupt politicians. Overall, however, the effect of corruption on aid allocations appears to be weak; Svensson (2000) finds no evidence that donors allocate aid towards the less corrupt, for example. This is one reason why the HIPCs, with their legacy of past aid loans, are found disproportionately among the worst performers in the Transparency International Index of Corruption (TIIC), with one (Chad) at the very bottom. Allowing the Republic of Congo (Congo-Brazzaville) to reach decision point status in 2006 was especially controversial: the IMF argued that extra resources from debt relief would enable Congo-Brazzaville to strengthen anti-corruption institutions, but the Fund is felt to be unduly optimistic, since the country's corruption appears to start at the very top (Moss 2006). To make progress on debt relief, 'post-conflict' Sierra Leone has to deal with its still-resilient corruption problem – otherwise the country will remain stuck at the HIPC pre-decision point indefinitely. (Another 'post-conflict' country, Liberia, was granted debt relief in 2007.)

Large amounts of oil revenue are 'missing' from the fiscal accounts of Nigeria and São Tomé and Príncipe, while Chad and the World Bank were recently in dispute over the revenue-allocating mechanism created as a condition of the Bank financing Chad's oil pipeline project. More of the revenue is going to the military to fend off an intensifying rebellion – interconnecting with the Darfur crisis in neighbouring Sudan – and Chad illustrates the point that the absence of a robust 'social contract' underlies weak policy and the debt problem (Addison and Rahman 2004).[12] For the oil producers, initiatives such as the Extractive Industries Transparency Initiative (EITI), which was championed by the Africa Commission, need more action on the 'supply-side' of corruption, including vigorous prosecution of those from the North who offer bribes in the South.

Debt relief and other instruments for poverty reduction

Debt relief, like other forms of development finance, is subject to diminishing returns. As we move down the HIPC list from the completion countries to the pre-decision countries (see Table 9.1), so the value of an additional dollar of debt relief to poverty reduction almost certainly falls, since essentially we slide down the scale of states that are 'development effective' (in particular, the quality of the fiscal system declines markedly). The marginal return to poverty reduction will be positive in Mozambique, Tanzania and Uganda, which are building their institutions (with budget support eventually taking over from project aid) but zero for Somalia, which has no internationally recognized state (it would merely be an accounting transfer within donor governments and international financial institutions) and close to zero (or even negative) in Myanmar, which has a predatory state.

Debt relief is a state-to-state transfer that is then *intermediated* into poverty reduction by a chain of institutions of varying effectiveness. In contrast, donor-funded micro-finance programmes use NGOs (or quasi-state bodies) as the intermediary, often with good results, including reaching some of the chronically poor (those stuck in deep and persistent poverty) (Hulme and Arun 2003). Micro-finance is also subject to diminishing returns (not all of the chronic poor are able to make good use of it, for example), but diminishing returns are likely to set in faster for debt relief, especially in very fragile states – which cannot cope with the allocation and disbursement of very large amounts of debt relief and ODA until institution-building progresses. In summary, neither micro-finance nor debt relief constitute miracle cures. Each has its strengths (micro-finance improves livelihoods, while debt relief funds services and infrastructure) and diminishing returns eventually set in for both.

Figure 9.1 illustrates the issue. Assume two uses of a fixed amount of donor money (measured by the horizontal axis along the distance $O_d \leftrightarrow O_m$). The respective vertical axes measure the rates of return (to poverty reduction) from debt relief (left axis) and an alternative use of the money, for example micro-finance (right axis). An efficient allocation of donor money will be

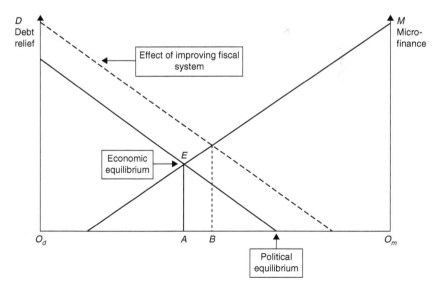

Figure 9.1 Allocating resources across debt relief versus an alternative (micro-insurance)

that which equalizes returns to debt relief and micro-finance at the margin; this is point E (which we label the 'economic equilibrium'). Of the total available funding, $O_d \rightarrow A$ is then allocated to debt relief and $A \leftarrow O_m$ to micro-finance. An improvement in intermediation can shift the schedules, raising the marginal return: in debt relief's case, constructing a better (pro-poor) fiscal system shifts the schedule right (shown by the dashed line) and a larger share ($O_d \rightarrow B$) can now be allocated to debt relief.

However, the debt agenda has become increasingly politically-driven, especially with the 2005 G8 summit taking relief beyond the level earlier identified as necessary to reach debt sustainability under the enhanced HIPC initiative – the political objective largely being to drive the debt stock of HIPCs down to zero, irrespective of whether there is a better use for the money. The 'political equilibrium' therefore probably lies to the right of the economic equilibrium in Figure 9.1, in the range where the marginal return to the alternative (micro-finance) exceeds that of debt relief, perhaps including the point at which further debt relief yields zero (economic) return.

The intention here is not to undermine the case for substantial and generous debt relief, nor to deny the importance of political considerations in determining debt relief. Rather, it is to emphasize the importance of keeping constantly in mind the alternative uses of donor money in the cause of poverty reduction – as more money is allocated to one intermediating instrument rather than to others. Mobilizing more development finance in total will ease the dilemmas of choice, but can never completely remove them. This point also relates to horizontal equity across poor countries. As stated earlier, debt relief for many of the pre-decision-point HIPCs will have limited impact: what Somalia needs now is not debt relief, but humanitarian assistance and effective international peace-keeping to support the eventual resurrection of the Somali state. But the allocation of resources (and attention) to this crucial set of tasks is minimal when set alongside the amount devoted to debt relief. This is true of other conflict and post-conflict countries as well.

Dangers and opportunities ahead

The HIPCs are overwhelmingly dependent on primary commodities for their export earnings, as are most of the non-HIPC debtors, including the sunset clause countries (with the exception of Bangladesh, which has significant manufacturing). Producers of oil and gas (for example, Bolivia, Congo-Brazzaville and São Tomé and Príncipe) as well as metals (for example, Tanzania and Zambia) are now experiencing a strong upturn in export prices after more than a decade of decline, with many agricultural commodity prices up as well. Optimists talk of a commodities 'super-cycle' lasting a decade at least, and driven by strong world demand. Pessimists note the propensity of such booms to collapse as rising prices eventually choke-off demand, as they did in the 1980s (and the terms of trade for net oil importers who export agricultural commodities or metals depends on the relative size of the different – import and export – price effects, and the overall balance of payments effect depends on the size of the supply and demand responses).

Countries have found it difficult to manage commodity-price booms (Botswana is the exception). At the time of the previous boom in the 1970s, many countries treated rising commodity prices as being a permanent feature rather than a temporary windfall, and spent unwisely (often consuming rather than investing), thereby causing macroeconomic disequilibrium – leaving economies in a precarious position when commodity prices inevitably turned down (Collier and Gunning 1999). If this is the start of a commodity super-cycle (which depends largely on China's future growth rate), then it represents an extraordinary opportunity, but also a dangerous moment, since past mistakes could be repeated – potentially on an even larger scale.

The last few years have been very favourable to sovereign borrowers; in early 2006, emerging market sovereign spreads over US Treasuries (as measured by JP Morgan's EMBI+ index of Emerging Market bonds) were less than 2 per cent, compared to 10 per cent in late 2002. But Africa, apart from South Africa, is largely absent from the portfolio of the typical bond fund. With better prospects for their export prices, poorer countries may become attractive to the international bond market that is 'reaching for yield' (although the political risks for lenders remain high). If such borrowing is invested wisely in human capital formation and well-chosen infrastructure it can accelerate growth and economic diversification, thereby facilitating debt service: but if it is wasted (as in the past) then countries will put themselves into an unsustainable position when, inevitably, commodity prices turn down again. And, for the oil producers, better macroeconomic management is imperative; the 'Dutch disease' effects of an oil boom can, by moving the real exchange rate against tradables, undermine external debt-service, as Nigeria demonstrated in the 1980s.[13] Managing Angola's oil boom is proving especially difficult, and the country has a history of ill-conceived borrowing using oil as collateral, dating from the civil war years.

Conclusions

The HIPCs that have reached their completion points account for 64 per cent of the HIPC initiative assistance to be delivered by creditors (IMF and World Bank 2006: 1). We are therefore much further down the road than just a few years ago, and the MDRI has recently added further impetus. Ultimately, debt is the product of a larger picture of global finance for poor countries, including the governance of the international aid architecture and the role of the Bretton Woods institutions, which we have only touched upon (see instead, Atkinson 2004, and Sagasti *et al.* 2005). And the main challenges going forward are scaling-up aid, reducing aid volatility, achieving increased aid effectiveness and – the overarching goal – improved governance, especially in the use of public money, whether provided by taxation, debt relief or new ODA.

Given the very high social returns from investing in primary education, basic health care, and safe water and sanitation – rates of return that exceed concessional, and indeed commercial, rates of interest – it makes sense to borrow both domestically and externally for poverty reduction and national development. Historically, no nation has developed without creating deep and liquid domestic markets for government debt, thereby facilitating non-inflationary financing of the fiscal deficit as well as better management of output and employment across the business cycle. As a government's credit profile improves, its debt denominated in domestic currency eventually finds a market with international investors, allowing it to expand beyond the initially narrow base of demand in its own financial system. And there are other benefits as well, not least the deepening of the financial sector that accompanies the creation of a larger and more liquid market for government debt, thereby allowing domestic banks, insurance companies and pension funds to match their assets and liabilities better. This in turn improves their ability to lend and invest in the private sector, the main motor for output and employment growth.

Therefore, the objective of action in the area of debt and development cannot be to 'end debt for ever'. To do so would have a very high opportunity cost in terms of poverty reduction and economic growth forgone. Rather, it must be to move countries out of their present impasse with creditors, make their debt positions sustainable (that is, enable debt to be serviced without endangering economic and social objectives) and to develop marketable debt instruments for sovereign, corporate and municipal borrowers that are attractive to both domestic and international investors. The history of the emerging economies shows that this can be done, but only by careful macroeconomic management, better governance, and the judicious use of well-targeted and generous international assistance.

Notes

This study was originally prepared for the Economic Council of Sweden Conference on 'Foreign Aid Policy', Stockholm, 15 May 2006. Originally published in the *Swedish Economic Policy Review* (2006, 13(2): 205–30) it is reproduced here with their kind permission. Comments from conference participants, especially Geske Dijkstra, were very helpful, as were comments by an anonymous referee of this chapter. Discussions with Mark McGillivray were also useful. The usual disclaimer applies.

1 'Fiscal Policy is sustainable if the time path of the debt/GDP ratio is bounded, i.e. does not continue to grow without limit' (see Cuddington 1997: 13).

2　Blend countries have access to both IDA and IBRD, but they are not eligible for grants (except for HIV/AIDS projects). Blend countries do not qualify for soft terms from the Paris Club and are automatically excluded from HIPC. Now that Nigeria has been reclassified, Zimbabwe is the only African blend country.

3　The MDRI is confined to debts owed to the three multilateral lenders, and therefore countries may still be left with some debt after the MDRI and enhanced HIPC Initiative processes are complete, since 'the MDRI does not propose any parallel debt relief on the part of official or private creditors, or of multilateral institutions beyond the IMF, IDA and the AfDF' (IMF 2006: 1).

4　While the MDRI is an initiative common to the three multilateral lenders, they can vary its coverage and implementation (IMF 2006).

5　The completion point is reached when a PRSP has been implemented for one year; a reform programme supported by an IMF Poverty Reduction and Growth Facility (PRGF) has shown at least six months of satisfactory performance; and all completion triggers have been met.

6　Iraq's official debt burden is US$120 billion, of which US$40 billion was held by Paris Club members prior to this year's debt relief.

7　OECD-DAC defines as ODA grants or loans to countries and territories on Part I of the DAC List of Aid Recipients (developing countries). These must be: (i) undertaken by the official sector; (ii) have economic development and welfare as their main objective; and (iii) be on concessional financial terms (for a loan having a grant element of at least 25 per cent). Technical co-operation is included in addition to financial flows but grants, loans and credits for military purposes, as well as transfer payments to private individuals, are generally excluded.

8　The data reported in this section of the chapter are from the IMF and World Bank (2005: 3).

9　The effect on the capital base of the regional development banks is also a concern. Bolivia has asked the Inter-American Development Bank (IDB) for relief, but Brazil and Mexico are concerned about the impact on their ownership stakes and have suggested that the US and the EU take responsibility for relieving most of the debt.

10　Bolivia's largest foreign investor, Petrobas (the state-owned Brazilian oil company) halted plans to invest US$5 billion in Bolivia's gas sector (it has invested US$1.5 billion to date) when the nationalization was announced, but the government's relations with foreign investors are now improving after it clarified its policy stance.

11　Malawi has a ratio of one doctor to 36,000 people; Manchester has one doctor to 550 people, according to WHO.

12　In April 2006, Sudan allegedly sponsored an invasion of Chad to overthrow President Déby, partly for granting some 200,000 of Darfur's refugees a safe haven in UN-run camps. Sudan is said to want to replace Déby with a warlord closely involved in the Darfur massacres, and the invasion force consisted of elements of Sudan's notorious janjaweed militias.

13　Some oil producers must also face adjustment to a decline in their oil endowment. Gabon has borrowed heavily and now faces a difficult adjustment as its oil supplies decline, implying a large (and unprecedented) shift into non-traditional exportables requiring, in turn, a sizeable real exchange rate adjustment (Söderling 2006).

References

ActionAid (2005) *Real Aid: An Agenda for Making Aid Work*, London: ActionAid.

Addison, T. and S. M. Murshed (2003) 'Debt Relief and Civil War', *Journal of Peace Research*, 40(2): 159–76.

Addison, T. and A. Rahman (2004) 'Resolving the HIPC Problem: Is Good Policy Enough?', in T. Addison, H. Hansen and F. Tarp (eds), *Debt Relief for Poor Countries*, Basingstoke: Palgrave Macmillan for UNU-WIDER.

Addison, T., H. Hansen and F. Tarp (eds) (2004) *Debt Relief for Poor Countries*, Basingstoke: Palgrave Macmillan for UNU-WIDER.

Atkinson A. B. (ed.) (2004) *New Sources of Development Finance*, Oxford: Oxford University Press for UNU-WIDER.

Birdsall, N. and B. Deese (2005) 'Beyond HIPC: Secure, Sustainable Debt Relief for Poor Countries', in F. Cheru and C. Bradford (eds), *The Millennium Development Goals: Raising the Resources to Tackle World Poverty*, London: Zed Books: 135–55.

Chauvin, N. and A. Kraay (2005) 'What Has 100 Billion Dollars Worth of Debt Relief Done for Low Income Countries?', Unpublished paper, Washington, DC: World Bank.

Claessens, S. (2005) 'Institutional Changes to Prevent the Recurrence of Debt Problems', in J. J. Teunissen and A. Akkerman (eds), *Helping the Poor? The IMF and Low-Income Countries*, The Hague: FONDAD: 139–51.

Cohen, D. (2000) *The HIPC Initiative: True and False Promises*, Technical Paper 166, Paris: OECD Development Centre.

Collier, P. and J. Gunning (eds) (1999) *Trade Shocks in Developing Countries: Volume 1 – Africa*, Oxford: Oxford University Press.

Crafts, N. (2006) 'The World Economy in the 1990s: A Long-Run Perspective', in P. W. Rhode and G. Toniolo (eds), *The Global Economy in the 1990s: A Long-Run Perspective*, Cambridge: Cambridge University Press: 21–42.

Cuddington, J. T. (1997) 'Analyzing the Sustainability of Fiscal Deficits in Developing Countries', Policy Research Working Paper 1784, Washington, DC: World Bank.

Easterly, W. (2001). *The Elusive Quest for Growth*, Cambridge, MA: MIT Press.

Eurodad (2006) *EU Aid: Genuine Leadership or Misleading Figures?*, Brussels: Eurodad.

Hansen, H. (2004) 'The Impact of External Aid and External Debt on Growth and Investment', in T. Addison, H. Hansen and F. Tarp (eds), *Debt Relief for Poor Countries*, Basingstoke: Palgrave Macmillan for UNU-WIDER.

Hulme, D. and T. Arun (2003) 'Balancing Supply and Demand: The Emerging Agenda for Microfinance Institutions', *Journal of Microfinance*, 5(2): 1–6.

IMF (2006) 'The Multilateral Debt Relief (MDRI)', Washington, DC: International Monetary Fund (March).

IMF and World Bank (2004) 'Heavily Indebted Poor Countries (HIPC) Initiative: Status of Implementation', Washington, DC: International Development Association and International Monetary Fund (22 August).

IMF and World Bank (2005) 'Note on the G-8 Debt Relief Proposal: Assessment of Costs, Implementation Issues, and Financing Options', Washington, DC, Development Assistance Committee, DC 2005-0023 (21 September).

IMF and World Bank (2006) 'Heavily Indebted Poor Countries (HIPC) Initiative – Statistical Update', Washington, DC: International Development Association and International Monetary Fund (22 March).

Jayachandran, S. and M. Kremer (2006) 'Odious Debt', *American Economic Review*, 96(1): 82–92.

Kanbur, R. (2000) 'Aid, Conditionality, and Debt in Africa', in F. Tarp (ed.), *Foreign Aid and Development: Lessons Learnt and Directions for the Future*, London: Routledge: 409–22.

Kayizzi-Mugerwa, S. (ed.) (2003) *Reforming Africa's Institutions: Ownership, Incentives and Capabilities*, Tokyo: UNU Press for UNU-WIDER.

Kraay, A. and V. Nehru (2006) 'When Is External Debt Sustainable?', *World Bank Economic Review*, 20(3): 341–65.

Moss, T. (2006) 'Congo-Brazzaville: Too Corrupt for Debt Relief or too Indebted to Fight Corruption?', Washington, DC: Center for Global Development. Available at http://blogs.cgdev.org/mt/mt-tb.cgi/335 (Accessed: 3 April 2006).

Moss, T., S. Standley and N. Birdsall (2005) 'Double Standards on IDA and Debt: The Case for Reclassifying Nigeria', Brief, Washington, DC: Center for Global Development.

Natsios, A. S. (2006) 'Five Debates on International Development: The US Perspective', *Development Policy Review*, 24(2): 131–9.

New Economics Foundation (2006) *Debt Relief as if People Mattered: A Rights Based Approach to Debt Sustainability*, London: New Economics Foundation.

Peel, M. (2005) 'Amnesia and Self-Interest Cloud Debate on Africa', *Financial Times*, 11 March. Available at: http://news.ft.com.

Reinikka, R. and J. Svensson (2002) *Beyond Debt Relief: Assessing Frontline Service Delivery*, Washington, DC: World Bank.

Sachs, J. (2002) 'Resolving the Debt Crisis of Low-Income Countries', *Brookings Papers on Economic Activity*, 1: 257–86.

Sagasti, F., K. Bezanson and F. Prada (2005) *The Future of Development Financing: Challenges and Strategic Choices*, Basingstoke: Palgrave Macmillan for the Ministry for Foreign Affairs, Sweden.

Söderling, L (2006) 'After the Oil: Challenges Ahead in Gabon', *Journal of African Economies*, 15(1): 117–48.

Stiglitz, J. (2005) 'Development Policies in a World of Globalization', in K. P. Gallagher (ed.), *Putting Development First: The Importance of Policy Space in the WTO and IFIs*, London: Zed Books: 15–32.

Svensson J. (2000) 'Foreign Aid and Rent-Seeking', *Journal of International Economics*, 51: 437–61.

Vallée, O. and S. Vallée (2005) 'The Poverty of Economic Policy: Is Debt Sustainability Really Sustainable?', *Journal of International Affairs*, 58(2): 177–92.

World Bank (2006) 'World Bank Approves US$37 Billion for Multilateral Debt Relief Initiative', Press Release 2006/327/PREM, Washington DC: World Bank.

10
Remittances and Financial Inclusion in Development

Helen S. Toxopeus and Robert Lensink

Introduction

Each year, millions of migrants send money earned abroad back to their country of origin. They participate in globalization by engaging in arbitrage in international labour markets, creating family bonds and obligations across countries. The development impact of migration and the ensuing international remittance flow have become increasingly the subject of research and policy discussions, once the vast scale of international 'people and money flows' became apparent. It is no longer uncommon for remittance inflows to constitute 5–10 per cent of total GDP in (small) developing countries (World Bank 2005b). Remittance inflows surpass official development flows in middle-income countries, and foreign direct investment in low-income countries. For 2005, the World Bank estimates the total flows to equal US$250 billion (including informal flows). This trend is unlikely to reverse in the medium to long term. Migration is expected to continue, and costs of remitting are falling, providing a lower threshold for migration. The World Bank (2005c: 92–3) expects that remittance flows will continue to grow at an annual rate of 7–8 per cent, similar to the growth rates of the 1990s (ibid.).

The effects of this large-scale movement of capital are many, both positive and negative (for a full discussion, see World Bank 2005c: 99–105). On the downside, a large inflow of remittances may lead to currency appreciation, thereby lowering competitiveness of export products (World Bank 2005c: 104). Some also argue that the work effort of remittance recipients may decrease, thus dampening growth (Chami *et al.* 2005). On the positive side, remittance inflows increase capital availability for consumption in the receiving countries, and can create in the local economies multiplier effects on GDP, job creation, consumption, income and investment (Stahl and Arnold 1986; De Vasconcelos 2005). Remittances also supply foreign exchange, complementing national savings and providing funding for investment, notably for small-scale projects, hence providing finance for output growth (Solimano 2003). Bugamelli and Paternò (2005) show that a large flow of remittances into a country can help to reduce the probability of current-account reversals, and thus reduce the chance of a financial crisis. Furthermore, remittances are a person-to-person flow of money without government intervention, often delivered directly to the lower-income segment of a country. They can therefore stimulate development without increasing debt or the administrative burden. Remittances are also supposed to improve financial inclusion by providing affordable financial services within the formal financial system to those who tend to be excluded. Remittances may therefore play a crucial role in the wider issue of access to finance.

There is now ample evidence that financial development in general, and banking development in particular, has a positive effect on economic growth (see, for example, Levine 2003). However, while available literature suggests that remittances may stimulate economic growth – for example, through improved financial inclusion – there is a lack of empirical studies to confirm this hypothesis. In this chapter, we take up the challenge to assess empirically the impact of remittance inflows on financial inclusion. More specifically, this chapter is the first to demonstrate the effect of remittance inflows on financial access and usage for a cross-country group of developing countries. We also provide new empirical evidence on the growth effects of remittances to developing countries through the improvement of financial inclusion.

Trends in remittances

The importance of workers' remittances is shown clearly by Figure 10.1(a). This figure indicates that, since 1997, remittance flows to the entire group of developing countries surpass the inflow of official development assistance (ODA). However, foreign direct investments (FDI) are still the most important inflow for the entire group of developing countries. The same holds for such country groups as the upper-middle-income countries (Figure 10.1(b)); the lower-middle-income countries (Figure 10.1(c)); and the regions of East Asia and the Pacific (Figure 10.1(e)), Latin America (Figure 10.1(f)) and Europe and Central Asia (Figure 10.1(g)).

In low-income countries (Figure 10.1(d)), remittances even now constitute the most important inflow, with ODA second in magnitude. The same pattern can be observed in the Middle East (Figure 10.1(h)) and South Asia (Figure 10.1(i)). In Sub-Saharan Africa (SSA), ODA flows dwarf both FDI and workers' remittances (Figure 10.1(j)). Remittances are the least important inflow only in this region, but even here we can see a steady increase.

The accuracy of the data presented above may vary among regions. There is considerable variation in how remittances are transferred through formal or informal channels, a fact that affects whether or not flows are recorded (for an overview of the players in the remittance market, see Orozco (2004)). The *Global Economic Prospects Report 2006* (World Bank 2005c) provides an

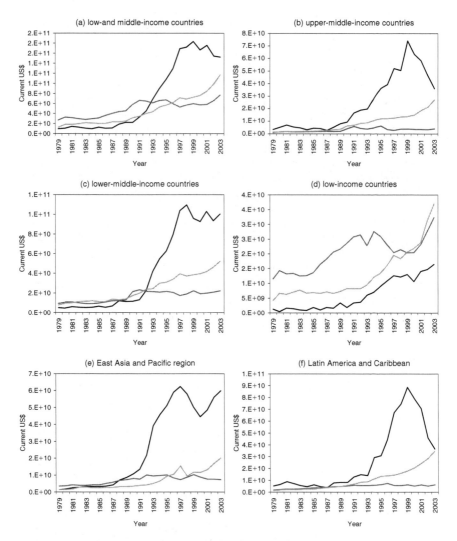

Figure 10.1   FDI, ODA and remittance inflows, 1979–2003

Notes: ——FDI, net inflows (BoP, current US$);   ——ODA and official aid (current US$); ——Worker remittances and employed compensation, received (US$).

Sources: (a) World Bank (2005a); (b)–(j) World Bank (2005a, 2005b).

overview of the different channels used for remittances at the country level. This varies from formal channels being used in the Dominican Republic in 96 per cent of the cases, to just 20 per cent in Uganda (World Bank (2005c: 91), based on World Bank household surveys). In SSA, for example, the use of

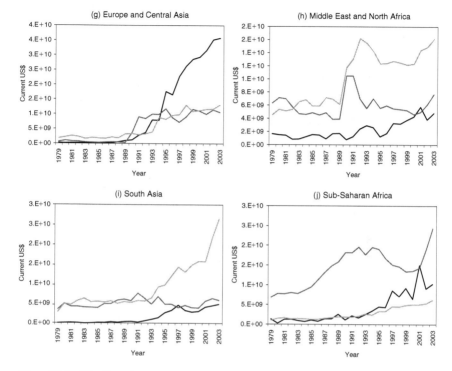

Figure 10.1 (Continued)

informal channels is more widespread, and thus is not well recorded (Sander 2003: 3–4). The current state of data on remittances is disadvantaged by this large variation in the channels used, and should be kept in mind.

By matching migration patterns worldwide, Harrison, *et al.* (2003) estimate the size of remittance flows for each continent and for selected countries (origin and destination) for the year 2000.[1] Table 10.1 shows the aggregate per continent. Remittances flows from North America to Latin America and the Caribbean (LAC) are large, at US$14.2 billion, but remittance flows between Asian countries are twice that size, displaying a large South–South remittance flow in Asia (within-Asia flows are US$29.3 billion if Japan is excluded). Remittance flows within Africa are estimated to be larger than those from both Europe and Asia. Other large magnitudes are directed from North America to Asia and within Europe.

When we look more closely at the flows within regions, they are not evenly distributed among countries. Table 10.2 gives more detail by listing all remittance flows in 2000 that exceeded US$300 million (Harrison *et al.* 2003).

Table 10.1   Size of remittance flows between continents, 2000

	Remittances going to:						
	Africa	Asia	Europe	LAC	North America	Oceania	Total[a]
Remittances coming from:							
Africa	3.7	0.5	0.1	0.0	0.0	0.0	4.3
Asia	3.4	31.5	3.4	0.5	0.2	0.0	39.0
Europe	2.6	3.2	9.5[b]	0.4	0.4	0.1	16.2
Latin America/ Caribbean	–	0.1	0.6	1.1	0.1	–	1.9
North America	0.7	7.9	5.7	14.2	0.9	0.1	29.5
Oceania	0	0.2	0.4	–	0	0.1	0.7
Totals	10.4	43.4	19.7	16.2	1.6	0.3	91.6

Note: [a] Totals may differ slightly in own calculations due to rounding.
  [b] US$24.1 million for European border-workers excluded.
Source: Harrison *et al.* (2003).

The flow from the US to Mexico is overwhelmingly the largest, account-ing for about half of all flows to LAC countries. The table also shows that remittance flows within Asia originate largely in Saudi Arabia, with Japan in second place. More than half of the Europe-to-Asia flows occur within the Germany–Turkey corridor. Although the largest flows are to developing countries, some developed countries also receive considerable amounts of remittances (Canada, Germany, UK and Italy). The sending countries are all developed OECD countries, with the exception of Saudi Arabia (developed, but not OECD). Despite these large flows originating in the developed coun-tries, about 30 per cent of all remittance flows are 'South–South' (if Saudi Arabia were classified as a developing country, this would raise South–South remittances to 45 per cent – World Bank 2005c: 111).

It is often claimed that remittance flows are more stable than other capital inflows. Using the *World Development Indicators 2005* (WDI) (World Bank 2005b) for developed countries as a whole, we calculate and compare the volatility of remittance flows, ODA and FDI over the period 1979–2003, meas-uring volatility in two ways. One is the coefficient of variation, calculated as the standard deviation divided by the mean (times 100). The coefficients of variation of the three capital flows indicate that the least volatile flow is ODA, followed by remittances, with FDI being the most volatile (see Table 10.3).

This variable, however, does not take into account increasing trends in the data. Since FDI and remittances show an increasing trend during this

Table 10.2   Largest remittance corridors, 2000 (in decreasing order)

From	To	Amount (US$ millions)
United States	Mexico	7,612.5
Saudi Arabia	India	3,609.7
Saudi Arabia	Pakistan	1,804.9
Saudi Arabia	Philippines	1.582.7
Saudi Arabia	Egypt	1,388.4
United States	China	1,350.5
Germany	Turkey	1,195.2
United States	Philippines	1,186.4
Japan	Korea	1,012.1
United States	India	977.7
Saudi Arabia	Indonesia	971.8
United States	Vietnam	837.9
Saudi Arabia	Bangladesh	694.2
France	Portugal	659.2
United States	Canada	658.2
United States	Germany	634.0
France	Morocco	600.1
United States	United Kingdom	595.1
France	Algeria	568.5
Japan	China	534.6
Switzerland	Italy	448.4
United States	Italy	437.9
United States	Poland	432.0
United States	Colombia	422.3
Japan	Brazil	405.3
Germany	Italy	370.2
United States	Russia	353.4

Source: Harrison *et al.* (2003).

Table 10.3   Measures of volatility for FDI, ODA and remittances

	FDI	ODA	Remittances
Coefficient of variation	95	32	65
Std dev. of residuals of a linear regression line	1.4E+11	3.7E+10	4.7E+10

Source: Own calculation based on data from World Bank (2005b).

period, we also want to measure volatility with a linear-trend assumption for each of the three capital flows. A steady increase in both remittances and FDI is therefore not included as part of volatility. We measure the best-fit trend line for the three capital flows, by regressing them individually against the period measured (per year), including a constant in the regression. We then calculate the standard deviation of the residuals of each regression as a measure of volatility (the square root of the sum of the squared residuals). Qualitatively, this measure yields similar results as the coefficient of variation: ODA is the least volatile flow followed by remittances and FDI.

The effect of remittances on financial inclusion

In this section we explore the exact channels in which changes that may cause remittances to increase financial inclusion are taking place. We look at demand, supply and policy factors, and apply the access frontier theory to financial markets in the developing countries.

Demand factors

Remittance senders, by definition, need at least one financial service: one that offers international payments. This demand can be an incentive for turning towards the banking sector or other financial institutions as a supplier. At the other end of the transaction, the need to *receive* remittances may induce people to look for the first time for financial services beyond their neighbourhood. The World Bank (2005c) notes that 'in contrast to cash transactions, remittances channelled through bank accounts may encourage savings and enable a better match for savings and investment in the economy'. Thus, for many, migration and the subsequent sending of remittance can be the first personal interaction with the global economy.

The migrant sending the remittances induces the recipient to contact the institution through which the money is being transmitted. If this institution is a bank offering supplementary financial products (compared to a money transfer organization or informal channel that offers remittance-sending services only), this interaction can create a demand for products such as savings, credit, mortgages and insurance. In this manner, the increased financial awareness of the migrant can be the driving force for increased literacy at the receiving end. Estimates show that around 10 per cent of remittance receipts are saved, invested and used for entrepreneurial activity (Orozco and Fedewa 2005: 4). The fact that some cash inflow is invested indicates that a demand for complementary financial products does exist among remittance receivers.

Some remittances are sent in kind, in order to stipulate the use of the remitted 'capital'. This implies that there is a certain need on the sender's side to influence the use of their money (such as sending an airline ticket or vouchers). Linking other financial products, such as different payout options or mortgages, to the remitted amount is a service that is already at times requested by customers. Increasing the possibilities in this manner for formal money transfer services could be a response to the existing demand (Sander and Maimbo 2005: 68).

Supply factors

A wide array of institutions exist to respond to the vast demand for remittance-sending services. In addition to many informal channels and the money-transfer organizations that capture a large share of the market, other financial institutions, more diversified and formal, also offer similar services. Commercial banks, recognizing the vast size of remittance flows,[2] however small individual amounts may be, are increasingly interested in targeting this new market segment. As well as capturing money flows, the remittance channel can be used to sell financial service packages geared towards low-income individuals. Hernández-Coss (2005) states that 'by developing formal remittance channels that are competitive with informal ones, the formal financial sector has an incentive to develop and benefit from the overall opportunity to grow and expand through the remittance market'. Credit unions worldwide have also focused on remittances and have collectively created a remittance service (IRnet) for sending money electronically. In the process, they offer other financial services to these users, such as savings accounts (see Grace 2005).

The perceived benefits of serving the low-income market have increased as a result of the demand by the poorer people for remittance services and the ensuing constant inflow of money. Regular remittances can reduce informational problems because the continual inflow of money from abroad allows the lower-income segment of the population to build a sound financial history with a financial institution. The earned income now needs some form of intermediation in order to transfer it to its destination. Banks can cross-sell to obtain new clients and enable them to build a financial history by offering international transfer services together with complementary services, such as savings or cheque accounts. Through the remittance inflow, the bank gains an insight into the client's income and expected future funds, thus indicating the potential creditworthiness of the recipient, since a constant (future) inflow can repay loans. In addition, as adverse circumstances at home generally increase remittances from abroad,[3] this can potentially lower a client's risk profile. Banks thus obtain information about prospective loan clients, reducing the problem of adverse selection. Furthermore, remittances are a relatively risk-free way of establishing contact with new clientele.[4] The bank can use this knowledge to base greater emphasis in its client analysis on 'soft' data, such as the reliability and character of the firm's owner.

The argument is similar for remittance inflows as a marketable collateral. Remittance inflows not only have an informational function, but they also convey direct value to the bank. When remittances go through a bank, clients can use both current and future inflows as 'collateral'. If the inflows are accepted by a bank as such, loans could be (partly) covered by remittance inflows, thus lowering the bank's risk, and motivating payback and optimal project management.

Finally, the direct income effect of remittances may affect supply. When a family member decides to migrate, he/she would, rationally speaking, do so only if the expected benefit from working abroad minus the extra costs of sustaining the individual abroad were larger than the family income before migration. Therefore, receiving families will in general move to a higher-income client group that is more attractive for the bank and may thus boost the supply of financial services for this group.

The access frontier

The access frontier can be applied to examine the relationship between remittance inflows and financial inclusion from a different angle. This method combines demand and supply arguments and is used by Porteous (2004) to look at how a financial market can 'work for the poor'. The access frontier can be defined as the maximum usage possible under existing structural conditions of technology, infrastructure and regulation (Porteous 2004: 8). He argues that the access frontier expands outwards until market development moves into a saturation and consolidation phase, where the market reaches a natural limit. Usage is at its maximum, and non-usage becomes a genuine choice, unhindered by income or supply constraints. Porteous investigates why the access frontier in developing countries is not yet at its maximum (natural limit).

We take the example of South Africa, cited by Porteous, to demonstrate how remittance inflows can move the access frontier outwards. In South Africa, 48 per cent of adults have a bank account. The two most frequently cited reasons for not having a bank account are the lack of either a regular income (35.6 per cent) or a job (59.8 per cent). According to the third most common reason, earnings are too scanty to make it worthwhile (11.4 per cent). Up to 6 per cent of people cite reasons such as having no identity documentation, not qualifying for an account, or not wanting to keep a minimum balance nor pay service fees.

The regular inflow of remittances may move the access frontier outwards by eliminating the reasons for non-usage. Remittance inflows can function as a substitution for a job or regular income. Since remittances in most cases are sent to sustain a family, the inflow is often regular, making it comparable to 'regular income'. Also, when a family member migrates, family earnings tend to increase, thereby reducing the income-effect problems of having a bank account. These make the recipients of remittances interesting clients for banks. If the obstacles to banking, whether demand-led or supply-led, are removed, the receipt of international remittances may trigger an outward move of the access frontier. Recipients become potential bank clients, and they themselves will also have a greater need to use banking services.

The effects mentioned above will depend on the ability and willingness of banks to adapt. If banks are interested in remittance inflows from abroad, their product packages should be expanded accordingly, by offering, for example, low-cost or free international transactions for clients who have a bank account with them. However, as Prahalad (2005: 8) notes, a dominant logic applies to private-sector businesses that may restrict their ability to see a dynamic and viable market opportunity at the 'bottom of the pyramid'. On the demand side, inadequate regulation and mistrust of banks can hinder the development of financial access considerably. Adequate government regulation and policy in this area will also play a part. These are discussed next.

Policy and regulatory issues

Through policy geared to integrating remittance senders with the formal economy, governments can create a more inclusive financial sector and a more efficient and formal economy. They can increase the financial depth of the economy and improve the monitoring of financial flows. Governments can influence access to formal financial services in a country by stimulating remittance sending through formal channels. This puts migrants and remittance recipients in touch with diversified financial institutions, and can lead to increased demand and supply of other financial products.

Governments can encourage transfers through formal channels by removing taxes on incoming remittances; relaxing exchange and capital controls; allowing domestic banks to operate overseas; providing ID cards for migrants; supporting hometown associations; providing matching grants, offering loan/pension schemes and bonds targeted at the diasporas, and by actively supporting the diaspora to help ensure the welfare of their citizens abroad (World Bank 2005c: 95). Also, educating the population on the benefits and processes of financial institutions can increase demand for formal financial services (World Bank 2003b). These measures make it more attractive for diversified financial institutions to enter the remittance market, and for the clientele to send money through formal channels. Two regulatory issues in moving towards formal channels need, however, to be highlighted: identification requirements for migrants and regulation on money laundering and the financing of terrorism.

Valid immigration status is often a problem when using formal channels to remit funds. Migrants without legal status lack adequate identification to open bank accounts abroad, or to use the banking system to transfer funds. Surveys of migrants in Los Angeles and New York show that they are discouraged from opening bank accounts by minimum balance requirements and strict identification regulations (Ratha 2003: 35). In these cases, migrants tend to resort to money transfer organizations or informal networks. With alternative, acceptable forms of identification available for opening bank accounts, more migrants are able to participate in the formal banking system and use this channel to transfer money abroad. The most prominent example of this measure is the 'matrícula consular' issued to Mexican migrants at consulates in the US (Hernández-Coss 2005: 12). As private banks become more interested in the remittance market, they will start to accept forms of identification other than those based on legal immigrant status. Much, however, depends on the immigration policies of the country. For security reasons, some authorities may disagree with this alternative form of identification, an issue related to the next topic.

Another factor driving the formalization of international capital flows is the increased regulations on money laundering and the financing of terrorist activities, which received a boost after 9/11. The US Patriot Act stipulates that banks and other financial institutions should endeavour to 'know their customers', or to be able to identify and monitor everyone depositing or transferring money through them (de Vasconcelos 2005). The small remittance organizations in the US that maintained bank accounts where money is pooled from various individual sources for transfers abroad have discontinued these accounts, because under the new regulation banks considered it too risky. This policy has almost certainly led to an increased demand for formal banking channels for remittances, particularly in those countries where measured inflows doubled or even tripled between 2001 and 2003 (World Bank 2005c: 91).

Preliminary evidence for a causal relationship

At the time of writing, the Inter-American Development Bank (2005) estimates that fewer than 10 per cent of remittance receivers have access to basic banking services, although this estimate varies widely among countries. Countries with a long migrant tradition, such as Portugal, Turkey and the Philippines, have developed financial institutions geared towards migrant populations, with banks capturing a large proportion of remittances. When people become bank clients at the receiving end, this affects the number of individuals who are bank clients in the home country, including returning migrants. Portuguese banks, for example, have developed full banking services in France, Germany and other emigrant destinations, thus encouraging emigrants to have bank accounts and use banking services (Orozco 2002: 14–15). The Turkish remittance market consists mainly of Turkish banks with efficient systems for transferring money to accounts maintained with head offices in the home country (Orozco 2002: 17). In the Philippines, banks have about a 71 per cent share of the remittance market (Philippines Census Bureau, quoted in Orozco 2002: 16). According to Orozco and Fedewa (2005),

Table 10.4 Percentage of population with bank accounts (remittance recipients and non-recipients), 2003 (per cent)

	Guatemala	Honduras	El Salvador	Mexico	Ecuador
Recipients	41	34	31	19	46
Non-recipients	17	16	19	16	34

Source: Orozco and Fedewa (2005).

remittance recipients in selected Latin-American countries are more likely to be banking individuals than non-recipients (Table 10.4).

The experience of credit unions affiliated to the World Council of Credit Unions (WOCCU) shows that on average 14 per cent to 28 per cent of the non-members who approach these institutions requesting transfer services through their IRnet eventually open an account (Maimbo and Ratha 2005: 9). Generally, credit unions are well equipped to serve the previously non-banking remittance senders and receivers, because of their good rural locations (Maimbo and Ratha 2005: 10).

Other factors affecting financial inclusion

The recent research paper by Beck *et al.* (2005) presents new indicators of banking sector penetration for ninety-nine countries, on both access and use, and shows the correlation between data on access to finance and other variables at a cross-country level, using various proxies for branch penetration, ATM penetration, number of loans and deposits.

Beck *et al.* (2005) observe a correlation between banking outreach and economic size, and with population density. More densely populated areas have a higher bank branch and ATM penetration; the relevance of the economic size of a country suggests that economies of scale play a part in banking services. Financial outreach, like financial development, is positively correlated with institutional quality. Effective credit information sharing also shows a correlation with increased banking penetration (outlets), though not necessarily with the number of loans.

The variable restrictions on bank activities is correlated negatively with branch penetration. The share of assets held by government-owned banks has a negative correlation with demographic branch and ATM penetration. The concentration ratio is positively associated with branch and ATM penetration, and with deposit taking. Finally, the communication and transportation infrastructure indicators have a positive correlation with all indicators used for access to, and use of, banking services. One more variable added in this discussion is average income level, to control for the possibility that a higher level of development does not influence the results.

Research design

As mentioned at the start of the chapter, our focus is on the impact of remittances on financial inclusion in developing countries. The set of developing countries included in the sample is based on data availability, and the variable with the poorest availability for developing countries is financial inclusion. Consequently, selection of the sample countries is based almost entirely on the data availability for this (dependent) variable. A few countries were later deleted because of a lack of remittance data, the main independent variable in the analysis.

One pitfall in using a sample based on data availability is that countries with a failing or unorganized government may be under-represented because of poor administrative systems. This would bias the sample towards developing countries with 'better' governments, thus possibly the higher-income developing countries. Comparing the sample to the country's population indicated that there is, indeed, a slight under-representation of low-income countries (only 24 per cent of the low-income countries are included) and an over-representation of lower-middle-income and upper-middle-income countries (54 per cent and 50 per cent, respectively). The total sample consists of 41 per cent of all nations classified as developing countries according to the World Bank Atlas Classification (2005d).

The regional representation of developing countries also varies; only 21 per cent of SSA developing countries are represented, compared to 70 per cent of those in Europe and Central Asia. Sub-Saharan Africa, Middle East–North Africa, and East Asia–Pacific regions are under-represented, whereas Europe and Central Asia, Latin America and the Caribbean, and South Asia are over-represented (see Table 10.5).

Table 10.5 Regional representation in sample

Region	No. of countries in		Proportion of countries in sample
	The sample	This region	
Europe and Central Asia	19	27	0.704
Latin America and Caribbean	19	32	0.594
Sub-Saharan Africa	10	48	0.208
South Asia	5	8	0.625
East Asia and Pacific	7	24	0.292
Middle East and North Africa	4	14	0.286
Total	64	153	0.418

Source: Authors' calculations using World Bank (2005d).

Data collection

Data on remittance flows are expected to under-report real flows systematically, as a result of lack of information on flows through informal channels, and inaccurate reporting by government bodies. Estimates on informal flows vary widely, between 50 per cent and 250 per cent of recorded flows (Freund and Spatafora 2005: 2). Thus, for a comparative analysis, it is difficult to use data that include estimates of informal flows.[5] A project on remittance data led by the World Bank, the IMF and the UN is under way at the time of writing to define remittances clearly and incorporate their measurement into worldwide household surveys (Hovinga 2005). To optimize the estimates of remittance flows, we are making a compromise between using a dataset that is most complete and most accurate. The balance of payments statistics of the IMF are the most commonly used data in this respect, and three categories are often compiled (see also Reinke and Patterson 2005):

(i) workers' remittances (credit); transfers by migrants living abroad for longer than one year;
(ii) employee compensation (credit); transfers by migrants abroad for less than one year; and
(iii) migrant transfers (credit); money that migrants take back home when they return indefinitely.

The first two are the most relevant for financial transfer services, since these flows are transmitted by means other than personal delivery. However, the distinction between these three categories is sometimes blurred in individual country reports to IMF. Some countries report the aggregate of all three categories under either worker remittances or employee compensation. Therefore, for comparability, the World Bank incorporates all three items together (World Bank 2005b; see Reinke and Patterson 2005 for more details). Since this is a cross-country comparative study, we use the dataset created by the World Bank, which also has the advantage that it has augmented the IMF data with estimates of remittances for countries with incomplete or missing data. The World Bank has also compiled figures per region and per income level, which is useful for a descriptive analysis of remittance flows worldwide.

Financial inclusion

Until recently, measuring financial inclusion at a cross-country level meant using proxies that were arguably more reflective of financial development than financial inclusion (see, for example, Beck, Levine and Loayza 1999. The dataset from Beck *et al.* (2005) introduces various indicators on access to financial services, use of deposits and loans, average deposit and loan size, and even predicted share of households with bank accounts. It provides a comprehensive country-level comparison for both developed and developing countries. To construct the predicted share of households with bank accounts, they use a smaller dataset from Claessens (2005) and Gasparini *et al.* (2005) on the share of households with bank accounts (*Sba*) and regress this on the log of deposit accounts per 100,000 people and log of average deposit account size in US$. Since this specific measure gives a direct indication of the usage of formal savings and transaction services (and not just banking penetration or number of loans/deposits), this seems to be the best indicator to use for measuring the utilization of financial services, and is therefore applied here.

Opting for this variable also determines the time dimension to be used. The time frame is just one year per country, allowing for a cross-sectional analysis only. Most data points are from 2003, though the years of data collection range from 2001 to 2005.

Measuring other variables

We include all factors that Beck *et al.* (2005) show as correlating with at least one proxy for financial access and/or use (see previous section). As mentioned above, we also include income level (GDP per capita) to control for income effects that might influence access to finance. The indicators used to measure these variables are listed in the Appendix, where we also present descriptive statistics of the dependent and independent variables (see Appendix Table 10.A1 on page 257).

Since we are looking for a causal effect of remittance inflows on financial inclusion, a time lag is built into the analysis, by including statistics for each country on remittances for the year preceding the financial inclusion data. This way, if a relationship is found, it is less likely to flow in the opposite direction. Thus, data for financial inclusion stem from the years 2001–5 and for remittances from 2000–3 (data from 2004 are not yet available). To be comparable across countries, remittance flows are computed per capita, using population figures from the WDI (World Bank 2005b).

Regression results

In order to test the effect of remittance inflows on financial inclusion, we use the general-to-specific approach. We start with a model in which all independent variables are included. This model is specified as follows:

$$
\begin{aligned}
\text{FININCL} = {} & \beta_1 + \beta_2\,(\text{LOG})\text{REMCAP} + \beta_3\,\text{GOVERN} + \beta_4\,\text{POPDENS} \\
& + \beta_5\,\text{LOG(GDP)} + \beta_6\,\text{GDPCAP} + \beta_7\,\text{COMINFR} + \beta_8\,\text{TRANSINFR} \\
& + \beta_9\,\text{CONCENTR} + \beta_{10}\,\text{CREDITINFO} + \beta_{11}\,\text{SHAREGOV} \\
& + \beta_{12}\,\text{RESTRICT} + \beta_{13}\,\text{ENTRYREQ} + e_t
\end{aligned}
$$

Abbreviations are:

FININCL = predicted share of households with bank accounts;
REMCAP = remittance inflow per capita;
GOVERN = governance index;
POPDENS = population density;
GDP = gross domestic product;
GDPCAP = GDP per capita;
COMINFR = communication infrastructure;
TRANSINFR = transportation infrastructure;
CONCENTR = concentration ratio;
CREDITINFO = credit information index;
SHAREGOV = share of assets in government-owned banks;
RESTRICT = restrictions on bank activities; and
ENTRYREQ = requirements for entry into banking.

Appendix Table 10.A2 (see page 258) gives the definitions, sources and the year of observation for all variables.

Next, we delete all insignificant variables one at a time, and end up with explanatory variables that have a significance level below 10 per cent. In order to examine the robustness of the outcomes, for the preferred equation we also present an estimate in which data for certain developed economies are included.

A matter of concern may be the possible collinearity between the independent variables. Therefore, in Appendix Table 10.A3 (see page 260), a correlation matrix is presented for all independent variables. This table shows that remittances per capita have no correlation with other variables higher than 0.27 (with population density). Looking at all the variables, none of the pairwise correlations is larger than 0.8, indicating that there are no potentially harmful collinear relationships. We also create an auxiliary regression with remittances per capita on the left-hand side and all the other independent variables on the right. The R^2 obtained is 0.28 (adjusted R^2 is -0.0075). We can therefore conclude that the variation in remittances per capita is not explained by variation in the other variables. Thus, collinearity does not have a harmful effect on the outcomes of the regressions.

We use two estimation techniques. First, we apply the ordinary least squares (OLS) estimation method. Second, since it is well known that least squares estimation results may be very sensitive to some possible outliers, especially for small samples, we also use the median estimator. Median regressions are much more resistant to possible outliers. The median estimator essentially forms a part of the non-parametric quantile regression technique. This technique determines the coefficients by minimizing the sum of absolute deviations. More specifically, the median linear regression parameters are given by the value of the vector β that minimizes $\sum_{i=1}^{n} \left| y_i - x_i'\beta \right| = \sum_{i=1}^{n} \left(0.5 - 1(y_i \geq x_i'\beta) \right) \left(y_i - x_i'\beta \right)$. All estimates are done with STATA. The regression results are given in Table 10.6.

Table 10.6 shows that, in all cases, remittances have a significantly positive effect on financial inclusion. Including all potentially relevant variables, and estimating with OLS, remittances per capita become the only significant variable at a 10 per cent level. When the median regression technique is used, remittances are significant at the 1 per cent level. Moreover, with this technique, all other variables appear to be significant as well. With a backward selection, remittances per capita enter significantly into the equation at a 1 per cent level, together with GDP at a 10 per cent level and the governance index at a 1 per cent level. The same results hold for the median regressor; here, however, GDP is no longer significant at the usual significance level.

When certain developed countries are included, remittances still appear to have a positive significant effect on financial inclusion, both in the OLS and the median estimator. When looking at the significance of the models as a whole, all models have a significant F-value. The adjusted R^2 varies between 0.28 and 0.8. The regression results also indicate that in some cases (see, for example Equation 2a in the tables) the residuals are not normally distributed, indicated by the values for the kurtosis and skewness. In these cases, the median estimator may be more reliable. The Ramsey reset test suggests that the equations are correctly specified, and that the functional form of the models is appropriate. Overall, the regression results clearly show the relevance of remittances in explaining financial inclusion.

Remittances, financial inclusion and economic growth

Although examination of the remittances–financial inclusion/economic growth nexus is not the main objective of this chapter, we end this section by presenting some new evidence on the topic. We assess the impact of remittances on the economic growth of developing countries by estimating a set of equations in which per capita economic growth and financial inclusion are the endogenous variables. The results are presented in Table 10.7.

Table 10.7 clearly shows that financial inclusion has a positive effect on per capita growth. In all regressions, our indicator for financial inclusion has a positive and significant impact on growth. Moreover, also in this set of system regressions, remittances have a significantly positive effect on financial inclusion. We tried several other specifications of the growth equation, by also introducing remittances directly in the growth equation. However, in none of these specifications do the additional variables appear to be significant. For reasons of space, these regression results are not presented. Most importantly, the regressions given in Table 10.7 empirically confirm our main

Table 10.6 Explaining the predicted share of households with bank accounts

	1a	1b	2a	2b	3a	3b
Constant	-0.22 (0.86)	-0.39 (0.00)	-0.393 (0.22)	-0.098 (0.78)	-0.364 (0.21)	-0.691 (0.01)
Lrencap	0.098 (0.08) [0.74]	0.057 (0.00)	0.052 (0.01) [0.42]	0.046 (0.00)	0.052 (0.00) [0.27]	0.058 (0.00)
Concentr	-0.209 (0.54) [-0.18]	0.123 (0.00)				
Cominfr	0.476 (0.49) [0.24]	0.193 (0.00)				
Creditinfo	0.012 (0.64) [0.11]	0.004 (0.00)				
Entryreq	-0.04 (0.43) [-0.25]	-0.06 (0.00)				
Lgdp	0.019 (0.70) [0.15]	0.032 (0.00)	0.022 (0.07) [0.19]	0.011 (0.46)	0.022 (0.06) [0.14]	0.034 (0.00)
Gdppc	0.000016 (0.84) [0.13]	-4.5e-06 (0.00)				
Govern	0.166 (0.34) [0.44]	0.072 (0.00)	0.244 (0.00) [0.63]	0.244 (0.00)	0.268 (0.00) [0.73]	0.254 (0.00)
Popdens	0.00004 (0.89) [0.05]	-0.0002 (0.00)				
Restrict	-0.013 (0.71) [-0.07]	0.007 (0.00)				

(Continued)

Table 10.6 (Continued)

	1a	1b	2a	2b	3a	3b
Sharegov	0.00012 [0.01]	-0.00047				
	(0.96)	(0.00)				
Transinfr	1.190 [0.16]	2.859				
	(0.64)	(0.00)				
N	22	22	37	37	47	47
Adj R²	0.28		0.51		0.80	
Pseudo R²		0.51		0.42		0.63
F	6.92		24.70		61.90	
	(0.003)		(0.00)		(0.00)	
Skewness	-0.044		0.638		0.625	
Kurtosis	2.32		5.599		5.44	
Rest test	F=0.15		F=0.76		F=1.16	
	(0.93)		(0.52)		(0.34)	
Method	OLS	MED	OLS	MED	OLS	MED

Notes: Figures in parentheses are p-values, based on White adjusted standard errors. Figures in brackets are standardized coefficients. Dependent variable is the predicted share of bank accounts (*Sba*). The sample for Equations 1 and 2 contains developing countries only. For Equation 3 we also added some (total of ten) developed economies for which data on the dependent and independent variables are available. OLS refers to the results from ordinary least squares regressions. MED refers to results from the quantile (median) regression technique.

Table 10.7 Remittances, financial inclusion and per capita growth

Dep. var.	1a Grow	1b Sba	2a Grow	2b Sba	3a Grow	3b Sba	4a Grow	4b Sba
Lgdppc	-0.005 (0.37)		-0.005 (0.25)		-0.006 (0.21)		-0.005 (0.29)	
Govc	-0.013 (0.01)		-0.0012 (0.01)		-0.0012 (0.01)		-0.0012 (0.01)	
Trade	-1.4e-06 (0.99)							
Invgdp	0.0002 (0.61)		0.00026 (0.52)					
Sba	0.077 (0.10)		0.059 (0.03)		0.064 (0.01)		0.061 (0.01)	
Concentr	0.02 (0.10)		0.018 (0.11)		0.198 (0.08)		0.019 (0.084)	
Govern	-0.006 (0.42)	0.257 (0.00)		0.263 (0.10)		0.265 (0.00)		0.244 (0.00)
Lremcap		0.055 (0.00)		0.055 (0.00)		0.055 (0.00)		0.051 (0.00)
Lgdp		0.028 (0.06)		0.026 (0.10)		0.027 (0.09)		0.029 (0.03)
Grow		-1.80 (0.64)		-2.88 (0.48)		-2.74 (0.51)		
Constant	0.030 (0.40)	-0.52 (-1.27)	0.037 (0.22)	-0.452 (0.26)	0.044 (0.13)	-0.471 (0.24)	0.039 (0.18)	-0.563 (0.10)
N	35	35	35	35	35	35	35	35
R²	0.39	0.49	0.41	0.42	0.40	0.43	0.40	0.58

Notes and Source: The sets of equations (1a and 1b; 2a and 2b; 3a and 3b) are estimated with three-stage least squares. P-values are in parentheses. *Grow* refers to the average GDP per capita growth rate of the 1990–2003 period. *Sba* refers to the percentage share of bank accounts (financial inclusion). *Lgdppc* is the initial value (1990) of GDP per capita. *Govc* is government consumption over GDP; *Trade* is net trade over GDP and *Invgdp* is investment over GDP. The last three variables refer to 1999 and are derived from World Bank (2005b).

hypothesis that remittances stimulate financial inclusion and, through this channel, stimulate per capita growth.

Conclusions

In this chapter we have focused on the relationship between remittance inflows and financial inclusion in developing countries. We have presented single-equation estimates on remittances, and financial inclusion and system estimates in which economic growth is explained by financial inclusion, for example, and financial inclusion by remittances inflows, for example. These regressions clearly confirm our main hypothesis that remittances have a development impact through their effect on financial inclusion.

Overall, the chapter indicates the importance of studying the effects of remittances in developing countries. Remittances in terms of size are not only one of the main capital inflows in developing countries – often even more substantial than ODA – but also seem to have a robust positive effect on economic growth. It is therefore surprising that empirical studies on remittance inflows lag behind, certainly when compared to the numerous studies dealing with the development impact of ODA.

We realize that more research is needed for a conclusive answer on the development impact of remittances. A drawback of our study – as well as of all other studies available – is that remittances data are still very limited. Therefore, data on remittance flows need to be improved and a method of recording remittance at the international level needs to be developed. From an academic point of view, quality data on remittances are essential for providing good policy guidance. Only then can the effects of remittance flows (not just on financial inclusion) be investigated more accurately. Measurement of informal flows in particular should be researched further, as is already happening (Freund and Spatafora 2005; Reinke and Patterson 2005). It would be interesting to analyse further what factors affect the use of formal as opposed to informal channels, since flows through formal channels are more likely to have a positive impact on financial inclusion. Also, the measure of financial inclusion needs to be improved. Building on the dataset created by Beck *et al.* (2005), the next step could be to create variables that measure access to, and usage of, financial services across the board, not just with regard to deposits and loans. In addition, research could also be improved further by including other characteristics of the sending migrants into the analysis, such as income level, since this is likely to play a role in the effect of remittances on financial usage. This would give a better insight into the categories of migrants who are banking; who become banking individuals because of remittances; and who are still not using any formal financial services. Policy can then be focused on the groups who are yet to become banking individuals.

Appendix

Table 10.A1 Descriptive statistics of dependent and independent variables

All variables	Predicted share of banking households	Remittance inflow/capita at $t-1$	Economic size (GDP)	Average income level (GDP per capita)	Governance index	Concentration ratio	Restrictions on bank activities
Mean	0.2632	64.3109	96,500,000,000	2217.7130	−0.2227	0.6416	1.7917
Median	0.2425	26.5304	18,200,000,000	1774.5740	−0.3503	0.6123	2.0000
Maximum	0.7860	562.9053	1,420,000,000,000	6794.8640	1.2456	1.0000	4.0000
Minimum	0.0010	0.1990	742,000,000	101.5248	−1.2112	0.2247	0.0000
Std dev.	0.1993	105.7897	215,000,000,000	1849.7400	0.6016	0.1909	1.1291
Skewness	0.6320	2.7632	4.31	1.0253	0.5736	0.2736	0.1476
Kurtosis	2.7441	10.9877	24.52	3.1526	2.4648	2.3660	2.1732
Jarque-Bera	2.6336	251.5869	1,433.22	11.2758	4.0736	1.7827	1.5414
Probability	0.2680	0.0000	0.00	0.0036	0.1304	0.4101	0.4627
Observations	38	64	64	64	61	61	48

	Communication infrastructure (telephone lines per capita)	Transportation infrastructure (railways per km²)	Population density	Share of assets in government-owned banks	Credit information index	Requirements for entry into banking
Mean	0.1462	0.0173	116.7910	24.5957	3.1667	7.3617
Median	0.1222	0.0081	72.2395	16.3000	3.5000	8.0000
Maximum	0.4172	0.1229	1060.7000	80.000	6.0000	8.0000
Minimum	0.0024	0.0000	3.0393	0.0000	0.0000	3.0000
Std dev.	0.1102	0.0221	162.2590	24.5717	2.0433	0.9874
Skewness	0.5388	2.6351	3.7558	0.7537	−0.3475	−2.1430
Kurtosis	2.3671	11.4366	20.2196	2.2759	1.9326	9.1315
Jarque-Bera	4.1645	239.1355	941.1710	5.3599	4.0558	109.5986
Probability	0.1246	0.0000	0.0000	0.0686	0.1316	0.0000
Observations	64	58	64	46	60	47

Note: See text for data sources.

Table 10.A2 Definitions, sources and year of observation of all variables

Variable	Definition	Source	Year
Demographic branch penetration	No. of bank branches per 100,000 people	Beck, Demirgüç-Kunt and Martinez Peria (2005)	Varies by country (2001–5)
Geographic branch penetration	No. of branches per 1,000 km^2	Beck, Demirgüç-Kunt and Martinez Peria (2005)	Varies by country (2001–5)
Demographic ATM penetration	No. of ATMs per 100,000 people	Beck, Demirgüç-Kunt and Martinez Peria (2005)	Varies by country (2001–5)
Geographic ATM penetration	No. of ATMs per 1,000 km^2	Beck, Demirgüç-Kunt and Martinez Peria (2005)	Varies by country (2001–5)
Loan accounts p.c.	Average loan size/GDP p.c.	Beck, Demirgüç-Kunt and Martinez Peria (2005)	Varies by country (2001–5)
Loan-income ratio	No. of loans per 1,000 people	Beck, Demirgüç-Kunt and Martinez Peria (2005)	Varies by country (2001–5)
Deposit accounts p.c.	Average deposit size/GDP p.c.	Beck, Demirgüç-Kunt and Martinez Peria (2005)	Varies by country (2001–5)
Deposit income ratio	No. of deposits per 1,000 people	Beck, Demirgüç-Kunt and Martinez Peria (2005)	Varies by country (2001–5)
Predicted household share with bank account	Calculated using data on share of households with bank accounts on the log of deposit accounts per 100,000 and the log of average deposit size (US$)	Beck, Demirgüç-Kunt and Martinez Peria (2005), with data from Claessens (2005) and Gasparini, Gutierrez and Porto (2005)	Varies by country (2001–5)
Remittance inflow p.c. at $t-1$	Remittance inflow/total population at $t-1$	World Bank (2005a) for remittances; (2005b) for developed countries and for GDP	Remittances and population at $t-1$

Economic size	GDP	World Bank (2005b)	2003
Average income level	GDP p.c. (constant 2000 US$)	World Bank (2005b)	2003
Governance index	Average score of six governance indicators, where high score implies better governance	Kaufmann, Kraay and Mastruzzi (2005)	2004
Concentration ratio	Assets of three largest banks as a share of assets of all commercial banks in the system	Fitch's bankscope database in Beck, Demirgüç and Levine (1999)	2003
Credit information index	Scored on 0–6 scale, score increasing with availability of credit information	Djankov, McLiesh and Shleifer (2004), adopted from La Porta et al. (1998)	2005 data; 2003–4 data not available online
Restrictions on bank activities	Sum of restrictions on banks owning real estate, insurance, securities and non-financial firms	World Bank Regulation and Supervision Database	2001
Entry requirements for banking	No. of requirements for banking licence	World Bank Regulation and Supervision Database	2001
Share of assets in government-owned banks	Percentage of banking system assets in banks with 50%+ share owned by government	World Bank Regulation and Supervision Database	2001
Communication infrastructure	Telephone lines p.c.	World Bank (2005b)	2003; 2002 for some
Transportation infrastructure	Railways per km^2	World Bank (2005b)	2002 and 2003
Population density	Total population/total land area	World Bank (2005b)	2003

Notes and Source: p.c. = per capita. Additional variables used in growth regressions: *Grow:* GDP per capita growth rate between 1990 and 2003. Calculated from GDP per capita figures in constant 2000 US$.* *Govc:* Government consumption over GDP, 1999.* *Invgdp:* Gross investment over GDP, 1999.* *Lgdp:* Ln GDP per capita of 1990.* *Trade:* Net trade over GDP, 1999 (source for * in notes, World Bank 2005b).

Table 10.A3 Pairwise correlation coefficients between all independent variables

	COMINFR	CONCENTR	CREDITINFO	ENTRYREQ	GDP	GDPCAP
COMINFR	1.000000	-0.099790	0.219836	-0.040053	0.126198	0.731847
CONCENTR	-0.099790	1.000000	-0.221936	0.096412	-0.264003	-0.023732
CREDITINFO	0.219836	-0.221936	1.000000	-0.066661	0.072580	0.452804
ENTRYREQ	-0.040053	0.096412	-0.066661	1.000000	-0.207876	-0.059795
GDP	0.126198	-0.264003	0.072580	-0.207876	1.000000	0.043252
GDPCAP	0.731847	-0.023732	0.452804	-0.059795	0.043252	1.000000
GOVERN	0.540971	0.076189	0.425651	-0.183370	-0.013865	0.765663
POPDENS	-0.106434	-0.177748	-0.136680	-0.220983	0.018302	-0.053917
REMCAP	0.111719	0.058276	0.024737	0.151785	-0.149840	0.181374
RESTRICT	-0.097490	0.002701	-0.057729	-0.092019	0.287350	-0.231934
SHAREGOV	0.014680	-0.204817	-0.199169	-0.183069	0.425331	-0.176688
TRANSINFR	0.621847	-0.038677	0.032291	0.019170	-0.051169	0.537903

	GOVERN	POPDENS	REMCAP	RESTRICT	SHAREGOV	TRANSINFR
COMINFR	0.540971	-0.106434	0.111719	-0.097490	0.014680	0.621847
CONCENTR	0.076189	-0.177748	0.058276	0.002701	-0.204817	-0.038677
CREDITINFO	0.425651	-0.136680	0.024737	-0.057729	-0.199169	0.032291
ENTRYREQ	-0.183370	-0.220983	0.151785	-0.092019	-0.183069	0.019170
GDP	-0.013865	0.018302	-0.149840	0.287350	0.425331	-0.051169
GDPCAP	0.765663	-0.053917	0.181374	-0.231934	-0.176688	0.537903
GOVERN	1.000000	-0.111593	-0.011880	-0.156725	-0.219176	0.382951
POPDENS	-0.111593	1.000000	0.267179	0.214463	0.202532	0.144333
REMCAP	-0.011880	0.267179	1.000000	0.068121	-0.185363	0.113073
RESTRICT	-0.156725	0.214463	0.068121	1.000000	0.252075	-0.091206
SHAREGOV	-0.219176	0.202532	-0.185363	0.252075	1.000000	0.071678
TRANSINFR	0.382951	0.144333	0.113073	-0.091206	0.071678	1.000000

Note: Abbreviations as Table 10.6, Equation 1.

Notes

We thank Niels Hermes for constructive comments on an earlier version of this chapter.

1 The data by Harrison *et al.* (2003) are not an exact match to the year 2000 data by the World Bank (2005b). Although categorized somewhat differently, Latin America–Caribbean flows reported here are smaller, while European and Asian flows are larger. Although both sets are based on the IMF balance-of-payment statistics, they have been augmented by the authors' own estimates for missing or badly recorded flows. This difference is a good indication of the need for improvements in remittance data.
2 Harris (2002) estimates that the average annual amount per sender is in the range of US$700–1,000 (quoted in Orozco 2003).
3 For evidence on counter-cyclicality of remittance flows, see World Bank (2005c: 99–100).
4 See Berger and Udell (2002) on relationship lending.
5 For methods on measuring informal remittances, see also Hernández-Coss (2005) and World Bank (2003a).

References

Beck, T., A. Demirgüç-Kunt and R. Levine (1999) 'A New Database on Financial Development and Structure', WB Policy Research Working Paper 2146, Washington, DC: World Bank.

Beck, T., R. Levine and N. Loayza (1999) 'Finance and the Sources of Growth', WB Policy Research Working Paper 2057, Washington, DC: World Bank.

Beck, T., A. Demirgüç-Kunt and M. Martinez Peria (2005) Reaching Out: Access to and Use of Banking Services Across Countries, Washington, DC: World Bank.

Berger, A. N. and G. F. Udell (2002) 'Small Business Credit Availability and Relationship Lending: The Importance of Bank Organisational Structure', *The Economic Journal*, 112 (February): F32–F53.

Bugamelli, M. and F. Paternò (2005) 'Do Workers' Remittances Reduce the Probability of Current Account Reversals?', WB Policy Research Working Paper 3766, Washington, DC: World Bank.

Chami, R., C. Fullenkamp and S. Jahjah (2005) 'Are Immigrant Remittance Flows a Source of Capital for Development?', *IMF Staff Papers*, 52(1), Washington, DC: IMF.

Claessens, S. (2005) 'Access to Financial Services: A Review of the Issues and Public Policy Objectives', WB Policy Research Paper 3589, Washington, DC: World Bank.

Djankov, S., C. McLiesh and A. Shleifer (2004), 'Private Credit around the World', Working Paper, Cambridge, Mass.: Department of Economics, Harvard University.

Freund, C. and N. Spatafora (2005) 'Remittances: Transaction Costs, Determinants, and Informal Flows', WB Policy Research Working Paper 3704, Washington, DC: World Bank.

Gasparini, L., F. Gutierrez and G. Porto (2005) 'Finance and Credit Variables in Household Surveys of Developing Countries', Mimeo, Washington, DC: World Bank.

Grace, D. (2005) 'Exploring the Credit Union Experience with Remittances in the Latin American Market', in S. M. Maimbo and D. Ratha (eds), *Remittances: Development Impact and Future Prospects*, Washington, DC: World Bank: 160–73.

Harris, N. (2002) *Thinking the Unthinkable: The Immigration Myth Exposed*, New York: I. B. Tauris & Co.

Harrison, A., T. Britton and A. Swanson (2003) 'Working Abroad: The Benefits Flowing from Nationals Working in Other Economies', Paper presented at the Round Table on Sustainable Development, 19 November, Paris: OECD.

Hernández-Coss, R. (2005) 'A Proposed Framework to Analyze Informal Funds Transfer Systems', in S. M. Maimbo and D. Ratha (eds), *Remittances: Development Impact and Future Prospects*, Washington, DC. World Bank: 244–74.

Hovinga, I. (2005) 'Presentation', Paper presented at the United Nations' Expert Group Meeting on International Migration and Development, 6–8 July, New York: UN.

Inter-American Development Bank (IDB) (2005) News Release. Available at: www.iadb.org (accessed 17 November 2005).

Kaufmann, D., A. Kraay and M. Mastruzzi (2005) 'Governance Matters IV: Governance Indictors for 1996–2004', WB Policy Research Paper 3630, Washington, DC: World Bank.

La Porta, R., F. Lopez-de-Silanes, A. Shleifer and R. Vishny (1998) 'Law and Finance', *Journal of Political Economy*, 106: 1113–55.

Levine, R. (2003) *Finance and Growth: Theory, Evidence and Mechanisms*, Minnesota: University of Minnesota and NBER.

Maimbo, S. M. and D. Ratha (2005) 'Remittances: Development Impact and Future Prospects', in S. M. Maimbo and D. Ratha (eds), *Remittances: Development Impact and Future Prospects*, Washington, DC: World Bank: 1–16.

Orozco, M. (2002) 'Worker Remittances: The Human Face of Globalization', Working paper commissioned by the Multilateral Investment Fund of the IDB, Washington, DC: Inter-American Dialogue.

Orozco, M. (2003) 'Worker Remittances: An International Comparison', Working Paper commissioned by the Multilateral Investment Fund of the IDB, Washington, DC: Inter-American Dialogue.

Orozco, M. (2004) 'The Remittance Marketplace: Prices, Policy and Financial Institutions', Pew Hispanic Center Report, Washington, DC: Pew Hispanic Center.

Orozco, M. and R. Fedewa (2005) 'Leveraging Efforts on Remittances and Financial Intermediation', Report commissioned by the IDB, Washington, DC: Inter-American Dialogue.

Porteous, D. (2004) 'Making Financial Markets Work for the Poor', Paper commissioned by FinMark Trust, 31 October. Available at: www.dfid.gov.uk/news/files/trade_news/adb-workshop-makingfinancial.pdf.

Prahalad, C. K. (2005) *The Fortune at the Bottom of the Pyramid*, Upper Saddle River, NJ: Wharton School Publishing.

Ratha, D. (2003), 'Workers' Remittances: An Important and Stable Source of Development Finance', in S. M. Maimbo and D. Ratha (eds), *Remittances: Development Impact and Future Prospects*, Washington, DC: World Bank: 19–52.

Reinke, J. and N. Patterson (2005) 'Remittances in the Balance of Payments Framework', Paper presented at the International Technical Meeting on Measuring Remittances, 24–25 January, Washington, DC: IMF.

Sander, C. (2003) 'Capturing a Market Share? Migrant Remittance Transfers and Commercialisation of Microfinance in Africa', Paper prepared for the conference on Current Issues in Microfinance, 12–14 August, Johannesburg, South Africa.

Sander, C. and S. M. Maimbo (2005) 'Migrant Remittances in Africa: A Regional Perspective', in S. M. Maimbo and D. Ratha (eds), *Remittances: Development Impact and Future Prospects*, Washington, DC: World Bank: 53–80.

Solimano, A. (2003) 'Remittances by Emigrants: Issues and Evidence', Paper presented at the UNU-WIDER workshop on Innovative Sources for Development Finance, 17–18 May, Helsinki: UNU-WIDER.

Stahl, C. W. and F. Arnold (1986) 'Overseas Workers' Remittances in Asian Development', *International Migration Review*, 20(4): 899–925.

De Vasconcelos, P. (2005) 'Improving the Development Impact of Remittances', Paper presented at United Nations' Expert Group Meeting on International Migration and Development, 6–8 July, New York.

World Bank (2003a) 'Informal Funds Transfer Systems in the APEC Region: Initial Findings and a Framework for Further Analysis', Paper presented at the APEC finance ministers meeting, 1–5 September, Washignton, DC.

World Bank (2003b) *Global Development Finance 2003*, Washington, DC: World Bank.

World Bank (2005a) *Global Development Finance 2005*, Washington, DC: World Bank.

World Bank (2005b) *World Development Indicators 2005*, Washington, DC: World Bank.

World Bank (2005c) *Global Economic Prospects Report 2006: Economic Implications of Remittances and Migration*, Washington, DC: World Bank.

World Bank (2005d) 'World Bank Atlas Classification'. Available at: web.worldbank.org/WBSITE/EXTERNAL/DATASTATISTICS/0,,contentMDK:20420458~menuPK:641331 56~pagePK:64133150~piPK:64133175~theSitePK:239419,00.html

World Bank (2007) 'Regulation and Supervision Database'. Washington, DC: World Bank. Available at: http://econ.worldbank.org/WBSITE/EXTERNAL/EXTDEC/EXTRESEARCH/0,, contentMDK:20345037~pagePK:64214825~piPK:64214943~theSitePK:469382,00. html

Index

Key: **bold**=extended discussion; b=box; f=figure; n=endnote/footnote; t=table.